DJDodds
October 93

Old-Fashioned

Gardens

Old-Fashioned Gardens

TREVOR NOTTLE

Photographs by RAY JARRATT

KANGAROO PRESS

PICTURE ACKNOWLEDGEMENTS

For those photographs not taken by Ray Jarratt, our thanks are due to the following photographers: Bernd Benthaak, pp. 11, 39, 42, 59; Neil Lorimer, p. 33; Trevor Nottle, pp. 128, 129, 141, 148, 149, 176, 177, 185; Keva North, pp. 51, 76, 121; Andrew Payne, pp. 14–15, 37, 88, 116, 120, 157, 164, 169; and the Australian Picture Library, pp. 17, 29, 34–35, 36, 65, 68, 77, 145.

For permission to reproduce photographs of the following items, we would like to thank:

National Library of Australia for S.T. Gill (1818–80): 'Spring' *c.* 1847, watercolour, 29.3 × 21.8 cm (p. 21 and on the back jacket) and 'January' *c.* 1847, watercolour, 21.8 × 18.3 cm (p. 20).

Alexander Turnbull Library, National Library of New Zealand, for Mrs King, *House of Captain King, R.A., Jermyn St. Auckland*, 1858, watercolour 14.7 × 24.2 cm, original in Alexander Turnbull Library A 128/7 (Ref.No.F126230½) on p. 8; 'Nelson, *c.* 1860 looking south-east from the centre of the town', photographer William Meluish (Ref. No.F96556½) on page 16, 'Lydia Williams in her garden, Napier, *c.* 1885' photographer William Williams, E.R. Williams Collection (Ref.No. G25644‡) on page 23; 'Lydia Williams, Napier, *c.* 1885', photographer William Williams, E.R. Williams Collection (Ref.No.G25646‡) on p. 106; 'Raupo whares and gardens, Karaka Bay, Wellington, 1879', photographer Henry Wright, *Evening Post* Collection (Ref.No.F9027¼) on p. 110;

'The camp, the cook and the cabbage', Wairarapa, *c.* 1894 (Ref.No.F224483½) on p. 111; and 'Lydia Williams, Napier *c.* 1885', photographer William Williams, E.R. Williams Collection (Ref.No. G25633‡) on page 146.

Mitchell Library, State Library of NSW, for Kerry, 'A Homestead, postcard' (SPF—Bush Life NSW, *c.* 1905) on p. 9; Holterman, 'House, bark roof, verticle timber slap walls & family' (ZPXA4999 Box 10 no.70154) on p. 23; Holterman, 'Large House weatherboard with shingling roof' (ZPXA Box 10 no.70150) on p. 13; and Holterman, 'House showing garden area, Hill End' (ZPXA4999 Box 10 no.70164) on p. 107.

Mortlock Library, State Library of SA, for 'Angmering House, Enfield' (B5629) on p. 19; John Glover, (1767–1849), *A View of the Artist's House and Garden in Mills Plains, Van Diemen's Land*, 1835, oil on canvas, 76.5 × 114.3 cm, Art Gallery of SA—Morgan Thomas Bequest Fund 1951 (0.1464) on page 48–49.

State Library of Tasmania for *Front View of Windsor Park* on pp. 2–3 and *Highfield, Circular-head* on p. 12.

State Library of Victoria for 'Farm on the Bass River, Gippsland', *c.* 1881, photographer Fred Kruger, (hta 154 f.42) on p. 1.

Nelson Provincial Museum Nelson, NZ, for A.S. Allan, *Residence of Captain Wakefield*, 1849, on p. 13.

Mrs Diana Cooper for photograph of topiary scrollwork, Mt Bischott, Tasmania, about 1900.

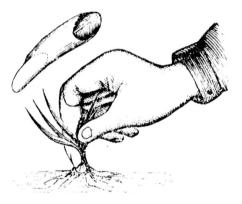

Breen's Patent Finger Spade

First published in 1992 by Kangaroo Press Pty Ltd
3 Whitehall Road (PO Box 75) Kenthurst NSW 2156
Printed in Singapore through Global Com Pte Ltd

ISBN 0 86417 436 5

Created and designed by Barbara Beckett Publishing
Illustrated garden plans by Amanda McPaul

Nottle, Trevor.
   Old-fashioned gardens.
   Bibliography.
   Includes index.
   ISBN 0 86417 436 5.
   1. Gardens—Australia—History—19th century.
   2. Cottage gardens, English—Australia.
   3. Gardens—Styles—History. 4. Plants,
Ornamental. I. Jarratt Ray. II. Title.
712.60994

HALF-TITLE PAGE
From the earliest times of our history the enclosure of gardens has been a significant theme. This early photograph of a settler's cottage in Gippsland, Victoria, vividly captures the sense of a garden as an enclosure where civilisation and security hold sway; outside the picket fence, Nature reigns in wild, awesome majesty.

PREVIOUS TWO PAGES
Front View of Windsor Park, 1854 by C.H.T. Constantini. A garden that was decorative and productive was a nice compromise between the demands of fashion and the fact of living in a colony where self-sufficiency was often necessary.

Contents

Budding's Patent Lawn Mower

Introduction

The influence of our gardening past is evident in almost every town and city. Old gardens and plants are once again enjoyed and valued by a wide cross-section of the community. Owners of elaborate Victorian mansions, stylish Italianate terraces, verandah'd villas and homely cottages are taking on the challenges of rejuvenating or re-creating the gardens around their old homes. Moreover, they are discovering for themselves the pleasures of gardening.

*Simplicity that works; hollyhocks, jade plant (*Portulacaria afra*) and statice (*Limonium perezii*) make a colourful garden show even during the driest seasons.*

LEFT

Tall agapanthus and the tracery of overhanging boughs and leaves create a sense of enclosure.

OPPOSITE PAGE

Abundant flowers that thrive together create a garden picture hard to beat for old-fashioned homeliness and charm.

The owner of a cottage may uncover under a 1950s lawn the edging tiles and gravel paths of a nineteenth-century garden. With enthusiasm fired by the find, further digging may well lead to an outline of the full garden and the growth of a plan to re-create the garden. Another gardener may find nothing but broken beer bottles, smashed crockery and mutton bones, but still the idea may take root that the old bungalow should have a garden to match its style and age. Excavations for a swimming pool may turn up the buried stones of a rockery and pond that once graced the gardens of a grand mansion. As a result, the owner's mind may turn towards finding an alternative spot for the pool so that the rockery and pond can be reinstated. These ideas occur to the owners of old houses and gardens because there is now a widespread public appreciation of our garden history. This has come about through the existence, activities and publications of garden history societies in Australia and New Zealand, the National Trust of Australia, the New Zealand Historic Trust and a host of other conservation groups, and through the dedication of many amateur gardeners.

We do not yet have a country-wide society dedicated to the preservation and propagation of old flowers such as the National Council for the Preservation of Plants and Gardens in the United Kingdom. A Victorian group, the Ornamental Plant Collections Association, based at the Royal Melbourne Botanic Gardens, has been formed to preserve the many fine garden flowers that have been raised in Australia, and it is to be hoped that similar associations will be formed in other states and regions. While none of the plants raised in Australia or New Zealand has the antiquity that can be attached to the garden flowers of England, France or even the United States of America, there are many hundreds of camellias, fuchsias, pelargoniums (regal and zonal), gladioli, roses, daffodils, chrysanthemums, orchids, dahlias and

House of Captain King, Jermyn Street, Auckland, New Zealand, *1858, by Mrs King. The spread of garden ideas worldwide was made possible in the nineteenth century by the advent of cheap printing and mass publication.*

other plants which form a part of our gardening history and which are still in the hands of a few collectors. These plants should be made secure against loss.

It would be a mistake, however, to think only of such plants as 'antiques' suitable for inclusion in the gardens of a few connoisseurs or as specimens limited to the gardens belonging to historic houses. Above all, the garden flowers of Australia and New Zealand are hardy plants raised and selected to suit our soils, climates and seasons, and they should be far more widely grown than they are at present. The roses and daffodils bred by Alister Clark at Bulla, Victoria, in the 1920s are prime examples. It is a curious fact that many garden flowers from overseas are introduced to

Australasian gardens every year, yet precious few pass the test of time to become firmly established as garden favourites, while equally colourful local versions pass unnoticed. Just think how many dozens of roses are introduced each season and then try to recall how few remain popular for more than a few years. Admittedly some nurserymen are now beginning to rework old favourites, but the number of these classic roses is trifling compared with the stream of novelties imported every year.

The term 'old-fashioned flowers' is a rather vague one, for there is a considerable difference between our understanding of it and the way in which it would be understood by a European or even an American gardener. English enthusiasts may well think back to plants popular in the sixteenth or seventeenth centuries, Americans may look to plants popular in the eighteenth century; we in Australia and New Zealand cannot look back beyond the nineteenth century unless we include plants attached by sentiment to the homelands of our forebears.

The role of sentiment was, and remains, an important one in deciding plant choices but is always modified by the influences of climate, soils, availability of water and the skills of the propagator. Tulips and primroses may have been

A Chinese gardener, c. *1890.*

fond favourites in cooler, wetter homelands, but they proved difficult in our climate and so have not entered so strongly into our garden making. The reverse has also operated, where plants thought delicate and cold-tender in Europe have revelled in our warm climate and prospered as popular

Perhaps closer to the nineteenth-century rustic style than the gardenesque designs favoured by the middle classes, this garden would today be regarded as a cottage garden. The rectangular plots with plants dotted hither and yon show that even the simplest homes could have been surrounded with colourful gardens if the owners so wished.

easy-going garden plants. In particular, plants from the Cape of Good Hope, California, southern China and even Chile were found to be perfectly hardy and have now passed into the lore of Australian and New Zealand gardeners as being old-fashioned. Other influences, particularly the mass migrations of Europeans, Californians and Chinese during the gold rushes of the mid-1800s, and the lesser movements of Germanic peoples as a result of religious persecution, would have introduced yet other plants to our gardens which may make for significant differences in our understanding of old-fashioned flowers as against that of English gardeners and collectors.

Our appreciation of old-fashioned plants is further expanded (or confused) by the recent importations of English cottage-garden flowers made by specialist growers and by the rejuvenated plantings around many historic homes—some made with academic accuracy, others based on more eclectic choices. Thus our present day 'palette' of old-fashioned flowers is enriched by many genera and species which were not grown here in the

early days, at least not so far as we know from the meagre surviving written records. Things such as astrantia, aconitum, asperula, a good many 'fancy' herbs, peonies, many 'new' old roses (e.g., these bred by David Austin) and many violets would have to be included here.

Historical accuracy need not be such a great problem, unless plants need to be selected purely on established fact for inclusion in important garden recreations. An example is Elizabeth Farm, near Parramatta, where every plant was related to contemporary family letters and to sketches and paintings of the period when the house was in the hands of the Macarthur family. In gardens where strict accuracy is not necessary, if indeed it ever is, these recently imported old-fashioned flowers may be included without agonising over their validity on the grounds of local history. Things tend to overlap in an old garden, and total change is rare from owner to owner, so the question becomes one not so much of accuracy as of the characteristics of the individual flowers.

The first characteristic that makes a flower old-fashioned in the eyes of modern gardeners is perhaps the most elusive and yet the most obvious —that is, the flower should be unsophisticated and look the way we think it should look. Therefore there will be no dahlias that look like waterlilies, no asters that look like chrysanthemums, no gladioli that look like rosebuds, no monster daffodils, no green hollyhocks, and no camellias that look like orchids; nor will there be any blue roses. There will certainly be a wide variety of flower forms, but they will all still strongly show the influence of the wild forms and simple variations such as doubling, quartering and hose-in-hose effects.

While the forms and colours will remain within these constraints, we must bear in mind other possibilities not often met in present-day gardening, especially the possibilities of particoloured, flaked, striped, rimmed and eyed flowers where contrasting colour zones and markings provide endless variety. In more leisure times such differences were keenly observed and cultivated. Scale is important too— generally there were few really gigantic flowers such as may be found among camellias, roses, dahlias and gladioli, although there were large flowers now little seen, especially sunflowers, tall mignonette and even the humble black-eyed susans (*Rudbeckia* sp.). Above all, there were no elaborately bred F_1 hybrids such as we have today dominating our annuals. No legions of identical petunias, violas and primulas. True, there were seed strains of very similar flowers, but minute differences were always present. Every now and again 'rogues' would appear to show again nature's careless consideration of man's attraction to conformity and uniformity.

This, then, is the background to our understanding of old-fashioned flowers, the things of our history which show in our gardens and in our garden making. Little has been said of perfume or colours, for these were perhaps secondary to the discovery of plants which would thrive in the range of Australian and New Zealand climates; however, they will be considered as individual flowers are discussed.

The examples given in this book serve to introduce the differences that distinguish old-fashioned flowers as grown in the colonies from those found in English and European gardens. Had space allowed, mention could have been made of even more exotic plants, tropical and semitropical, cultivated in the gardens of colonial Queensland. Some useful references to these will be found in Ellis Rowan's *A Flower Hunter in Queensland and New Zealand* (1898). But these were restricted to the heated 'stoves' of a wealthy few in the southern population centres, and most colonists were content with hardy flowers.

Towards a Distinctive Garden Style

There is something deep inside almost everyone that binds us to the soil. We need to grow things, to dig and plant, to tend and harvest. For many people, myself included, this involvement stirs and satisfies a sense of being a part of the scheme of things. Through gardening we can be in touch with the rhythms of the seasons and the forces that nuture growing things.

Gardening also brings us in touch with each other as we swap plants, share ideas, enjoy each other's triumphs and contemplate our failures across the back fence, while out walking, or when we meet at the local nursery. The advent of garden visiting has also served gardeners well as a means of meeting and befriending like-minded folk. From other people's gardens we can gather ideas, make mental notes for future reference about garden design and plants, and learn from each other's experiences. The diversity of old-fashioned gardens offers a rich field for exploration; there are many styles, designs and plants to discuss, seek out and consider. In revisiting them and trying to meld them to our present circumstances we are, even if unconsciously, moving towards the gardens of tomorrow.

Although all our garden styles have been imported, we seem at last to be reviewing their influence from the perspective gained by two hundred years' residence and assessing future

A low hedge of clipped box adds authentic charm to this old-fashioned mixed border of perennials and shrubs. Stiffness and stuffiness have been artfully avoided by letting some plants spill over the hedge onto the grass.

Towering tree ferns and a background of mature gum trees are all that remain of the temperate rainforest in which this garden was made.

directions. This process is possible only because of the widespread interest in the gardens of yesteryear. Without the many examples of well-cared-for old gardens, both rejuvenated and re-created, our perspective of our garden heritage would be confined to the dim, misty plates of early photographers, a few early paintings and some sketchy written records.

The development of a distinctive national garden style, one that would be instantly recognisable, may never happen. However, re-creating an old-fashioned garden will bring for most of us pleasurable work, a few frustrations and many enjoyable rewards. My aim in writing this book is to share with you my own experiences and enthusiasm for old-fashioned plants and gardens.

Highfield, Circular-head, Stanley, Tasmania, *1840.*
The young garden of this villa is set out to show each plant to advantage. The approach to garden design that treats each plant as a specimen in a collection is an attempt at gardenesque design as advocated by the great garden writer of the Victorian age, John Claudius Loudon.

ABOVE
A palisade of pickets surrounds this sixteenth-century garden of rectangular beds, demonstrating that enclosure and regularity have had a long and pervasive influence on the way we make gardens.

TOP
Surrounded by bush, a garden and house made a statement of civilisation and possession for many settlers. Within its clearly defined boundaries a little bit of Home could be made — at least to the extent that climate, leisure and available water allowed.

ABOVE
Shelter from retained native trees or from plantations of imported exotics was a first consideration for many colonial garden makers. Long-term replacement programs are needed to keep the shelter going into the twenty-first century.

NEXT TWO PAGES
With its neat border, lush girdle of shrubs and background of tall gums, this croquet lawn would inspire any player.

Part 1
Gardens and Gardening

1 The Nineteenth-Century Colonial Garden

The notion of an old-fashioned garden has its foundations in a mixture of ideas about the past which have been formed by existing gardens, our memories, books, pictures and a degree of sentimentalism. Our history has been too short and our population too mobile for the strong traditions of the cottager to have had a profound effect on our gardening traditions, yet there is an undeniable influence underlying every old-fashioned garden.

An old-fashioned garden is a fairly uncomplicated structure based on a grid of straight paths and a wide selection of flowering plants—shrubs, bulbs, annuals, biennials, perennials and climbers—planted with no particular regard to flowering season or stature and with an unsophisticated colour scheme. Less influential is the mixture of vegetables, fruit and nut trees, raspberries and other soft fruits which are commonplace in the English originals from which our own old-fashioned gardens have derived. Even less consideration is given to the

numerous outbuildings which once typified a self-sufficient household—the pigsty, cow byre, bee skeps, stable, pigeon loft and hen run; all these have given way to lawns, swimming pools and patios. Thus, while the majority of Australasian gardens

ABOVE
Nelson, c. 1860. Barren hills and distant neighbours focused many family interests on the home and garden making.
RIGHT
Modern cool storage and bulb production methods can produce spectacular displays in warm climates.

have always been small ones, those which have locally been thought of as cottage gardens have not evolved directly through a long history of self-sufficient rural workers as have the cottage gardens of England. Other powerful social forces have caused the cottage garden tradition to be reinterpreted in a colonial vernacular.

In the Beginning

The first small gardens made after the settlement of each Antipodean colony seem to have had remarkable similarities wherever they were made. Essentially they were gardens for survival, so we may guess that in the main they grew vegetables, grains and fruits and maybe some herbs and simple medicinal plants. Enclosure was a first requirement, as a protection against the depredations of wild animals, thieves, straying cattle, sheep and horses, and in some cases against the attacks of native warriors. Simply constructed paling fences or hurdles woven from pliable saplings are often the only significant garden detail found in early drawings and paintings. Aside from their protective role, these also served as boundary markers for individual properties. Inside, the enclosed ground was usually divided into rectangular beds, the size being determined by the arm and hoe reach of the gardener.

Apple trees and a scattered carpet of flowers bedeck this fifteenth-century garden enclosed with a fence made of woven 'wattle' hurdles.

The overall size of most gardens was determined by the number of people available to cultivate the soil. The usual plot was large enough to be managed by two adults—generally a quarter-acre or so in area. In warm, dry climates this meant a great deal of water carrying and irrigation as well as weeding, tilling and pest control. Although it

was often expected that a family would be made self-supporting for food on land this size, it must have taken an intense effort by skilled gardeners even in the best conditions. We know from history how ill-prepared many settlers were for becoming self-sufficient.

Often the earliest colonial survival gardens are shown as being made up of long rows. Pathways were strictly no-nonsense, leading straight from the gate to the door and connecting the house, the well, the outhouse and stable. Such an arrangement is embedded deep in our memory. Enclosure and direct lines of access are part of the cultural baggage we carry with us in our innermost being. Given a bare block of land and a need to make a garden, a first-time garden maker of today, with no conscious knowledge of garden making, will usually sense the need for enclosure and regularity and will lay out a garden that harks back to ancient traditions. Pictorial evidence from the fifteenth century onwards shows how long established these traditional patterns of garden making are; it is scarcely any cause for wonder then that we do not feel truly comfortable with other more recent and alien styles of garden design.

Later nineteenth-century developments of this basic rectangular style allowed for variations on the theme which broke up the pattern with other simple geometric shapes while retaining an overall regularity of design and axial layout. The path to the front door may have been diverted around a central garden bed, but the sight line to the threshold stayed true as ever.

A Time of Change

Colonial gardens were established at a time when rapid changes in the British social order, in work patterns, lifestyle and the distribution of wealth, were accompanied by equally rapid developments in many branches of technology. New techniques made sheet glass much cheaper, and coupled with the new engineering skills of prefabrication and large-scale metal casting, the mass production of glasshouses was possible in a range of sizes. New mining techniques produced cheap coal which could be burned to produce steam-heated conservatories and vast propagating houses. Improved transport over the new railway systems and better postal services allowed plants to be delivered safely over long distances. The domestic gardener benefited from all these improvements in having access to many new and comparatively cheap plants. There were also direct technological benefits in the form of numerous handy inventions to make the home gardener's chores easier—the most famous being Budding's Patent Lawn Mower (1830). There were many

Angmering House, Enfield, c. 1860. Travelling halfway around the world to make homes, settlers brought with them many plants for their new gardens. Agaves from central America and bulbs from the Cape mingle with native trees and shrubs and vegetables in this garden.

others too, including all shapes and sizes of sprayers, puffers, secateurs, saws and implements of amazing design for just about every garden operation, for example, Breen's Patent Finger Spade, a scoop-like attachment for the index finger to help in pricking out seedlings.

Alongside all these improvements, subsidiary industries arose as by-products from the new heavy industries to support the gardener with chemical fertilisers (slag and coke breeze, nitrates, etc.) and chemical insecticides, fumigants and fungicides. Expanded world trade also brought about the ready availability of such wondrous stuff as Peruvian guano, Abrolhos guano, Colonial guano and even Kangaroo Island guano. The marvels of the Polynesian rock phosphate and superphosphate of lime produced by the Colonial Sugar Refining Co. in the 1890s were new additions to the home gardener's battery of aids. Was it any wonder that horticulture flourished as never before?

In order to establish their new gardens, many people consulted books and magazines; cheap, printed in large numbers, and heavily illustrated, these were distributed to all corners of the British Empire. They were full of new plant discoveries, new equipment, fertilisers, pesticides and ideas for making gardens. The ideas of John Claudius

Loudon were published in his magazine, *The Gardener's Magazine* (1826–43), and in several books —*Encyclopedia of Gardening* (1822) and *The Suburban Gardener and Villa Companion* (1838), which were most popular and widely read. His enthusiasm for new plants and technological advances gave rise to a style of gardening termed 'gardenesque', which in essence allowed 'gardeners and botanical amateurs to display their trees and flowers to the greatest advantage'. His equally talented wife, Jane Loudon, besides writing horror stories (e.g., *The Mummy*) wrote three gardening books for a new emerging group—leisured middle class women. The books were *Gardening for Ladies, The Ladies' Flower Garden* (4 vols) and *A Lady's Country Companion*. All of these books were available in the colonies.

J. Shirley Hibberd was another gardening publisher whose works were widely circulated and read; his periodical *The Floral World and Garden Guide* (1858–75) was highly successful, as were his books *Rustic Adornments for Homes of Taste* (1856), *The Amateur's Flower Garden, The Amateur's Rose Book, The Amateur's Greenhouse, The Fern Garden* (1869), and *The Ivy* (1872).

What was important about all these books was that they took plants out of their role as necessary components of a landscape and firmly established them as objects worthy of individual study and display. These influential imports were supplemented by many local papers and books which also reflected the new enthusiasm for flower gardening; among these were Daniel Bunce's *The Manual of Practical Gardening Adapted to the Climate*

of *Van Diemen's Land* (1837–38), James Sinclair's
The Gardener's Magazine (1855), Thomas Cole's
Gardening in Victoria (1860) and George McEwin's
The South Australian Vigneron & Gardener's Manual
(1843).

As the century advanced and Australia and New
Zealand changed from rural outposts of the British
Empire to increasingly urbanised countries, other

ABOVE

The Months of the Year in Australia—Adelaide,
'January', c. *1847, by S.T. Gill. Plants grew easily in the
new soils and warm climates of the colonies. Melons and other
plants that required cultivation under glass at Home flourished
outdoors and could be grown by everybody.*

RIGHT

The Four Seasons in Australia—Adelaide, 'Spring',
c. *1847, by S.T. Gill.*

books appeared which furthered the transformation of the cottage garden into the flower garden. Principal among them were the books of William Robinson—*Alpine Flowers for English Gardens* (1870). *The Wild Garden* (1870) and *The English Flower Garden* (1883). His magazine *The Garden* founded in (1871) is still in publication today under the aegis of the Royal Horticultural Society. Contemporaneous with these were works by local authors such as Mrs Rolf Boldrewood, whose *The Flower Garden in Australia— A Book for Ladies and Amateurs* (1893) tended to be less authoritative but nonetheless influential.

By the end of the century the flower garden was well established as the prime domestic pursuit of the middle classes and was beginning to be seen among the urban working classes of the big cities and towns. The transformation would be completed in the twentieth century by writers such as Gertrude Jekyll, Mrs C. W. Earle, Eleanor Sinclair-Rohde, Rose Kingsley, Vita Sackville-West and more recent writers such as Marjory Fish and Beth Chatto. Local authors who carried on the developing trend to flower gardening were C. Bogue Luffmann, *The Principles of Gardening in Australia* (1903), Mrs Arthur Tuckett, *A Year in My Garden* (1905) and later by Edna Walling in her books.

Botanical Exploration and Plant Breeding

Evidence of the floral richness that existed in gardens in nineteenth-century colonial times is to be found in nursery catalogues and garden magazines of the period. English magazines such as the *Gardener's Magazine*, the *Gardener's Chronicle*, the *Floricultural Cabinet*, the *Garden and the Field* and *Gardening Illustrated* were widely circulated, even as far afield as the Antipodes, and available at popular prices. Scarcely an issue appeared without at least passing reference to the newest plant arrivals from faraway Japan, China, Tibet, Peru, Patagonia, Siberia or Australia. Even the home amateurs got into the plant collection game, and the correspondence columns of these horticultural papers are full of letters from folk recently returned from Greece, Italy, the Bahamas, the Alps or the Pyrenees laden with all manner of botanical acquisitions which they transplanted to their gardens, with mixed success. This floral explosion was not limited to England. Similar, though perhaps less pervasive, forces were at work in the homelands of the other colonial powers, France and Germany.

The seemingly endless flow of seeds, bulbs,

tubers, roots and plants was received by the big nurseries and wealthy private collectors, who subscribed to the plant-hunting expeditions in return for a share in the floral booty. But it was usually not long before the hardy plants among them were propagated and distributed widely.

Parallel to this rapid expansion of available plant species was the development of plant breeding. By today's standards of knowledge, nineteenth-century plant breeding was crude and unscientific, but the pollen-daubers of those days knew that by cross-pollinating two different plants in the same genus, improved forms could be obtained. The number of such improvements was quite staggering, as may be seen by perusing the seedsmen's catalogues of the period. From abutilon to zinnia via ferns, geraniums, asters, violets, lilacs, clematis, all manner of alpines, roses, shrubs and

trees, the home gardener could select from hundreds of species and cultivars. Not only in floral lines did the nurseries offer an enormous choice, but also in fruit and nut trees, soft fruits and vegetables, with hundreds of apple and pear cultivars and dozens of gooseberries and cabbage strains to choose from.

The impact of this immense, even staggering, volume of plant material on colonial gardeners was not to overwhelm them. They took it all in their stride, eagerly welcoming news of the latest discoveries and productions. Each novelty was enthusiastically received, assessed for the value of its flowers, foliage and habit by the pundits of the day, and assigned a number of potential garden uses in the columns of the horticultural press. Mention might be made here that some of these uses are looked on today as being little more than freakish: multiple grafting and in-arching to produce

outlandish specimens, for example. The more extravagant forms of topiary and the excesses of the outlandish bedding-out schemes executed in public gardens and the mansions of the super-rich all draw rather derisive comment in these more enlightened times. But what is important is not what the

ABOVE

Petasites japonicus 'Giganteus' from the Yokohama Nursery Co. catalogue of 1895. Printed in English and distributed widely in Europe, North America and Australia, the catalogue introduced many Japanese and Chinese plants to Western gardeners by direct marketing.

LEFT

Wardian case illustrated by Louisa Johnson in Every Lady Her Own Flower Gardener, *1845 edition. Invented by Dr Nathaniel Ward of London, the Wardian case was a simple, tight-closing miniature glasshouse used for transporting plants over long distances.*

gardeners of the time did with plants but their *atttitude* to gardens and plants.

From reading the books, magazines and catalogues of the period one gains the impression that the prevalent nineteenth-century attitudes towards horticulture were those of enthusiasm, experimentation, and enjoyment in the exuberant use of the floral treasure chest that was being opened by plant hunters and breeders. To recapture

Photographed relaxing in her garden surrounded by well-established fruit trees and neat flower beds, this banjo-plucking colonist shows the folks at home that life was not all hard work in the Land of the Long White Cloud.

some of these attitudes must be the aim of any gardener seeking to re-create the atmosphere of a nineteenth-century cottage or villa garden. For while the economic strictures of working-class life ruled out the wholesale adoption of such grandiose pieces of Victoriana as alpine gardens, pinetums, rhododendron glades, heated conservatories, Chinese gardens and araucaria avenues, small gardeners nevertheless did make bold, imaginative and colourful use of plants. They were keen to try new plants and acquire as many as their means would allow, displaying them in gay profusion and appreciating them individually.

The Advent of Lawns

Towards the end of the nineteenth century, as towns and cities grew larger and reticulated water supplies were established, lawns became more common. Previously, only very magnificent

Success in the colonies. A proud family show off their home, garden and family in this early photograph.

ABOVE

Every old-fashioned garden should have a relaxed, quiet air about it. A seat such as this offers an opportunity to sit and contemplate.

RIGHT

A lawn, even a small narrow one, can act as an open space and a means of directing attention from one part of a garden to another. Here the disappearing curve of grass leads the eye, and maybe the body, into the unknown garden out of sight.

OPPOSITE PAGE, TOP

An old-fashioned 'dipping pool' and fountain. The small raised pool could have been used as a source of water for pot plants and nearby garden flowers.

OPPOSITE PAGE, BOTTOM LEFT

A broad or deep grassy patch uninterrupted by trees and shrubs and well sheltered around the boundary makes a useful and private place for picnics, games or quiet contemplation.

OPPOSITE PAGE, BOTTOM RIGHT

Uncomplicated shapes are best for garden pools. Here a circular pool with waterlilies near one side so their beautiful flowers can be seen close-up and with a large area of open water to reflect the sky proves the value of simple designs.

establishments could boast a genuine greensward; others made do with roughly scythed native pasture grasses which browned off in dry seasons. Most people preferred to use their garden plots for more important and favoured plants such as vegetables, fruit trees and treasured flowers. The arrival of piped water happily coincided with the introduction in Australia of hardy perennial grasses from South Africa, and, the two events enabled gardeners to plant patches of grass in areas too hot and dry for fine turf. Couch, buffalo grass and kikuyu were widely advertised and hailed as a major development for gardeners. A variegated form of buffalo grass was even known, such was the fascination with exotic grass. If only they hadn't been quite so enthusiastic we should have been saved a great deal of bother eradicating such things as kikuyu grass, paspalum grass and the whole tribe of couch grasses!

Of course, the newfangled lawns needed a swag of gadgetry to keep them going: India-rubber hoses were essential, as well as grass shears, scythes and maybe even one of Mr Budding's new hand-propelled, feather-light cast-iron lawnmowers. By and large, lawns occupied shapes that had existed previously as garden beds. Towards the end of the period, as lawns took up a larger part of the garden and lawnmowers improved in design and became more widely owned, garden beds became much simpler in shape to make mowing easier. Another aspect of maintenance which helped to simplify garden layout was the need to keep the lawns within bounds. The couch, kikuyu and buffalo grew just as vigorously as they do today, and the

conventional edgings to beds proved quite ineffectual in containing them. More drastic measures were needed to control such willing growers. There were those who favoured lawns edged with stout jarrah slats to hold in the running grasses, but regular chopping with a hatchet was still needed to keep things under control. A cheaper and more common method was to deeply trench the lawn edges with a sharp spade. The resulting dry moat was considered reasonably effective, even though strenuous hatchet work was still needed now and then to keep the edges neat. Fortunately, we no longer need to use such rampant growers to make a patch of grass, so unless you are really determined to be authentic, the niceties of such hatchet handiwork need not concern you.

Water, a Treasured Resource

Water has always been in short supply in Australian gardens and except in a few very high-rainfall areas has played a small part as a decorative feature in garden making. The earliest gardens followed English and European precedents and gathered rainwater in wooden butts (barrels) placed to catch the run-off from gutters and downpipes. The practical importance of these far outweighed any idea of them as decorative garden features. Horse troughs and watering tanks for livestock may have also been included on the perimeter of a garden to save the trouble of toting water long distances. It is

Water as a decorative feature in gardens has always been valued, whether for making a cascade among rockwork or something as simple as a small dipping well.

It is not necessary to turn on splendid fountains to create old-fashioned gardens; a small pool and a trickle of water are all that are needed to enjoy the magic qualities of sound, light and movement that water alone can give.

possible that goldfish and waterlilies could have been introduced in the larger tanks to give family members a little pleasure. Farm ponds and natural creeks may have been included in gardens. Again they were most often at the boundaries, close enough for the convenient supply of water but not wholly included as important parts of the layout.

In a few gardens, purely decorative pools would have been included in the flower garden or shade house. A common design was a simple circular pool, built of brick and rendered with cement and raised above ground level. In many cases pools like this had a broad, flat rim wide enough to sit on or to hold a collection of potted ferns, begonias, palms, camellias and other plants; it served as a dipping well to water the plants. Water was usually supplied by a hand pump connected to a well or by bucketing water as required to maintain the level.

Later nineteenth-century gardens could make greater use of water, as windmills and deeper wells, larger dams and piped water supplies made access more reliable and less labour intensive. Decorative pools and rockeries sported cast-iron or bronze fountains, jets, sprays and cascades and may have included small streams constructed from lava, lumps of crystalline rock, fossilised rocks, pieces of stalagmites and stalactites, and other interesting geological specimens. Larger gardens were able to form and fill large ponds and lakes which were treated in the Romantic 'natural' style rimmed with willows and reeds, decked with waterlilies and pickerel weed (*Pontederia cordata*), and equipped with a Gothic boathouse or bathing pavilion.

Occasionally Japanese gardens were made, following the precepts set down by Josiah Conder in *Landscape Gardening in Japan* (1893). Plants for

these gardens were often supplied by companies such as the Yokohama Nursery Company Ltd, which exported all manner of Oriental plants. Meandering rockwork streams, cascades, bronze cranes, Japanese lanterns of stone or bronze, Dogs of Fo (stone temple guardians), half-moon bridges, stepping stones across the water and bamboo and thatch summerhouses enjoyed a brief vogue among those who could afford them. To catch the mood, the Yokohama Nursery Company (and others) were happy to supply tree peonies, bamboos in variety, camellias, liliums dug fresh from the mountain sides, bonsai, Japanese irises, Japanese cherries, the sacred lotus (*Nelumbo nucifera*), conifers and cycads, Japanese maples and vegetable oddities such as the giant butter burr (*Petasites japonicus* 'Giganteus'). Enhancing the exotic effects, local nurseries supplied rhododendrons, azaleas, grasses, hydrangeas, elephant's ears (*Colocasia* sp.) ferns and tree ferns, and more curiosities like the Chilean giant rhubarb (*Gunnera manicata*).

Re-establishing an Old Garden

The hardest part of any garden reconstruction is not the physical labour or the search for the hard-to-find plant; it is to visualise a garden in its youth. In cottage and villa gardens, visual interest came not so much from architectural and built features such as walls, steps and waterworks as from a prolific and varied planting. Looking at old

ABOVE
A small three-tiered copper fountain with simple scrolled decoration adds a touch of sophistication to a narrow rectangular pool. The water trickles from the spouts and cools the surrounding air on hot days.

LEFT
A few fresh flowers floated in an old urn show the hand of an unseen but attentive gardener who appreciates visitors to the garden.

RIGHT
Small lake or large pond? Whatever term you choose, the possibilities for planting a water garden offer the enjoyment of a whole new range of plants to most gardeners; an experience novel to many who garden in warm, dry climates.

gardens today, we see only the barest bones of their structure and the toughest, most vigorous survivors. Standing in an overgrown Victorian garden it is easy to imagine that it was always thus: vast towering shrubs, overblown and frowzy, backed by dolorous, dusty conifers with an understory of leaf litter, toadstools, and flowerless, scraggy shrublets. It is easy to let such scenes colour our view of nineteenth-century gardens. By and large, we think of folk in those times as being sombre, serious and sober, and looking at their gardens today we frequently see in them a reflection of these values. Such impressions are easily bolstered by common knowledge of Victorian times; their love of mourning jewellery, their fondness for the widowed Queen, their meticulous habit of marking every possible event with some sort of monument and their passion for religious enterprises all lead the unknowing to consider the Victorians a rather dull lot. How far from the truth!

flower beds in the lawns of large mansions were translated into square and circular beds in cottage and villa gardens. Common signs which may help you to decide on the likely layout of your old garden are clumps of jonquils, agapanthus, belladonnas or other bulbs laid out in rows, or regular arrangements of shrubs, roses or small trees.

While these path patterns may have been outlined with tiles, bricks or cut stone, it was far more usual to use rough rocks or hardwood laths laid on edge and held in place by wooden pegs. The most common surfacing was pea-gravel, though bricks, slate and even cobbles were not uncommon in areas where they could be obtained cheaply and easily.

In most cases it is not too hard to settle on an appropriate path and bed layout, guided by the position of doors and gateways with access to sheds and outhouses, as well as by existing plants. Bear in mind the basic rule to keep things relatively simple. Cottage and villa gardens were usually maintained by their owners and thus should be within the

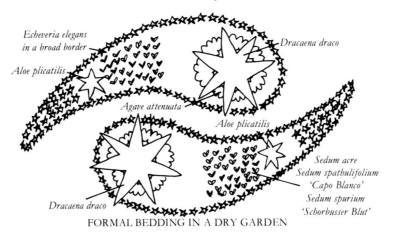

Echeveria elegans in a broad border

Aloe plicatilis

Dracaena draco

Agave attenuata

Aloe plicatilis

Sedum acre
Sedum spathulifolium 'Capo Blanco'
Sedum spurium 'Schorbusser Blut'

Dracaena draco

FORMAL BEDDING IN A DRY GARDEN

*Two spectacular dragon's blood trees (*Dracaena draco*) from the Canary Islands add a genuine old-fashioned air to this dry garden. Underneath their elephantine trunks and fantastic top growth of silvery succulent leaves, more plants*

*from arid places continue the exotic theme. Dot plants of the fan-leaved aloe (*Aloe plicatilis*) add to the paisley pattern and counterpoint the larger forms of the trees. Overall, the garden would be approximately 9 m by 6 m.*

To discover what the Victorian or nineteenth-century gardeners were like, we have to look a little deeper than the evidence offered to our eyes by the remains of their gardens which we may find today. A little detective work is a lot of fun and usually leads to a few surprises.

Starting at the house, the first step is to survey the garden, making notes on what you have to start with in the way of plant life, and to make an approximate plan of any pathways that are in existence. As gardens are liable to change with each new owner, it pays to keep an eye out for telltale signs of paths that may have been turned over to garden. Likewise, be aware that in small gardens the general tendency was to create simplified versions of the current fashions in large gardens and to make changes in small ways; so the star and crescent

maintenance time available to gardener-owners of today.

To rediscover the rich diversity of plants that once filled in the spaces between and under these remnant trees and shrubs, we must look to surviving records. Searching the literature and archival records is the second phase of the detective work involved in re-establishing an old garden. The most accessible resources are the major public libraries, where information can be located in a variety of sections. Obvious places to search are the gardening, horticultural and landscape categories. Less obvious places are the national or state collections, which try to assemble as much as possible of the material published since publications were first printed, and the archival photographic collections. The libraries attached

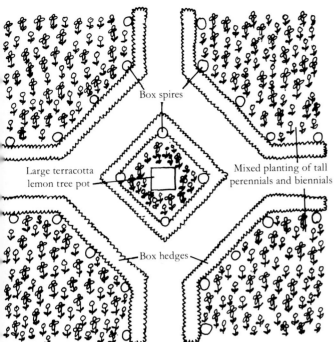

Box spires

Large terracotta
lemon tree pot

Mixed planting of tall
perennials and biennials

Box hedges

AN ITALIANATE EDWARDIAN GARDEN

*This garden has strong vertical lines imposed by a series of
tall, narrow spires cut from box. These are echoed in the
choice of plants to fill the beds that are surrounded by low box
hedges from which the spires rocket skyward. Foxgloves,
verbascums,* Macleaya microcarpa, Galtonia candicans,
Campanula pyramidalis *'Alba' and* Kniphophia *'Maid
of Orleans' lead the eye upward and are supported by*
Eryngium planum, Crambe cordifolia, Salvia
transcaucasica, S. forskaohlei, S. azurea *and* S. sclarea.
*The hedging should be kept low (approximately 50 cm) and
the spires should reach about 2 m tall. The central square
should feature a large terracotta pot in the Italian manner.*

to botanic gardens, horticultural colleges and
agricultural colleges also hold extensive collections
of specialised literature. Sometimes local council
libraries also hold useful collections related to
their community. Historical societies, too, are
worthwhile avenues of investigation, particularly
as they frequently keep extensive photographic
collections and may have accumulated local
information based on interviews with old residents
or nurserymen.

You should take every opportunity to talk to any
old gardeners and nurserymen you may meet so that
you can gather your own evidence relevant to your
own situation. Often these people have records in
the form of old catalogues, stock lists and
magazines which go back many years. Usually they
are happy to talk over their memories and show
their keepsakes to anyone who evinces an interest.

Second-hand shops are worth rummaging
through in your search for material relevant to
gardens of the late nineteenth century. Books,
postcards, nursery catalogues, gardening magazines,
watercolour paintings and sketches, prints and

photographs are all worth poring over and
thumbing through for items of interest. Among all
the junk, there may well be some useful items
showing garden details and plant types.

The Secrets of Recreating Old-Fashioned Gardens

'What is the secret of your lovely old garden?'
visitors often ask. They may admire the flowers and
ask where the unusual plants came from. They may
recall other gardens where these things once grew.
But, more than anything, people visiting old
gardens sense something magical about them.
Setting aside the possibility that horticulturally
inclined gnomes come out at night to dig and delve
and make old gardens sparkle with fairy dew, what
are the secrets of old gardens?

The first secret is one that is often sensed but
less often understood. Standing in an old garden a
feeling of comfort seems to prevail; somehow the
garden seems right, it feels right. How is this
feeling of 'rightness' created? The feeling is created
by the garden being scaled in such a way by the
plants and objects it contains that we feel part of it
but not the dominant feature. This is best explained
by looking at the difference between old gardens
and new gardens. New gardens are open to the
world, something deliberately so in order to display
wealth and fashion; the plants are small, and the
house and even the human figure loom large
physically. Old gardens are enclosed by trees and

A NEW COTTAGE HERBER

mints

strawberries

chives and thymes

parsley

dianthus

oregano and marjoram

*This design draws on the traditional orchard layout but adds
more formal notes in having brick edging and defined gravelled
pathways. The plantings are much more varied and colourful
than the simple flowers of an orchard garden: herbs chosen for
culinary use, making potpourri, for foliage and colour or for
their historical associations. Old varieties of fruit trees, crab-
apples,* Judas trees (Cercis siliquastrum) *or bauhinias*
(Bauhinia galpinii *or* B. variegata) *form the orchard.*

ABOVE
A background of mature trees is a great asset to any garden plan, but their strong, far-reaching roots mean that new lawns and flower plantings need special measures to ensure success.

RIGHT
At the end of a short grove an inviting seat offers a chance for sitting in the warm sun out of sight.

OPPOSITE PAGE, TOP
Massive old trees add a magical touch to any garden. Such precious treasures are worth every care and attention.

OPPOSITE PAGE, BOTTOM
Large gardens have room for large trees set in informal plantations, especially around the perimeter. Plant big trees for the enjoyment of future generations.

shrubs; the house is much less dominant—it may not be seen at all—and the human figure takes on a less imposing stature against the mature trees and thicketing bushes.

The first steps in making an old-fashioned garden are to plan and plant so that a feeling of enclosure and a sense of scale can be developed as quickly as possible. A wide open garden design that aims to show off the house as an object for public admiration can never allow that to happen. The plan must enclose the house in banks and screens of trees and shrubs, or at least create the feeling that the garden encloses the house. This does not necessarily mean that the house must be surrounded by a dense, impenetrable jungle. Rather the trees

and shrubs should be trained to prevent that happening. Enclosure does not need to imply isolation.

'Let all be revealed, but gradually' should be a rule observed by those who would make an old-fashioned garden. Even the smallest city garden open to view to every passer-by can have a sense of mystery by the simple fact of a shadowy tunnel of grape vines running down the side leading to who knows what? Where not even this is possible, a low hedge and some framing trees can cause people to stop and look over and through. So try to have something special to look at, say, an urn filled with silver-leaved plants, gay with annuals and plants with colourful leaves or green with ferns. Those who have larger gardens will be able to experiment with the same ideas but will also be able to make internal hedges, grow filigreed screens of shrubs and small trees, build garden walls with half-open doors or archways swagged with a curtain of ivy, or make paths that disappear around corners into deep shade or appear half-blocked by shrubs. Even if all that is out of sight is the neighbour's laundry, the curiosity aroused by unseen possibilities adds much to the enchantment of a garden.

TRAINING

Training trees and shrubs and climbers is perhaps the most critical part of creating an old-fashioned garden, for it requires consistent effort over a period of time. This is not so much to achieve any particular style of old garden but rather to make the plants themselves appear old and to create the feeling of enclosure without ending in a deadly tangle of badly overgrown plants. All too often people plant trees, shrubs and climbers and think that is all there is to making a garden. The plants are left to get on with growing and are never interfered with. People have been led into thinking that low-maintenance gardens are no-maintenance gardens. This is not so. Gardens must have gardeners, and the gardeners must know what effects they want to create with plants and set about achieving them. Trees, shrubs and climbers need to be trained and maintained; they cannot do it themselves, nor do they read landscape designs, garden plans or even the pretty pictures in glossy magazines.

How is this training done? It is done from the outset, from the moment the plant goes in the ground. Instead of planting a tree and watching it

A shallow reflecting pool built as part of a large rockery typical of a grand old-fashioned garden. The water reflecting the sky is the important feature here, so it is important that the plants do not overshadow the pool or that water plants do not cover the mirror surface.

grow for ten years before deciding that its branches are too low and have to be cut off, the tree is pruned carefully from the beginning so that such drastic tree surgery is not necessary. Many gardeners feel diffident about doing this, but it is not hard; it does take a little time and some energy, and you must know what it is your want the tree to do and what it is capable of doing.

What do you want a tree to do to give a garden an established feeling? Basically it should be tall and have a definite trunk, or trunks, and this is how it must be trained. To start, a stong, tall pole—a pole, not a tomato stake—is required. It must be firmly set in the ground at the time the young tree is planted. The training is simple enough, the side shoots of the tree must gradually be pruned off as the tree grows until the trunk has reached the desired height. The growing tree will look somewhat ungainly for several years and will need to be carefully tied to the supporting pole while it is a stripling, but it will quickly develop a good crown once it is tall and heavy pruning ceases. A good height of trunk to aim for is somewhere between two and three metres, more if the tree is naturally

ABOVE
A tunnel of interlaced trees trained and pruned to create an enclosed vista to a distant garden also provides summer shade.

RIGHT
A rustic archway weighed down with rambling roses frames an old cottage. The open gate bids us welcome.

LEFT
A chinoiserie gazebo sheltered by a grove of Japanese maples makes a complete picture in itself. The sunny aspect and the serene composition demand no further decoration.

LEFT, TOP
Traditional cottage-garden shrubs and flowers make up this garden; where cool-climate plants do not flourish, you can use plants from climates similar to that of your own region.

HOW A BOX STANDARD IS MADE

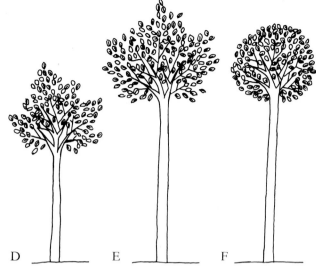

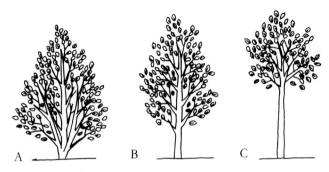

(A) Buy and plant an advanced size box tree.

(B) Trim unwanted side branches back to the bare stem.

(C) Trim the branches upward until a small head of top growth remains. Rub off new side shoots.

(D) During the second year of growth, repeat the process, keeping a small head of top growth.

(E) In the third year the box standard should reach a good height. Repeat the training program.

(F) Once new leaves of the head growth have hardened off (usually about midsummer), the plant can be given its first clipping and made into a finished standard box ball. Fertilise very six months and clip growth every year.

pendant, as, for example, the coloured-leaf forms of *Gleditsia triacanthos.*

This tough basic training is especially appropriate with the fashionable *Pyrus salicifolia* 'Pendula'—the weeping silver pear. It is by habit very sloppy, growing in all directions at once and quickly making a bird's nest of interlocking branches with no clear leading growth. Put to the stake and trimmed of side growths, it will make a handsome small tree. But it must have firm guidance from the gardener. Trees with clear trunks not only look mature; they also allow other 'layers' of shrubs, perennials and bulbs to be planted underneath, and this 'layered' appearance is another sign of an old-fashioned garden.

ACHIEVING THE LAYERED LOOK

Often shrubs can be made to appear well established by training them as multi-trunked small trees. Sometimes small trees can be treated the same way, though this method of training should not be used with conifers which make a strong central growth, because it would spoil their lovely pyramidal shape. In this case the young shrubs should also be pruned up so that other plants can find a home underneath; but instead of allowing only one stem to take the lead, several stems can be selected to make the framework of exposed mini-trunks that will create the impression of age. This method also works well with shrubs that are old and overgrown. I have

LEFT

A birdbath used as an eye-catcher is at the centre of a garden filled with interesting flowers. The abundant blooms next catch the attention and draw viewers into the design.

The simple lines of this pergola allow the wistaria vines to show off their sinuous branches and long chains of flowers.

used it successfully with firethorns (*Pyracantha* species), Butterfly bushes such as *Buddleia alternifolia, B. lindleyana* and *B. salvifolia,* and a variety of large *Cotoneaster* species. By carefully removing low growth and trimming out excess branches, the branch structure of the bush can be revealed, maintaining the screening effect without the dreary mass of leaves hiding everything.

As a rule, shrubs and small trees treated this way do not need staking. Once this has been done and the soil appropriately prepared, an understory of perennials and bulbs that enjoy light shade can be planted. A few light climbers such as *Clematis viticella* or *Maurandia barclayana* could be planted too.

CLIMBERS, NOT STRANGLERS

Climbers, particularly wistarias, also benefit from a strictly disciplined upbringing. How often do wistarias, once planted, threaten to take over whole rooftops, tear apart pergolas and smother fully grown trees! All for the want of a firm hand to start with. Having provided a climber with a structure to climb on, it is not enough to simply leave it to do its best. It will! And you will pay in hard work for letting it have its way.

Allow only one or two stems to reach skyward. Tie them to (but do not twine them around) the upright of the verandah or pergola, and when they reach the roof line (or other desired level) nip out the growing tip and allow the side shoots to spread. This alone will not be enough. Wistarias are wilful things and need harsh discipline to check their

This simple cottage garden is entirely appropriate to the house it surrounds. The addition of any more decorative features would risk its integrity and appeal.

Semicircular random stone steps lead down a path under a pergola to a pool. The garden has a lot of hard construction, but it is scarcely noticeable because of the dense planting.
RIGHT
By some happy accident this creeper has fallen across a path and its heavily laden trails block the passage. Enjoy the flowers while they last. Cut the creeper back when its blooms have faded.

determined ways. Left to their own devices at this tender stage they simply romp madly in all directions. No flowers, just metres and metres of long ropy growths that reach out relentlessly searching for something to get a stranglehold on. Each side shoot that is not needed to achieve coverage of the pergola (or to stretch along the verandah) must be cut back hard so that only two or three leaves remain on each tender young, branch. With any luck the plant will respond by growing short side shoots which will flower. However, the plant may also send out another crop of long, strong growth shoots; these need to be pruned hard once again. Eventually the plant will send out fewer growth shoots and more side shoots and then the work load is greatly lessened. Care

must still be taken to watch out for, and remove, any unwanted growths that may shoot away from the base of the vine or from within the crown of flowering side shoots. Trained this way, wistarias will become beautiful garden plants instead of the massive delinquents so often seen when they are left to grow waywardly.

If a standard wistaria is wanted, the same principles apply, but discipline has to be even more firmly applied. There must be only one trunk. It must be trained to an upright stance without twining and twisting around its supporting pole and the crown of short flowering growths must be kept short, short, short or the whole thing will become top-heavy and topple over. Strong new growths must be snipped back smartly or completely removed in order to maintain the required neat appearance of a standard. Well done, the results will be well worth the work involved.

INTRODUCING NEW OR UNUSUAL PLANTS

Unusual plants can add that touch of distinction that is often the hallmark of an old-fashioned garden. By this I do not mean the very latest gigantic Hawaiian hibiscus with startling neon-coloured flowers the size of meat plates; I mean plants that have character without being gaudy or grandiose. New plants like *Chrysanthemum pacificum* and *Dendromecon rigidum* are fine; they have attractive foliage, small flowers and neat habits;

others with lacklustre foliage, gross flowers and graceless habits should be firmly rejected. The ability to spot good plants comes with experience gained from garden visiting and talking to other keen gardeners and plant collectors. It is the kind of gardening confidence that enables a gardener to say 'This spot needs a clump of something grassy to set off all the broad-leaved plants. I'll get so-and-so from the nursery and see how it goes.' It is the same confident handling of plants that enables people to get away with a potful of succulents somewhere prominent when everyone else finds them all too unfashionably prickly or just plain weird. These planned touches are closely allied to the next secret of making old-fashioned gardens: happy accidents.

HAPPY ACCIDENTS AND SLIGHT IMPERFECTIONS

It takes practice to recognize happy accidents and a deal of self-control to allow them to remain. All old-fashioned gardens have some slight imperfections that add to the feeling of age they create; hedges may have a few bumps and lumps, lawns may be mossy, small flowers may have self-sown into gravelled paths, shrubs may almost block off a rarely used pathway, apples may lie

Plants in rich variety decorate this hillside shrubbery. Between the mounds of flowering bushes, small paths and dry-stone walls crisscross the garden, allowing close enjoyment of individual plants and providing a means of holding the soil.

This secret garden shelters within a cluster of large almost tree-sized shrubs. The floor of the garden is kept free of bushy growth so that carpets of rock plants can scramble in the sunlit paving. The bird bath will mean that songbirds come often to the garden.

LEFT

A small open space gives room for a special kind of garden, in this case a show of plants with silver and grey-blue foliage that revel in full exposure to the sun.

where the have fallen (at least for a while), daisies may spangle a lawn instead of being poisoned out of existence, rose bushes may grow into shrubs, flower profusely and set large crops of hips without being pruned to within an inch of their lives, a seedling pumpkin may climb into a plum tree, a vegetable (like an artichoke) or a culinary herb may make an appearance in a flower garden. Anything can happen when plants come up where they are not expected, or when plans go slightly awry. Instead of immediately setting out to right these small wrongs, take a step back and with half-closed eyes see the possibilities for creating an interesting garden picture that chance may have presented.

ABOVE
Golden filigree leaves and rough, dark bark give eye-pleasing delight even to non-gardeners.

ABOVE RIGHT
The dark silhouette of the pergola and the shadows cast by trees in the foreground focus attention on the garden beyond.

LEFT
Deep foreground shadows, a strong silhouette and a sunlit urn against a dark background establish the changing play of light and shade as a major theme in sunny gardens.

LET THERE BE LIGHT, AND SHADE

It is only in old-fashioned gardens that light and shade are an important element in creating an atmosphere which establishes the mood that we recognise as separating old gardens from those that are new and modern. Old trees, tall shrubs, climbers and lower-growing plants all work together to create the magic that is found in old gardens. The patterns of shade that are cast constantly change the appearance of an old garden. In bright sunlight the shadows are intensified and the sunlit spaces highlighted; dappled shade gives way to deeper, darker, cooler tunnels, while elsewhere stark shafts of hard sunshine spotlight flowery patches. The varied micro-climates that are created in an old-fashioned garden allow a greater variety of plants to be grown, and this in itself adds to the feeling. Long hours of sunlight are needed for many everyday flowers to succeed; but when shade is introduced, many more plants of distinction will flourish.

Large trees effectively enclose and define a garden space with a framework of low, sweeping branches. Selective thinning of the canopy gives enough light at ground level for hardy perennials and ground cover to flourish.

THE EBB AND FLOW OF SEASONS

Old-fashioned gardens change with the seasons. Unlike many modern gardens, they make no attempt to be pretty much the same year-round with maybe a slight change in a few areas produced by annuals in rotation: spring, primulas; summer, petunias; autumn, African marigolds; winter, pansies. In old-fashioned gardens the changes are much more marked; in fact, they are celebrated. Trees, shrubs, climbers, perennials, bulbs and annuals grow and flower and fade according to their season. There is always something in flower, something about to flower, something producing seed-heads or pods, and something to be planted, divided or trimmed. There is a season for everything in an old-fashioned garden.

GARDEN ORNAMENTS

To look old-fashioned, a garden does not need any particular hardware. The look can be achieved by plants alone, by the ways in which they are planted and grown together, by the variety of plants that are used and by the ways they are trained. In some gardens anything more would not ring true; garden furniture and other bits and pieces would be too fussy, too out of place, too decorative.

However, there is a very wide choice of garden ornament that may be suitable for old-fashioned gardens. A shopping list could include a glasshouse, conservatory, shade house, summerhouse, gazebo, tennis or pool pavilion, fountain, pond, formal pool, cascade, dovecote, sundial, swing seat, garden seats, urns, large Italian terracotta pots, sculptures, bronze cranes, Japanese lanterns, edging tiles, garden lamps, rustic furniture, wrought-iron archway, cast-iron furniture, pergola, well head, aviary, bird feeding table, tubs, hanging baskets, hooped garden edging and wire-work plant stands. The questions to be answered are 'Which ones are appropriate?' and 'How many is too many?' In small gardens especially, restraint must be the guiding rule. The term usually applied to overdone old-fashioned gardens is *gentrified*. This simply

means that what once may have been a
working-man's cottage has been developed with so
many decorative items that it has taken on many of
the outward signs of a gentleman's residence; it has
become middle-class. Begin with only one or two
simple decorative items, consider each new idea
very carefully, reject things that appear too ornate
for the style of your house and garden, make haste
slowly. Keep it simple.

SHOPPING FOR PLANTS

Thinking up new ideas for making gardens,
gathering planting schemes from gardens seen in
magazines and on your travels and working out
what works and doesn't work for you requires
above every other consideration that a good
selection of plants is available to put your ideas into
action. It is necessary, therefore, to develop a list of
nurseries and mail-order plant specialists who will
be able to provide the range of plants you need.
The number of plants in cultivation is enormous,
far too many for any one nursery to carry any more
than a tiny fraction of the total; so keep a file of lists
and catalogues that will help bring your plans to
life. When you see plants that interest you, find out
where they came from. If you want something in
particular, keep asking and writing until you find a
supplier; not every stock item is advertised in lists.
Always reject plants that are not well grown,
vigorous and healthy. Let your supplier know if
you are not satisfied.

Key guidelines. Spend as much on preparing the
hole as you do on buying the plant that goes in it.
Grow only the best varieties for your purposes. If
your ideas don't work out, try something else. If a
plant doesn't thrive get rid of it. Keep it simple.

An Emerging Style

With the information that is available it is possible
to imagine what a colonial garden was like. It was
usually small enough to be managed by one family;
it was formal and fairly simple in design in accord
with the time and money that could be spent on it;
it frequently made a significant contribution to the
food eaten by the owners and their family; its care
often took up much of their leisure time; and it was
planted partly with old favourite plants from the
northern hemisphere, but it was also likely to
contain many 'new' plants that were suited to the
warmer climatic conditions of the colonies.
Reflecting the influence of settlement and
colonialisation, many gardens were enclosed and
inward looking, protecting their owners and plants
alike from an unpredictable and sometimes harsh
environment. Within this framework the garden
contained a profusion of plants which, as
settlements prospered and colonial exploration and
trade expanded, grew ever more luxuriant and
diverse.

Let us now go into an imaginary old-fashioned
garden and explore it more fully.

2   The Front Garden

What more perfect old-fashioned front garden could be found than in John Glover's painting 'A View of the Artist's House and Garden, Mills Plains, Van Diemen's Land' (1835)? Overflowing with a marvellous array of flowers and shrubs, beamed on by a benevolent golden sun and serenely pastoral, it surely represents what we are all seeking when we make a garden. It has a strong sense of place, a settled and comfortable 'homey' feeling. It is prolific, abundant and productive—there is a large orchard of young fruit trees in the background and a glazed propagating frame just outside his studio door.

A Postcard from Arcadia

Keen-eyed observers will quickly realise that the many flowers shown could not have been flowering at one time; Glover had adopted the habit developed by the old Dutch flower painters of including flowers of different seasons in one picture. More than likely this was done partly to show off

what he had acclimatised in his Antipodean garden so remote from the civilised world, but it was also to suggest the Arcadian paradise in which he had made his home. As an established artist Glover had given up his glittering patrons and the urbane, artistic world of London to migrate with his grown-up family to the new colony of Van Diemen's Land. With a substantial fortune raised by

A View of the Artist's House and Garden, Mills Plains, Van Diemen's Land, *John Glover's painting of Patterdale, his property near Launceston, where he lived from 1832 to 1849.*

selling his collection of paintings, he went first to Hobart and then to Launceston, where he bought land and built a farmhouse and studio. He named his property Patterdale.

Unlike many other paintings of the period, Glover's does not attempt to rearrange the Australian landscape to imitate European conventions, nor does it show the landscape as an interesting, freakish collection of plants and landforms. It shows a settled, civilised and comfortable Arcadia in which the artist and his family obviously felt at ease and at home. In many ways the garden is the archetype of an old-fashioned colonial garden.

Close inspection of the painting, which exemplifies Glover's love of detail, reveals that the garden contained many favourite old-fashioned flowers: roses, hollyhocks, Madonna lilies, granny's

bonnets, broom, mulleins, geraniums, Chinese hibiscus, heather, rosemary, and laurestinus. Regretably the garden no longer exists; the house remains derelict and surrounded by rough pasture.

What can we learn from this most perfect front garden? Aside from the profusion of the planting, the use of favourite old flowers and the random scatter of flowering shrubs, perennials, bulbs and other plants, the most important lesson by far is the simplicity of the design.

The Garden Path

Glover's garden shows how effective a simple straight path can be in establishing the atmosphere of an old-fashioned garden. The sanded path runs straight and true to the front door, but its edges are so softened by the profusion of flowers that they are nowhere visible. It is most likely that the path was made from sand or fine gravel from a creek bed. Rolled with a heavy roller and possibly contained within an edging of sawn timber, it would have made a serviceable and long-lasting walking surface.

Making good paths is not so well understood as it once was; another of the arts of gardening that has largely been lost. Yet it is not so difficult that it cannot be tackled over a couple of weekends. Having chosen the site for the path, it is necessary to excavate it to a depth of 15 to 20 centimetres, with a deeper drainage channel along each side. Just how deep this needs to be will be determined by how much rain falls in your area and how quickly the soil absorbs the run-off from showers. The best paths have a camber, a slight curve that dips downward at each side of the path. Constructing this can be time consuming, but is worth the trouble, as it vastly improves drainage from the path. Old-timers made their paths on a foundation of coarse gravel, small rocks, broken bricks or coarse cinders. This was rolled carefully to preserve a surface camber and then covered with a layer of finer material such as coarse sand or crushed dolomite. Following a good dousing with a hose or sprinkler, or a good overnight shower, this layer was rolled and rolled until it was compacted and solid. Finally a surface layer was put in place. This could be gravel chippings or screenings, sand, shellgrit or fine pebbles, and it too would have to be rolled several times to make a smooth, stable surface.

After this careful construction, the path could be expected to last many years. The surface may need to be topped now and again, but the underneath layers should rarely need attention. The most arduous work will be to keep small weeds under control and to rake the surface to clean off leaves and keep it tidy. Many modern gardeners, and

probably earlier ones as well, prefer to let flowers self-sow in the verges of their paths. This adds to the charm of the garden, softens the hard edges and is sometimes the place where plants do best. Gardening in gravel brings many unexpected rewards—naturalised plants, attractive 'chance' flower combinations and a welcoming air of relaxed informality.

DEFINING THE EDGES

Sometimes the idea of a more formal point of arrival at the front door takes root in the gardener's mind. Without going overboard for full-scale formality, a degree of homely tidiness can be introduced along a pathway by defining the edges with an informal hedge of lavender, lavender cotton (*Santolina pectinata*) or even low-mounding perennials such as dianthus or thrift (*Armeria* sp.).

Where lavender is concerned, the choice is extremely wide; from the low, compact forms of Italian lavender (*Lavandula stoechas*) and English lavender (*L. angustifolia*) to the larger, denser forms of Mitcham lavender (*L. dentata* 'Allardii'), French lavender (*L. dentata*), woolly lavender (*L. lanata*) and named forms such as 'Seal' and 'Hidcote Giant'. Although all lavenders are comparatively easy to grow, my choice would be for Mitcham lavender or woolly lavender. The former is particularly robust, long-lived and tolerant of hard conditions; it also produces masses of heavily

ABOVE
Grey gravel and stone walls make a foil for a cottage garden mix of roses, hollyhocks, nasturtiums and pink oenotheras.
BELOW
Rock gardens are a feature of many old gardens, but the cultivation of alpine plants with which to adorn them is difficult in warm, dry climates.

ABOVE
Low plantings of pink oenotheras, coreopsis and roses allow the tree's branch structure to show against the sky while still drawing the eye along the drive to the house.

RIGHT
Where garden plants and the surrounding bushland merge, pavings and edges can be less formal. Low plants are used to soften the strong retaining wall.

OPPOSITE PAGE
Successful plant associations repeated and designed simply create a strong sense of style. Confident use of bold foliage forms and large plant masses render bright colours and striking features unnecessary.

ABOVE

A simple cottage garden path runs straight and true. Its sense of purpose is not lessened by the overgrowth of nearby plants.

BELOW

Where the area of paving is large, small planting holes should be left here and there so that low sprawling and mat-forming plants can be inserted to break up the harshness of the surface.

RIGHT

Random slate paving inset into smooth lawn makes an unusual and attractive side path in a garden of flowers. The design depends for its impact on being kept trim and smart.

BELOW

Brick edgings and large paving stones add just the right note of long-established sensibility.

perfumed bloom spikes which are ideal for picking and drying. The latter has broad silver leaves and dark purple flowers. These plants are naturally bushy and need little pruning to keep them as neat rounded, bumpy and lumpy informal hedges.

Such pruning as needs to be done is easily achieved by clipping over the bushes once the flowers begin to fade. In this case it is not necessary to clip the bushes to a uniform shape; some bushes will spread more than others, and others will grow taller. These differences can be used to advantage if small annuals such as alyssum or forget-me-nots are sown in front of the hedge, or if small scramblers such as the blue pea (*Lathyrus sativus*) or *Lathyrus niger* are sown behind and allowed to lightly trail over the hedge top.

All lavenders need sunny conditions and well-drained soils. The most drought-tolerant form of lavender is Italian lavender, which has become naturalised in my own countryside, an area that usually gets no rain for the three hottest months of the year. If this is your choice, then look out for *L. stoechas* 'Pedunculata'. Its flower spikes are topped with striking purple bracts that set it apart from others of its kind as distinctly more colourful.

My reason for not suggesting any other lavenders for making hedges is that I find their growth and habits to be less reliable when used in this way. Individual plants may give great pleasure in mixed borders, shrubberies and herb gardens, but there is little so dismaying to a gardener than a hedge that is patchy through parts failing to thrive or dying unexpectedly, such as some of these may do.

A RESUMÉ OF LAVENDERS

Lavandula angustifolia (English Lavender) Plain, almost needle-like leaves and neat spikes of purple flowers. The new leaves are silver-grey but gradually turn to grey-green as they mature. There are many variations and selected cultivars available from specialist nurseries. Dwarf varieties: 'Munstead' (purple), 'Dwarf White' and 'Rosea' (pink) are widely distributed. Small varieties: 'Hidcote' (purple), 'Twickel Purple'. Taller varieties: *L. angustifolia* 'Alba' (white).

Lavandula lanata (Woolly Lavender) Broad, plain leaves which are covered in a dense silver white felting. The small heads of dark purple flowers are carried well above the bush. This plant will not tolerate shaded growing conditions and needs well-drained soil.

LEFT

*A delightful hedge of Mitcham lavender (*Lavandula dentata 'Allardii'*) separates one part of a back garden from another with an archway over a path leading between the two. Just the place to dry the handkerchiefs.*

Lavandula stoechas (Italian Lavender) The plant is very widely known. The bushes are extremely hardy and have naturalised widely in warm, dry climates. Growth is compact and the foliage simple grey-green. The flower heads distinguish this lavender; a topknot of showy lilac or purple bracts surmounts each plump flower spike. One variety with exceptionally long bracts is especially attractive. It is *L. stoechas* 'Pedunculata'.

Lavandula viridis (Green Lavender) This is, strictly speaking, a very close relative of *Lavandula stoechas* as is shown by its also having a topknot of bracts on having each spike of flowers. In this case the whole flower, and the foliage, is apple green. The flowers still bear a strong lavender perfume.

A rough pathway of random stones and short grasses lined with hardy sub-shrubs such as lavender is all that is needed to transform out-of-the-way corners into links in a garden walk that join up more intensively gardened areas.

Lavandula dentata (French Lavender) This variety also has a topknot above each flowering spike, but it is easily distinguished by the slight toothed indentations on the margins of each silver-grey leaf. Overall the bush gives the impression of being more solidly built than many of the other kinds; it appears altogether larger and heavier in all its parts.

Lavandula dentata 'Allardii' (Mitcham Lavender) The largest growing lavender. When well grown, not necessarily with liberal watering and feeding, it can easily grow to more than 1.3 m tall and spread for 1.5 m or more. The foliage is large, broad, silver-grey and irregularly toothed (often about midway along each lead), and the flowers are held high on exceptionally long stems. The flower colour is a strong purple and the perfume is excellent.

ABOVE
More intensive styles of flower gardening call for more work but also give greater rewards in flowers for picking.

TOP
The hard edge of this brick path is softened by the thick overgrowth of flowers that have been encouraged to lean over it.

Lavandula pinnata A new lavender as far as cultivation in gardens goes but one worth seeking out, for it has some very special qualities that make it a good garden shrub. The foliage is much divided and almost ferny in appearance, and it is heavily felted silver-white. The perfume is of spicy cedar-wood rather than lavender, but it is still very pleasant to the nose. Needs very well-drained soil.

***Lavandula canariensis* (Canary Islands Lavender)** A handsome mound of ferny greenery, with aromatic foliage and small spikes of intensely dark purple flowers. Rather frost tender and needs well-drained soil.

Profusion, Diversity and Informality

Behind the lavender bushes, the garden should follow the example set by Glover's garden: repeated use of plants in the design, informality, and, above all, profusion. The list of flowers shows that the garden contained no great rarities or novelties, yet the appearance is rich, colourful and satisfying. The same effect can be obtained today by following the same ideas. Prolific use of plants is most important. No garden looks convincingly established if the use of plants has been skimped. So always plant close and use lots of plants to achieve that desired sensation of long-settled luxuriance. This is not the place to show off a few expensive special plants; save them for a spot where they can be lingered over and studied closely. This is the welcome home for masses of scented-leaf geraniums, mock orange, shrub roses, herby things—things to pluck, crush, rub and smell.

Keeping a garden informal, especially when it is a pair of borders either side of a pathway, takes a degree of careful planning to make sure that it does in fact come out looking casual. Unless you have an eye for this sort of thing, it is best to plan such a garden on paper, even if not to scale. By this means you can make certain that, while the plants used to make the garden may be repeated throughout the design, they are deployed in such a way that they do not become monotonous. Whether laying out the garden on paper or on the ground, you should watch that there are no obvious lines or rows. Plants may be set backward or forward of an imaginary line and shifted within that band so that spacing is not regular. Smaller plants, used to fill the spaces between the larger ones which informally define the boundaries of the garden, also may be repeated throughout the design or, in the case of small perennials, annuals and bulbs may be used in larger clumps to carpet the ground.

ABOVE

A brilliant mix of annuals, perennials, shrubs and trees.

TOP

What a welcoming garden this is. Massed plants jostle cheerfully beside a neat pathway that offers many interesting flowery incidents along its way.

ABOVE

A woodland walk meandering among flowering shrubs and trees provides a 'wilderness' of apparently naturalised plants to enjoy. The flowering season has been extended by planting a carpet of bulbs under the larger plants.

ABOVE
The layered look creates visual interest at different levels.
TOP
This old urn has been thoughtfully planted so that its curving shape is not hidden by the plants in the background.
LEFT
A variety of foliage forms create a satisfying picture in green.
OPPOSITE PAGE
A colourful border of perennials and shrubby plants occupies a long, narrow space.

The weeping elm, the curving border of low dianthus plants and the curving grass walk combine to lead the viewer of this garden to walk on around the corner.

MORE ELABORATE PATTERNS

As a result of changes in fashion, the simple straight pathway to the front door typical of early colonial gardens was gradually transformed, by a series of simple variations based on plain geometric shapes, into something more elaborate. Surviving nineteenth-century gardens and plans published by John Loudon (*The Suburban Gardener and Villa Companion*), J. Shirley Hibberd (*Rustic Adornment for Homes of Taste*) and others show how the transformation took place. Essentially these 'improved' designs added extra beds to the garden. These might take a central position in the overall plan of a front garden, in which case the path had to skirt around them before reuniting before the front door, or they might be paired at either side of the central path. In larger gardens there might be repeated patterns of circles, squares or lozenges (i.e., diamond shaped).

To make these designs more apparent, the way they were planted became more formal. Plants were selected, trimmed and trained to conform with an overall design that increasingly had less and less to do with their natural habits and associations. By the end of the nineteenth-century the whole idea was out of control and running wildly into three-dimensional garden beds that were built of chicken wire and compost and stuffed with all manner of small, colourful plants in order to replicate Imperial Crowns, gigantic wine bottles and goblets, and other fantastic constructions. What started out simply as a means of creating a sense of arrival ended up so confused and stressed that a good design idea was almost lost for ever. Eventually the elaborate fashion collapsed and was swept aside.

Survivors from Old Front Gardens

The most prominent features surviving in front gardens from the nineteenth century are the palms

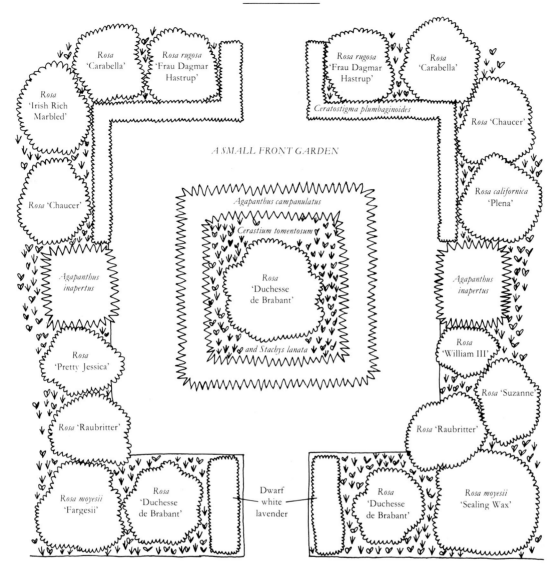

Rosa 'Carabella'

Rosa rugosa 'Frau Dagmar Hastrup'

Rosa rugosa 'Frau Dagmar Hastrup'

Rosa 'Carabella'

Rosa 'Irish Rich Marbled'

Ceratostigma plumbaginoides

Rosa 'Chaucer'

A SMALL FRONT GARDEN

Rosa 'Chaucer'

Agapanthus campanulatus

Rosa californica 'Plena'

Cerastium tomentosum

Agapanthus inapertus

Rosa 'Duchesse de Brabant'

Agapanthus inapertus

Rosa 'William III'

and Stachys lanata

Rosa 'Pretty Jessica'

Rosa 'Suzanne'

Rosa 'Raubritter'

Rosa 'Raubritter'

Rosa moyesii 'Fargesii'

Rosa 'Duchesse de Brabant'

Dwarf white lavender

Rosa 'Duchesse de Brabant'

Rosa moyesii 'Sealing Wax'

and conifers that were frequently the central forms of their designs. Whether in paired beds or in centrally placed isolation, *Livistona australis* (cabbage tree palm), *Roystonea regia* (royal palm), *Phoenix canariensis* (Phoenix palm) and even the date palm or assorted araucarias (Norfolk Island pines) or monkey-puzzle trees formed the centrepieces of relatively formal planting schemes; less frequently other conspicuous trees were used, camellias, dragon trees (*Dracaena* spp.) and wine palms (*Jubea spectabilis*) being quite popular. In favourable areas, rhododendrons might be preferred, while pomegranates were a favourite in warm, drier areas.

No doubt you will have heard horror stories of the expense of removing some of these overgrown monsters from present-day gardens. And not even for the sake of purity would I urge you to plant them today in any but the largest gardens. However, there are a small group of palm-like plants which make authentic and acceptable centrepieces—the cycads. These grow very slowly, have lovely palmy foliage and were favoured by colonials and their English cousins as tender pot

This small front garden has an emphasis on roses. A garden such as this will need plenty of sunshine—at least four to five hours each day to keep the roses healthy and blooming well. The roses are a mixture of old European roses, wild roses, shrub roses and modern David Austin hybrids. They are readily available from many good garden centres and specialist nurseries. Nearest the house a narrow border of bright blue Ceratostigma plumbaginoides *begins and ends with a clump of darkest blue* Agapanthus inapertus, *while low-growing roses 'William III' and 'Raubritter' merge with carpets of snow-in-summer (*Cerastium tomentosum*) and lamb's tongues (*Stachys lanata*) in the foreground plantings. A low hedge of dwarf white lavender leads into the garden, and the central bed is rimmed with the pale blue miniature* Agapanthus campanulatus. *Roses are heavy feeders, so a good dressing of stable litter and pelletised manure should be applied in early spring. The roots of the agapanthus will need to be 'pruned' yearly to keep them from competing too strongly with the roses and smaller plants. It is a simple matter to chop them spade deep at the edge of their leaf spread. For an inner-city garden the background to this design would ideally be trellis work 2 m tall on two sides with a picket fence on the street front.*

Really old flowering shrubs can make spectacular displays that bespeak old-fashioned style.

OPPOSITE PAGE
Banks of hydrangeas under established trees give welcome colour at Christmas.

plants. We know now that cycads, like camellias, do not need cosseting in shade houses. They can be purchased (and they are quite expensive) and planted with confidence, for they will grow slowly and stay a convenient size for very many years.

Older rhododendrons and camellias, genuine survivors since the 1880s, can still be found in considerable numbers. By consulting any specialist nursery you should be able to obtain some suited to your needs. Some distinction does need to be made between rhododendrons and azaleas, which were frequently listed as separate entries in catalogues and journals. Rhododendrons were generally regarded as large-leaved, large evergreen shrubs which were generally limited to the 'hill stations' of colonial society such as Mount Wilson (NSW),

Mount Macedon (Vic.) and Mount Lofty (SA). Really tough forms such as *Rhododendron ponticum* and its many variants were also tried with some success in favoured suburban locations in Melbourne and Sydney. Azaleas, by and large, were of the *indica* group—low shrubs, semi-deciduous and prodigious bloomers. Being low growers, they could more easily be found in places of shelter in suburban gardens than rhododendrons; thus they were widely cultivated in suburban gardens where soil conditions were acidic.

Following the Form

If you accept my argument that nineteenth-century gardeners enthusiastically cultivated the latest improvements, you may possibly feel you are not obliged to use only plants from the period. Before dashing off to indulge in a careless spend-up on the latest novelties, I should strongly recommend that you consider the form of the particular flower before you buy. This applies particularly to camellias and roses, which will be dealt with more thoroughly in later chapters. These two have been changed considerably by recent breeding developments. Camellias have become much bigger and more open, particularly those bred in California and those bred from *C. reticulata*. These modern blooms would be quite out of sympathy with the feeling I would be trying to re-create in my old-fashioned period garden, but you must make your own choice.

Other recent developments in the camellia world, however, might be considered very attractive inclusions in a garden restoration. I had a pair of *C. lutchuensis* grafted on 1.5 m standards; their weeping bronzy green foliage and masses of tiny white perfumed flowers seemed to be just right. *C. salicifolia* is very similar and would do just as well. *C.* 'Tiny Princess', with pale pink semi-double boutonnières, can also be treated as a standard most successfully. Less well suited, though more freely available, would be *C. rosaeflora*. The growth is too open and foliage too sparse for my liking, however—it doesn't look comfortable enough for the period. The reticulate camellia 'Captain Rawes' was known in nineteenth-century times, but it was a great rarity and regarded solely as a cool shade-house resident, or as a large tub plant; I would suggest the inclusion of this type be limited to similar usage in restoration projects.

After all these warnings, don't be put off. There are still hundreds to choose from among the *japonica* group: reds, pinks, whites, flakes, particoloured, formal, informal, semi-double or single; our grandparents had them all. Their preference was for the formal double, but many others were available. The choice is yours.

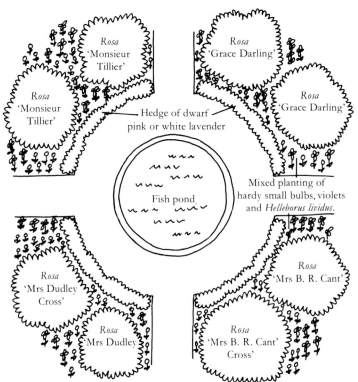

Rosa 'Monsieur Tillier'

Rosa 'Monsieur Tillier'

Rosa 'Grace Darling'

Rosa 'Grace Darling'

Hedge of dwarf pink or white lavender

Fish pond

Mixed planting of hardy small bulbs, violets and *Helleborus lividus*.

Rosa 'Mrs Dudley Cross'

Rosa 'Mrs Dudley Cross'

Rosa 'Mrs B. R. Cant'

Rosa 'Mrs B. R. Cant' Cross'

A BOWER OF TEA ROSES AROUND A RAISED FISH POND

Tea roses in pairs surround a small, raised fish pond of very simple design. A wide coping around the edge of the pond provides a place to sit comfortably to feed and watch goldfish and to enjoy the bower of tall old roses which enclose the garden. Pairs of roses will give plenty of buds and flowers for picking. Pruned to grow high on strong branches and allowed to spread, each pair could interlock and make a wall of foliage around the garden. The central rondel of low dwarf lavender in white or pink would be an added delight. The roses are underplanted with a rich variety of small plants. The outer edges of the garden are planted with taller plants with scented foliage.

The Rose—The Queen of Flowers

In summer gardens and where soil and water were suited, roses were the most popular choice. Of all flowers beloved of nineteenth-century gardeners, the rose was surely the best loved. Even today we still hark back to the old roses for standards of perfume, charm and cosy homeliness. In our mind's eye we see that queen of flowers, the *Rosa perfecta*; an elegantly plump bud adorned with a neatly turned plume of calyx tips which opens to display a rich pink flower tightly packed with hundreds of perfect petals. Layer upon layer will turn back until the fully developed bloom shows us the full beauty of its quartered centre. Nothing but Queen Victoria herself could be more reminiscent of the age.

We are indeed very lucky to have a large selection of nineteenth-century roses still available today. They have not always been so, for they fell

from grace in the 1920s and were rudely spurned by most rosarians and garden writers of the time. The rapid rise in popularity of the perpetually blooming hybrid teas swept all other roses aside. In a few gardens, however, the older beauties were still loved and kept going.

Even way back then, enthusiasts were busy collecting old roses from cottage gardens, churchyards and laneways, a pursuit stil popular today. Through Ireland, France and the countryside of England and eastern America, intrepid lady gardeners traversed the lanes and byways ever alert for a glimpse of some ancient rosy treasure. Lovingly transplanted and shared around, they have come down to us today—a profusion of moss roses, gallicas, albas, centifolias, damasks, burnets and roses of Provence. I rather doubt the accuracy of many of the names they now bear, suspecting that they have been assigned by a process of comparison with illustrations in old books and from the brief descriptions in old nursery lists. Nevertheless, both the roses and the names are full of the romance of a more gracious age, and their appeal is not lessened by the academic nomenclature arguments tossed around in rose journals by old-rose buffs.

Early in the history of the colonies these old rose familiars from the homelands were brought here in great numbers for sale, being listed simply under headings such as: 'Moss roses—assorted colours; Damasks, Albas, etc. ditto.' Intending purchasers were usually invited to specify colour preferences or to leave the selection up to the nursery's skilled staff.

After the 1860s, catalogues began to list larger and larger selections of the new classes of roses bred from new introductions from China. Boursaults, hybrid perpetuals and teas were the main groups that caught the eyes of the gardening enthusiasts. The main attractions of these new classes of roses were the vastly increased colour range, which for the first time included shades of flame, orange and coral, and the repeat-blooming habit of some cultivars.

The old European varieties, by and large, made rather compact thickets from one to two metres in height (e.g., gallicas, Burnets) or taller open shrubs (damasks and centifolias) which could be planted in hedge-like banks or as specimen flowering shrubs. Often plants were grown as standards or half-standards, but as they were comparatively expensive, it is unlikely they were much used in cottage gardens unless the owner was able to do the budding. The new introductions, Bourbons, hybrid perpetuals, etc., were more like modern roses in their growth patterns and habits. The significant difference was that many of the older roses had long willowy canes, where the roses of today have a more compact, erect habit.

This difference meant that the old roses could be grown in a variety of ways which would have given gardens an appearance quite foreign to modern rosarians. The long flexible canes could be trained around posts to make pillar roses; they could be spread low and tied down to pegs—a procedure known as pegging down; or the long canes could be interwoven to create a series of loops. The object of these various treatments was to produce flowering stems from most of the dormant buds along the canes. Of course, many roses were grown as regular bushes and standards too. (For more about roses, see chapter 8.)

A PLEASAUNCE OF WILD ROSES

In medieval times, pleasure gardens were made using plants taken from their natural habitats and transplanted to the garden of castle and manor house. Wild roses, violets, periwinkles, primroses, cowslips and other wild flowers were used to make gardens of delight. This idea is translated here into a smaller, more intimate version of an orchard garden. Tall, arching wild roses take the place of trees, and underneath a carpet of a thousand flowers can be made. The roses could be in shades of pink and rose as shown, or for a change, a garden of wild yellow roses could be made. Increase the rustic quality of the garden by introducing decorative grasses and herbs, or by adding a variety of small bulbs. Strengthen the definition of each bed with low hedges of lavender, dwarf berberis or dianthus; the paving could also be changed from grass to gravel, cobblestones bordered with bricks or cut paving stone. The size of such a garden would need to be approximately 6 m square to allow room for the roses to grow high, wide and handsome.

ABOVE

Rosa x *'Micrugosa'* is a low, dense shrub liberally sprinkled with rosy pink blooms over a long season.

TOP

Many shrub roses can be used to make flowering hedges in sunny side gardens. Trained along wires, they can be especially useful in screening ugly fences or the groundworks of tennis courts.

ABOVE LEFT

Roses make their best contribution to a garden when planted in groups of associated colours, or when individual blooms can be seen close up and smelled.

LEFT

Some modern roses, such as 'Duet', are prolific bloomers and suitable for old-fashioned gardens.

FAR LEFT

Tall and arching or low and spreading, old roses blend well with the complimentary colours of perennials and annuals and with silver foliage such as iris and Stachys lanata.

Front-Garden Favourites

Besides roses and rhododendrons, the front garden was frequently populated with a wide selection of flowering shrubs, perennials, bulbs and annuals. Whether displayed in the packed profusion of a simple cottage garden or in the more formal setting of a villa garden, the planting was usually more varied in foliage, colour and mixture than is usual today. Planted with the shrubs could be found datura, in white, rosy orange and lilac; and fuchsia, especially the shrubby species such as *Fuchsia magellanica*, *F. arborescens*, *F. cordifolia*, *F. boliviana*, *F. corymbiflora alba* and the new hybrids such as 'Erecta Novelty', 'Swanley Gem' and 'Swanley Orange'. Lilacs were also extremely popular, with many new hybrids appearing towards the end of the century; by and large the same cultivars are the mainstream varieties today. Deutzia, philadelphus, buddleia and sambucus were also popular choices for interplanting.

Around these shrubs were planted an assortment of hardy perennials, bulbs, annuals and sub-shrubs. In cottage gardens these could have been planted higgledy-piggledy or in very simple regular arrangements such as ribbon planting or block planting. In the latter two the plants, all of a kind, were planted out in lines or blocks in a manner still seen in some public parks and gardens (see chapter 13). In villa gardens the style of planting generally leant towards the more formal; perhaps a reflection of the current fashion for the Italianate, which was made popular by Victoria and Albert at Osborne.

When it comes to choosing from the annuals available today to plant out in a reconstructed colonial garden, there is little point in trying to buy the varieties known in the age of Queen Victoria, for almost certainly few named strains have survived. There is, however, ample evidence from old seed lists that there were many parallels with the seed lines available today in the old plant families. In petunias, for instance, there were double, frilled, pendant, brush-throated and colour strains just as there are today. Dianthus and picotees are a little more difficult, and the perennial sorts will have to be sought from specialist nurseries dealing in cottage plants and herbs. The annual picotees can usually be bought from nursery outlets and seedsmen. You will not be able to get the old named seed strains such as 'Crimson Belle', 'Mourning Cloak' or 'Pheasant Eye', but you will be able to get modern equivalents of these frilled, laced, eyed and deeply cut flowers. It is more than anything else a matter of keeping your eyes open and getting slips, seeds, etc. of whatever plants meet these descriptions as you visit the gardens of friends and strangers.

Other popular flowers were sweet william, wallflowers, clarkias, godetias and sweet peas, which were all available in separate colour strains. Of these, only sweet peas can still be had in separate strains, such as the 'Gawler' strains originated by the Harkness family of South Australia. China asters were also much favoured. Varieties such as 'Betteridge's Quilled', 'Boltze's Dwarf Bouquet' and 'Truffaut's Paeony-flowered Perfection (Improved)' were popular in the 1880s. Today's gardeners would be lucky to find more than one strain available. You must look to the big overseas seed houses if you wish to improve your selection.

Zinnias with names such as 'Tom Thumb', 'Double Striped', 'Dwarf Double' and 'Zebra Zinnias' tell us that colonial gardeners used a more varied range of forms than are usual today, though the smaller *Zinnia linearis* and 'Mexicana' strains would make likely substitutes.

FANCY FLORISTRY

One particular group of flowers was classed by gardeners of the 1800s as 'florists' flowers' (see also chapter 5). These were grown for display in cool glasshouses. Such flowers are still to be seen in spring and early summer in some public gardens. Among the most popular plants for these purposes were cinerarias, primulas, mimulus, gloxinias, cyclamen and calceolarias. Although amateurs no doubt included some of the hardiest of these in their gardens, they were largely the province of professional gardeners and therefore not really fitted to cottage gardens.

One florists' flower was universally popular with exhibitors, professional gardeners and cottage folk alike; it was the pansy. The enthusiastic colonial gardener could select from a treasure chest of superlative strains: 'Bugnot's Superb Blotched Exhibition', 'Non Plus Ultra', 'Giant Trimardeau', 'King of Blacks', 'Cardinal', 'Gold Lace' and 'Silver Edge', to name but a few. Happily, pansies seem to be making something of a comeback, especially the tufted violets (now called violas), where you can find 'Bowles Black', 'Maggie Mott', 'Prince Henry', 'Prince John', 'Blue Gem', 'Chantryland' and the modern 'Space Crystals' strain in yellow, blue, white and apricot. The bigger pansies, too, are enjoying a vogue, with at least half a dozen different sorts to choose from at many nurseries. It is hardly of great import, but nonetheless interesting, to ponder whether or not the present 'Butterfly' (or 'Papillon') strain is a descendant of 'Bugnot's Super Blotched Exhibition' or 'Cassier's Very Large Flowered Blotched' or some similar form.

BULBS AND ALMOST BULBS

Bulbs, too, played their part in making the show which colonial gardeners were so keen to see. They were especially valued for their hardiness in the drier areas, and everywhere much admired. This was especially true for bulbs from the Cape of Good Hope. Babianas, ixias, sparaxis, tritonias, watsonias, freesias, belladonnas, nerines and veltheimias were regarded in the Old World as tender subjects, yet in the Antipodes they grew perfectly well outside, multiplying and flowering with a freedom unknown in the Old World. Even such rarities as elephant's tongue (*Haemanthus*) and the cartwheel lily (*Brunsvigia josephinae*) could be grown to perfection outside.

Other much loved South Africans were the agapanthus, which came in several shades of blue and white as well as a silver variegated form and a gold variegated form (now very rare). There were also dwarf forms, a double blue, a pinkish form and a deep blue deciduous form. Naturally these were all blessed with Latin names, but great is the confusion of them, so I won't add to it. Nonetheless, most are still to be had if you look for them; the double blue seems to be the rarest.

Cliveas and strelitzias were other popular South African 'almost bulbs' which were well known to colonial gardeners. In those days, cliveas were called *Imantophyllum*, and a rare cream form and one with cream margins around the leaves were known to enthusiasts, as well as the well-known apricot and orange forms. The cream form is now becoming more widely available.

A beautiful bulb not often seen these days is *Galtonia candicans*—the summer hyacinth. In the 1860s it was recommended to gardeners then for its 'elegant, pure white, bell-shaped flowers'. It is perfectly hardy and easy to multiply from seed.

One last South African family of bulbs must be mentioned—the gladiolus tribe, a wide and varied group very different in the nineteenth century from the tall spikes of symmetrical ruffled flowers we know today. Among the varieties in trade in the last century are a few that can still be found today, though you are more likely to find them growing naturalised along the roadside than in the catalogues of gladiolus specialists. Some are very colourful, others curious, but all are hardy; they include *Gladiolus byzantinus* (bright purple), *G. colvillii* (lavender), *G. colvillii rubra* (brilliant red), *G. colvillii* 'The Bride' (pure white), *G. tristis* (greenish) and *G. undulatus* (spidery green).

South America was represented by jockey's caps (*Tigridia* spp.) in brilliant colours, sacred lily of the Incas (*Ismene festalis*), the brilliant blue walking iris (*Neomarica*); and from Mexico came the dahlia— already highly developed in the nineteenth century, firstly by the French and then by the British.

Bulbous treasures poured out of Chinese, Indian and Japanese ports, sealed in barrels of moss or sawdust for the long voyages to England or Australia. The choice is hardly any greater now than it was in the 1890s, when gardeners could choose *Lilium auratum*, *L. tigrinum* and its double form, *L. lancifolium rubrum* and *album* (now *L. speciosum*), as well as lesser things such as irises, *Funkia* (syn. *Hosta*) and *Hemerocallis*. An earlier introduction from India was the canna, which had been extensively hybridised in Europe—to the stage where catalogues in faraway Australia could boast in excess of forty named sorts. Customers were advised that 'fine colour plates of these [cannas] could be seen on application'.

European bulbs were immensely popular, and some would seem highly desirable now, for example, the range of double hyacinths—black, dark blue, porcelain blue, scarlet, pink, rose, red, white and yellow—all available as named varieties. Tulips could be had in variety, in 'Single Early', 'Early Doubles', 'Show' ('Byblomen', 'Bizarre' and 'Rembrandt', all striped groups) and 'Parrot' classes. In 1889, prices in C.F. Newman and Sons' catalogue were all four shillings per dozen for named sorts, or 2/6 per dozen mixed.

The Madonna lily (*Lilium candidum*), the very essence of a cottage garden ('Where else would they grow?' was the oft-heard wail of gardeners of the upper classes), is still essential today. You may be lucky to find them in a neighbourhood garden or growing wild, especially in the old goldmining districts, or you can raise them easily from seed. Try the Salonika form or the 'Cascade' strain. Solomon's seal (*Polygonatum vulgaris*) was a popular root for planting in shady areas, while tuberoses, Jacobean lily (*Sprekelia formosissima*) and vallota lily (*Vallota speciosa*) were popular for sunny spots. The unusual pineapple lily (*Eucomis punctata*) found a favoured spot in many gardens and also made a hardy tub plant. In cooler areas, snowdrops and snowflakes were sentimental favourites too, along with lily-of-the-valley and crocus.

During the middle and later years of the nineteenth century, the daffodil underwent profound changes in the hands of English, Irish and Scottish breeders, and many hundreds of new hybrids were introduced to a receptive and enthusiastic gardening public. A number of readers will no doubt know of places where many sorts of older daffodils can be found naturalised. Collecting bulbs to take home to include in your new re-creation will be easy, but identifying many of them will prove most frustrating—but don't let that put you off an attractive bloom. Jonquils, too, are a very confused group when it comes to names but are certainly a necessary inclusion in any nineteenth-century garden. Among the available jonquils and tazettas (larger and later than the

ABOVE
Spires make a nice change from the more common rounded dome shapes of many plants.

TOP
A cluster of daisy bushes seems to dictate the form of the path in this garden.

RIGHT
Massed roses of all kinds announce that here is the home of a garden lover.

OPPOSITE PAGE
A neat stone path gives access to a wide garden bed, enabling flowers to be picked and needful tasks attended to.

former) are 'Double Roman', 'Paper white', 'Soleil d'Or', 'Geranium' (white and red), 'Xerxes' (yellow and red), 'Pleiades' (white and yellow) and 'Silver Chimes' (pure white)—not all genuinely old but every one of them with an air and scent which is purely cottage garden (see chapter 12). The main daffodil groups were the large trumpets (Ajax group) of which the double yellow 'Van Sion', 'Bicolor' and the Tenby daffodil may still be had; the medium trumpet group (Leedsii and Incomparabilis groups) with many old doubles such as 'Butter and Eggs', 'Codlins and Cream' and 'Eggs and Bacon', and the small trumpet (Poeticus) group with a host of similar and confusing starry-flowered forms still to be found growing in many old gardens.

PERENNIALS GALORE

The other important contributors to the floral tapestry which made up the cottage garden were the perennial plants. So great was their number and such their variety that one hardly knows where to begin. Some have already been listed (agapanthus, hostas, cliveas, etc.), but there were hundreds of other hardy plants to choose from. Picture in your mind's eye a cottage flower border. Beginning at the back, some perennial favourites were red-hot pokers (then *Tritomas*, now *Kniphofia*), *Wachendorfia thrysiflorus* (an elegant South African with pleated leaves and tall spikes of rich yellow flowers); *Dietes*, the butterfly iris (*D. bicolor*, yellow and brown, and *D. iridoides*, white and blue), and Lord Howe Island wedding iris (*D. robinsoniana*, pure white and now rare in cultivation) and the ever popular calla lilies in white, yellow and rose pink. Less common now, but featured in many late nineteenth-century catalogues, were *Baptisia* (wild indigo), lavender shower (*Thalictrum*) and ornamental grasses such as the zebra grass (*Miscanthus japonica* 'Zebrina'). For a touch of tropical luxury, unknown in the frosty homelands, tender things such as *Alpinia* (shell ginger) and *Hedychium* were available to colonial gardeners; provided frost-free situations and adequate water supplies were given, these added a richness of foliage and perfume unseen in European gardens.

In the middle of our imaginary herbaceous border of cottagy things were such well-loved favourites as peonies, asters, shasta daisies, day lilies, balloon flowers (*Platycodon*), all members of the iris family (from Spurias to Siberians, Japanese, German, Dutch, English and Spanish), as well as less common things such as hostas, globe thistle (*Echinops*), *Artemisia gnaphaloides*, *Salvia leucantha*, *S. guaranitica*, *S. uliginosa* and *S. grahamii*. Granny's bonnets (*Aquilegia*) fitted in the middle ranks too, in shades of rosy-mauve, deep pink, pale pink, dark

maroons, purple and white. There were also double forms and a maroon and green form called 'Nora Barlow'. They can still be found today, although being a promiscuous lot, they give very mixed seedlings. In a cottage garden, of course, that is just the effect being striven for.

The front of this marvellous, ever-blooming border-of-the-mind can be packed with a myriad of colourful delights. Alongside the pansies, picotees, violas, bulbs, etc., already mentioned, we will have to poke in just a few cranesbills (*Geranium sanguineum*, *G. magnificum*, *G. wallichianum* or others), some alliums (*Allium moly*, *A. sicculum*, *A. sphaerocephalum*, *A. albopilosum*, to name a few), the very beautiful *Tovara virginiana*, with leaves brilliantly marked with a rusty red chevron, and maybe some campanulas such as *Campanula betulifolia*, *C. vidalii* and *C. muralis*.

This small sample demonstrates the immense variety of perennials that were available to gardeners by the end of last century. It was the variety and the profusion with which they were used that created the special effects, so well loved, of gaiety and abundance in cottage and villa gardens.

TEN NEW PERENNIALS YOU SHOULD KNOW ABOUT

Trillium chloracanthum   Large shamrock leaves top a solid stem about 50 cm tall. From the centre of each leaf cluster springs an almost white flower made of three narrow petals. Rather unusual and quietly becoming for a cool, shady spot. The plant slowly increases by short suckers from the thick tuberous roots. *T. sessile* is similar but has dark reddish flowers and the foliage is stained with the same colour.

Polygonatum hookeri   A dwarf Solomon's Seal with pale blue bells instead of the usual white. It grows to about 10 cm but colonises well and makes a good ground cover in a damp, shady spot. It is very hardy but because of its diminutive size can easily get swamped by more vigorous plants.

Hosta sieboldiana 'Elegans'   Despite all the hostas now coming onto the market, this oldie can still deliver the goods when it comes to vigour and its ability to keep looking good all through the summer. It makes very large leaves, broad and tapering to a point, each one puckered like seersucker and covered with a dense silver-blue meal. Established clumps will easily cover a square metre or more. Plants need good water supplies while the new leaves are growing, but after that less is required. Dappled shade will protect the leaves from sun scorch. Keep plants away from the competing root systems of large trees.

Crambe cordifolia A monster of the cabbage family that has finally arrived in nurseries following the craze for English flower gardens. Even without adopting the Anglophile trend, you can enjoy an amazing floral performance from this plant. Large dark green leaves, long and roughly toothed like those of horseradish, come up annually and in a few years from planting support a soaring candelabrum of flowering branches. Individual flowers are small, white and sweetly scented; massed over the framework of the 2 m flower spike they are a spectacular flight of butterflies. A sunny position is needed.

Salvia munzii This is one of the sagebrushes of California. The lavender-like foliage is strongly perfumed with a heady, spicy fragrance. Flower spikes of intense deep blue appear in midsummer. My trials show this plant to be exceptionally drought tolerant. It has the potential to be used as a hedge in a manner similar to lavender or rosemary.

Salvia spathacaea Another Californian sage, this one forms a low spreading shrublet with bright acid-green arrowhead-shaped leaves. From spring onwards blunt thick spikes develop which carry deep red blooms and bracts. Scrambling down banks or over rockwork, this plant would look at home and has the constitution to thrive in difficult sunny situations.

Salvia canariensis This large soft-wooded shrub from the Canary Islands is not yet used widely enough in our gardens. It easily grows to two metres tall and spreads just as wide. Very large sagitate leaves (shaped like arrowheads) are covered in a thick silver 'fur'. At midsummer large terminal flower heads appear. These have bracts and flowers coloured in rosy-purple tones and lilac—a mixture of desert sunset shades. The bracts remain long after the flowers have fallen, keeping the colour going for months. In my experience the plant responds well to very hard pruning in late winter. Cut almost to the ground, it quickly puts out fresh new growth. It thrives in a sunny position in gravelly dry soil.

Phlomis russelliana An old-fashioned perennial which for some reason has never taken off with gardeners, maybe because they were dazzled by delphiniums, dahlias and other whizz-bang performers. Its time has now come. Large felted heart-shaped leaves make a dense gound-covering mound from which emerges 1 m tall spires with whorls of soft yellow hooded flowers. Tolerant of dry conditions in sun or light shade.

Phlomis italica A Mediterranean sub-shrub with running stems that thread their way sparsely through other plants. The stems and narrow leaves are covered with a silver felt. During late spring, summer and autumn, whorls of hooded lavender-pink flowers appear on spikes that reach 50 cm tall. Although it is modestly invasive, it never becomes a pest and can be easily controlled, if needed, by pulling up unwanted suckers. It will grow in light shade or sun and can prosper in dry sites.

***Phygelius aequalis* (Yellow Trumpet)** This is a colour variation on the better-known Cape figwort, which has smoky red tubular flowers. In this case the flowers are a soft creamy yellow. The shrubby growth is well covered in glossy leaves, and the sprays of flowers which appear at the top of each stem will stand up to 1 m tall. The plant flowers in summer, autumn and early winter. It can be cut hard and will grow in full sun or a little shade. It makes a few runners at just below the surface of the soil and by these means can be easily propagated.

About Hedges

A piece of garden outside my study window is set within a simple framework of straight paths. Each plot is planted informally with a mixture of shrub roses, herbs, plants with scented leaves, bulbs, perennials, climbers and self-sowing annuals. In spring it is gay with flowers; in summer it is coolly coloured with shades of green; in autumn there are more flowers along with seed pods, rose hips and grasses. But in winter it is dull, dull, dull. After I have cleaned away the growth of dead and dying flowers and done such pruning as is needed, the sight from my window is, for three months, boring. To answer this I settled on some pieces of formal hedging to give the garden a stronger form throughout the year and especially in winter.

I chose box for the purpose. Plain box (*Buxus sempervirens*) seemed the best choice. It is hardy, compact and easy to get cheaply in quantity. There are other kinds, dwarf box (*B. sempervirens* var. *suffruticosa*) and Korean box (*B. microphylla* var. *koreana*) among them. Dwarf box is very small, low and compact; it is also very, very slow and intolerant of hot, dry conditions. The Korean box is large and spreading, so that keeping it in good shape requires extra trimming. They have their places, but not here. Nor would I choose myrtle (*Myrtus communis*), orange jessamine (*Murraya exotica*) or plumbago (*Plumbago capensis*). They all require too much trimming, and in doing that most of their flowering growths must be cut off. A shrubby honeysuckle, *Lonicera nitida* 'Baggesen's Gold', is often suggested for the purpose of making low hedges too. Again, it requires much trimming; worse, it sometimes collapses in patches, spoiling

ABOVE
Bright spring colour will be replaced by summer greenery. Plants such as ferns, hostas, irises, grasses and many perennials will add the pleasures of varied leaf forms to the garden over a long season from spring to autumn.

ABOVE RIGHT
Sheltered between a high stone wall and a tall thick hedge, this garden walk acts as a sun trap in a garden where winter winds chill the marrow. The warmth held captive in the garden allows many special plants to be grown and also concentrates the perfumes of the choice scented plants grown there.

RIGHT
Strong, hot colours can work together if they are used with confidence. A theme as simple as the one shown could easily be built on by adding more plants of similar colouring. Plants with coloured foliage can add a surprising dimension to such colour schemes.

OPPOSITE PAGE
This springtime garden is filled with colour and interesting plants. Thoughtful selection of plants with bold foliage and a variety of green shades will ensure that summertime interest will also be provided.

the whole effect. Rosemary is likewise afflicted and is best avoided for this purpose.

Early photographs show that a variety of other low plants were sometimes used to define edges in a hedgelike way. Dianthuses such as 'Mrs Sinkins' or 'Mrs Gullan' could be used. Their growth is compact and very neat. Once over with the shears after the flowers have faded will keep them that way. Ivy, too, was sometimes clipped hard to create tight, low hedges. Algerian ivy (*Hedera colchica*), English ivy (*H. helix*) and Canary Island ivy (*H. canariensis*) are the toughest and were the most often used. Plain dark green forms would be the most effective foil for the informal plantings in the border behind. Ivy treated this way would need careful attention to make sure it did not get out of control, and it would need renewing from time to time to maintain a good cover of leaves. To get started, simply plant out runners of ivy along the edge of the path and twine the growths into each other parallel to the path. Pegging down the trails of growth with hairpins, short lengths of bent wire or small forked sticks will cause extra roots to be made, and the hedge will quickly thicken up. The best time to trim ivy hedges is in late winter just before new growth begins to break. Like all hedges, ivy needs feeding at this time. It is also a good time to lay snail baits, or to hunt them out as you prune.

HEDGE CARE

Hedges are a long-term investment in any garden. They contribute much to creating shelter and privacy and giving a sense of enclosure. They also serve to give garden spaces definition and a permanent framework within which floral displays are set off as the seasons progress. As a hedge will be in place a long time and needs always to look good, a few basic rules should be attended to from the beginning:

Soil preparation. Prepare the ground for a hedge as well as would be done for any other part of the garden. Drainage should be good, the soil should be broken down to a fine tilth by thorough digging. If the hedge is to abut other gardens, a root barrier is a good idea. By sinking a layer of construction strength builder's plastic a metre or more into the soil along the line of the hedge the spread of roots into other garden beds can be significantly lessened.

Fertilising and watering. Hedges are hungry feeders and users of water. Root barriers will help to control the spread of roots, but there will still be a need to feed the hedge by using artificial fertilisers or by mulching with compost and animal manures. A line of 'drippers' (micro-irrigation system outlets) will help the hedge to grow well and help to train the roots to stay where the water is. A handful of slow-release fertiliser in the bottom of each planting hole is a great start for any hedge. Annual applications of fertilisers should be applied a few weeks before the major annual growth spurt. This spurt of growth usually happens just after flowering time or when the warm weather begins.

Planting. Hedges can be planted from pot-grown plants at any time provided the water supply is adequate. Plants purchased bare-rooted can provide some cost savings but must be attended to smartly; although planting in the depths of winter can be a chore, it cannot be set aside waiting for better weather. Use a string line or bamboo stakes to establish and check the line of the hedge before planting begins. Spacing of plants will depend on how large they will eventually become and on how quickly results are required. As a general rule of thumb, plant about one-third the distance covered by the spread of a mature plant (check this with the supplier) or closer if an effect is wanted quickly. Where hedge plants are deliberately set very close together to achieve a quick result, it will sometimes be necessary to remove some plants as the hedge matures. It seems to me that it would be better to be a little patient, although I know this is easier said than done.

Trimming and after care. The best time to trim a hedge is following the main growing season. As this is often in the hottest months, care must be taken, especially with box hedges, to minimise the risk of the newly cut foliage and stems getting sun scorch. Keep an eye on the weather; when a cool, cloudy spell is expected, set to work. Should a scorcher follow, have ready some shading material, hessian or light-grade shade cloth, ready to throw over the box plants until the exposed leaves have had a chance to toughen. Fortunately, box seems to be the only hedging plant where severe scorching can be a problem. Should hedges be flat on their sides or slightly raked (sloped) towards the top? The theory is that by trimming a hedge with raked sides sunlight will reach all parts of the hedge and encourage it to grow evenly, instead of the top overshadowing the lower parts and causing legginess and showing bare 'ankles' at the base. The advice comes down as hedge lore from England and Europe; it seems to be less of a problem in warmer, sunnier climates.

Old age seems to be a greater cause of hedges failing to grow down to ground level, especially in situations where they become overshadowed by nearby trees or where their tops overgrow their lower parts through being poorly maintained and infrequently trimmed. In most cases bare ankles and overgrown tops can be fixed by hard pruning. Photinia, holly, yew, box, bay, coprosma, laurestinus, plumbago (blue and white), Natal plum (*Carissa macrocarpa*), lion's paw (*Leonitis leonuris,* orange and white) and Cape honeysuckle (*Tecomaria capensis*, orange and yellow) are all old-fashioned hedge plants which respond well to hard cutting from time to time to rejuvenate growth and keep them within bounds. Rosemary, lavender, cypress and pittosporum resent hard pruning and often fail to thrive afterwards; indeed, they often develop patches of dieback. Cypress hedges need particular care to see that trimming does not cut into old wood that will not throw out new growth. Even parts of hedges that are covered temporarily by 'For Sale' signs will not recover if the foliage underneath turns brown and dies.

Can you plant right up to a hedge? No, the roots will compete too strongly with other garden plants for water and food. Large hedges will also overshadow other plants, causing them to grow awkwardly. A narrow pathway at the base of a large hedge permits access for trimming and allows aggressive weeds such as ivy and blackberry, spread by birds, to be painted with poison or grubbed out easily.

The Inner-City Front Garden

Those people restoring a nineteenth-century terrace house or semi-detached cottage in an inner-city area will have very little garden area to plant. Furthermore, what is planted will need to look good for as long as possible and to stand up to the exhaust fumes, smoke and smog that seem these days to plague city living. Although the space may be small and the number of plants grown few, an inner-city garden demands a high level of care to keep it shipshape. A few weeds or dusty leaves in a large garden go unnoticed, but in a city garden every small detail, including unlovely thistles and grime-besmirched foliage, attract immediate attention. This is because everything is seen at close range by everyone who comes up the garden path and often by everyone who passes down the street.

More than diligence over pulling out stray rye grasses and dusting the daisies is needed to make small city gardens attractive. First the soil must be well looked after; all too often it is exhausted of all goodness and treated more as a scrap heap than as a garden. Set this to rights, and things will begin to look up. Large street trees and overgrown shrubs cast deep and gloomy shadows that are anathema to many plants and deadly if their aggressive root systems have formed an impenetrable mass under the whole garden. Dealing with these presents difficult problems which call for drastic solutions.

COPING WITH STREET TREES

If you are determined to make a flower garden, then the roots of street trees must be severely discouraged. Root pruning is called for. Check first about the general state of health of the tree to be dealt with; the shock of root pruning could be too much for a decrepit street tree to survive. If the tree is vigorous and healthy, it is safe to go ahead. Uncertain? Consult a tree surgeon. Working in the confined space of a city garden means that mechanised equipment is often out of the question. Root pruning can be done very effectively with a narrow trench digger, but terrace owners will most likely find that they must do it by hand digging. At least the likelihood of ripping through gas mains, electricity cables, water and sewerage lines is much less. Using a pick and shovel, and a sharp saw to cut tree roots, a trench about one metre deep should be dug along the fence line. Invasive roots can be discouraged by any form of barrier laid against the outermost wall of the trench; some times backfilling with rubble and rocks will do the trick, but more often a solid barrier such as sheets of corrugated iron or builders-strength plastic sheeting is used. It works even better if the neighbours can be persuaded to extend the barrier along their front fence-lines. A word of warning: root pruning should not come any closer to the trunk of a tree than 2.5 metres. Where possible, a greater distance should be allowed.

Is all this hard work necessary? If it is not possible to root prune, alternatives may be found in growing plants in pots sunk in the soil or treated as a decorative feature, or shallow planting beds may be built over the root-filled existing soil. Care must be taken to make sure that the soil does not come up to the trunks of established trees and shrubs, as there is a great danger of them developing bark rot. A good many trees also respond adversely to changes in the quantities of water they receive and to alterations in natural drainage patterns. It is wise to consult a tree surgeon about proposed landscaping projects that may effect trees.

DEALING WITH OVERGROWN SHRUBS

Overgrown shrubs are a challenge to many gardeners who garden in small spaces. The shrubs are dominant and limit what can be done; yet to remove them would often expose the house to the prying eyes of every passer-by. The best solution is to turn the shrub into a small tree. This is easily done but should not be rushed. Take a good look at the shrub: from a distance, so you can see its overall shape, and from inside, so you understand how the branch structure works. First cut away the lowest 'skirts' to a height of about two metres. This will leave you with a cluster of branches holding up a canopy of leaves and twigs. Look again and imagine in your mind's eye what the 'tree' would look like if certain branches were removed and half a dozen or

TOP

Massive hedges create shelter from strong winds. The lumpy, bumpy shapes of old hedges enhance their appeal.

LEFT

A rondel of low hedging encloses a garden of random paving stones interplanted with thymes and other low carpeters.

Hedges need not be straight and cut square to achieve a powerful impact. Is there any doubt that this curved and rounded hedge leads to somewhere important?

so retained to make a multi-trunked tree. There is no hurry about this; consider all the possibilities before setting to work. When finished, the shrub will have been turned into an ancient-looking small tree with twisted trunks full of character. As the canopy will have been thinned when the branches were removed, there will be more light and space under the tree which can be gardened with flowers and plants.

REVIVING EXHAUSTED SOIL

How can you boost tired inner-city soil? Deep digging, double trenching can be a good start. It has a remarkable effect on hyperactive teenage boys too, especially if they want to earn money towards a car. Digging out soil to two spade depths is back-breaking work and time consuming, but it throughly breaks up soil that may have been compacted severely for a hundred years or more. It also gives an opportunity to uncover unusual aspects of local history. You didn't know your cottage was once a slaughter-house, did you? Who knows what bounty deep digging may uncover— a treasure trove of holey dollars, a rare antique tile, a piece of broken china, a stack of mutton bones, a handful of worn-out horseshoes, a button, a broken Matchbox toy car. Even if it is dug over to only one spade depth, the soil texture and aeration must be improved. Rotary hoeing does not really achieve the same effect unless the soil is very sandy; in heavy, compacted soils the blades tend to skip over the surface, leaving work still to be done by hand.

Once the soil has been broken up and as much junk as possible removed, it is time to begin rebuilding soil fertility. Chemical or natural fertilisers and composts, or a combination of both, can be used. My own method, if it could be called

that, is to use as much natural material as I can. I may do things backwards, but this works for me. First I make sure there are no perennial weeds such as dock, couch grass, kikuyu, sorrel, sour sobs or convolvulus by spraying carefully with one of the glyphosate weedkillers. Any strays are painted with poison using a child's paintbrush kept in the poisons cupboard for the purpose. My next step is to plant the garden and to sprinkle a light dressing of 'Complete D' or some similar chemical fertiliser on the soil. Then a good thick layer of stable litter —straw plus some manure—goes over the entire garden. Sometimes other materials are used to make a mulch about 20 cm thick. Pea straw, buzzer shavings and sawdust, wheaten or oaten straw, poultry litter, shredded tree and shrub prunings, pine needles and leaves from deciduous trees. If perennial weeds are likely to prove difficult to eradicate, a layer of old newspapers opened flat and laid six to eight pages thick goes down first. This will almost certainly stifle any regrowth, with the exception of blackberries. This layer of fertilising mulch is added to continually with lawn clippings and more of the other goodies as they are available. It is more or less a no-dig approach to gardening. For the owners of very small gardens the advantage is that the soil-building program goes on continuously without having bare patches and gaps in the garden.

PLANTING

With the tree roots taken care of and soil quality improved, garden making can go ahead with a fair chance of good results. The whole idea with very small gardens is to keep up a continuous display year-round. This need not mean a glorious riot of colour for twelve months; a combination of

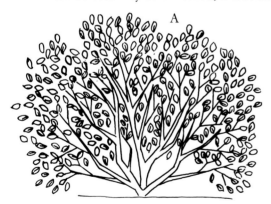

A　　　　　B　　　　　C

HOW A LARGE SHRUB BECOMES A SMALL TREE
(A) The first step is to cut away the lowest 'skirts' of the shrub and look inside the plant for significant and shapely branches which will form the 'bones' of the new tree.
(B) Consider the structure of the shrub and select branches that will be retained and those that will be removed. Work slowly; cut branches cannot be put back. Raise the canopy of the emerging tree by trimming the lowest twigs and small

branches until there is at least 2 m of clear space underneath.
(C) Consider the density of the remaining canopy. More light may be needed under the tree to allow new plants and ground cover to become established. Carefully thin the canopy by removing small branches and dead wood. Removing these growths also reveals more strongly the characteristic structure of the tree. By choosing to leave some crooked branches, the new tree can give the impression of great age.

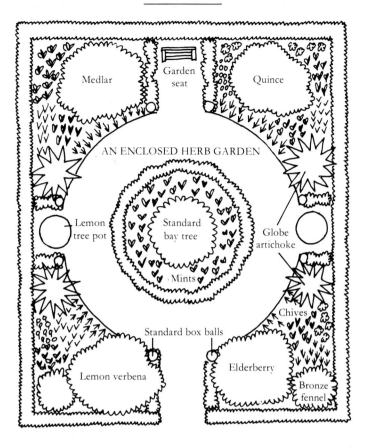

Within the garden diagram:

Medlar

Garden seat

Quince

AN ENCLOSED HERB GARDEN

Lemon tree pot

Standard bay tree

Globe artichoke

Mints

Chives

Standard box balls

Lemon verbena

Elderberry

Bronze fennel

*Tall outer hedges of box (about 1.5 m high five years after planting) enclose a small herb garden. Inner 'arms' of box and a central rondel, each clipped to about 60 cm high, add further to the old-fashioned appearance, while eight standard box balls introduce a note of formality. Small trees of quince, medlar, elderberry and lemon verbena (*Aloysia triphylla*) trained high give height and allow low herbs and scented shrubs to be grown underneath. At the centre of the garden a standard bay tree (*Laurus nobilis*) clipped to an umbrella shape provides fresh leaves for cooking. These formal touches contrast with the vigorous upright growth of clumps of bronze fennel and the arching silver leaves of globe artichokes that predominate in sunny corners of the design. A pair of large terracotta lemon tree pots establish a Mediterranean feeling even without being planted with cumquats, limes or lemons. The central rondel is filled with eau-de-Cologne mint, but spearmint, peppermint, apple mint or a mixture of mints would suit as well. The outer edges of the circular path are lined with a broad band of chives; behind this the ground between the 'key' plants of artichoke and fennel is filled with a* bouquet garni *of sage, lovage, garlic, garlic chives, oregano, parsleys (curled and flat-leaf) and thymes, all planted in patches of sufficient size to supply the table. Colourful forms such as golden oregano, purple-leaved basil and tricoloured sage are included for extra interest and for salad decoration.*

interesting foliage and flowers works even better than flowers alone. Depending on the situation, plants with attractive leaves could include coleus, hostas, succulents, *Colocasia*, ferns, camellias, *Plectranthus*; plants with purple, silver or variegated leaves, pelargoniums, geraniums; plants with scented leaves, *Iresene*, ivies, herbs—almost anything has potential if you develop an eye for attractive combinations. You can get ideas by visiting garden open days and just walking around the neighbourhood looking at gardens.

With a really small garden, the same general rules apply but greater reliance has to be placed on one of two schemes: (1) a very formal approach, with a strong framework of permanent plantings, such as low hedges or borders or with edging tiles or rock work backed up with centrally placed urns, large pots or tripods; (2) much greater use of 'throw away' plants which are bedded out already in flower and removed as soon as they begin to fade, to be replaced with more plants coming into flower. Pots, urns, tubs and the like need daily grooming (and watering in many situations) to keep them at a peak of perfection, and the plants in them need frequent replacing as they outgrow their allotted positions or finish flowering. Dreaming up new combinations of upright and trailing plants and of flowers and foliage can pass many pleasant hours. Some of the most stimulating ideas may well be found in overseas magazines, but use them as a jumping-off point for your own ideas rather than as models to be slavishly copied. Try to match the scope of your plantings to the style of your terrace or semi-detached cottage. Simple architectural styles call for simple gardens; more elaborate Gothic or Italianate designs call for more ambitious schemes.

ABOVE
A small inner-city garden need not be cramped in feeling or limited in what it contains. The features of cottage-garden style—profusion, variety and informality within a structured framework—can work well on a small scale.

LEFT
Terrace houses and maisonettes with very small gardens can best be treated formally, especially where the style of the building is decorative Victorian architecture rather than simple, plain colonial construction. The important trick is to keep everything in tip-top condition.

RIGHT
Strong lines created by an old carved font, paving and trellis work are softened by the luxuriant growth of sweet-scented herbs, low perennials and potted plants.

3   The Side Gardens

*The problem of which side of the garden to enter first can be a delightful choice or
a doubtful pleasure, depending on whether your particular piece of the nineteenth
century has a 'garden at the side' or a 'side-garden'!*
*The side-garden is the big problem for any modern urban gardener and was no less
a one for the gardener of yesteryear. What can be done with a space two metres
wide and fifteen metres long? By the time the necessary path has made its passage
from end to end, there is precious little room left for any sort of gardening. The
most common solution to these narrow windtraps has been to ignore them as garden
spaces and to treat them solely as utilitarian routes from front to back. In some
inner-city areas, such spaces were so small and overshadowed that they were left
quite alone.*

There are a few possibilities, however, that can
change such problem areas into attractive gardens.
Walls and fence-lines can be planted with various
vines or creepers to add refreshing greenery and
flowers to liven dull spaces. A simple pergola can
serve to screen out neighbours or to shade the
house walls from summer sun and heat. Large tubs
can provide room to grow flowers and can direct
foot traffic safely where smaller pots would be
dangerous objects that cause trips and stumbles.

ABOVE

Tall, thin plants such as hollyhocks lend an air of importance to an otherwise average small garden. Achieving height adds a dimension to a garden that is often overlooked.

LEFT

The garden in winter is a consideration rarely attended to but one that can add to our sense of the passage of the seasons if plants are chosen which reflect the progress of the changing year.

ABOVE LEFT

With just enough room for a pathway and a ribbon of garden, extra value can be had from pots planted with attractive flowering plants. The pots should be large enough to be in scale with the building, and the plants chosen for them should have bold foliage to look good against the walls.

OPPOSITE PAGE

Driveways are often visually the most important aspects of many small gardens. Incorporating them so that they are not barren, ugly and dominant requires consideration. Welcoming clumps of flowers, pots of greenery and the repeated strips of lawn relieve the vast area of paving, and the greenery of the climbers scales down the mass of the drive.

Wall Gardening

High walls are among the most difficult challenges a gardener can face. Successfully solving the problems of what to plant and how to grow things can lead to the most boring spaces becoming positive garden assets. First consideration is usually given to some sort of self-clinging vine, such as ivy, Boston ivy (*Ampelopsis veitchii* syn. *Parthenocissus tricuspidata*) or Virginia creeper (*Parthenocissus quinquefolia*). Each has its charms, despite the last two being deciduous, but they all tend to be rather suburban in effect because they have been relentlessly over-used. Creeping fig (*Ficus pumila*) is also often suggested as a good cover for unsightly walls, but like many ivies it grows rank with age and in the meantime wheedles its way into every vent and cranny, into wall cavities and under eaves.

A smarter looking way of covering walls is to train creepers or pliable shrubs along wires or wooden battens. The most effective designs are achieved using a grid pattern, at least 30 cm square, set either diagonally to make a diamond shape or on the square. Small-leaved ivies, Chinese star jasmine (*Trachelospermum jasminoides*) or firethorn (*Pyracantha atalantioides* 'Aurea', with yellow berries, or *P. coccinea* 'Lalandei', with red berries) are evergreens suited to the task. The firethorns are rather slower in growth than the other two.

If you are a patient gardener, a wonderful effect can be achieved, and a dull space vastly improved, by training a sasanqua camellia espalier-fashion against a wall. Choose varieties with fairly dense foliage, such as 'Shishi Gashira', 'Chansonette', 'Plantation Pink', 'Setsugekka', 'Lucinda' or 'Mine No Yuki'. Strong leading growths should be tied loosely to the wires or battens and side growths clipped or nipped to make a compact mass of leaves and twigs. Plants grown espalier-style need good feeding and watering to look their best.

On walls that are not exposed to the full blast of the summer sun, potted plants can be suspended by means of wrought-iron pot rings set into the wall. Filled with geraniums, ivy geraniums and annuals, and even ferns in cool situations, they can look charming. Choose a vibrant cottagey mixture of colours, or plan combinations of complimentary colours. A short stepladder, a hose and watering rose, regular watering and light applications of liquid fertiliser are all that is needed to make this very European display.

ABOVE
The simplest effects are often the best, and quite often not consciously planned. It is the seat that makes this a garden.

RIGHT
A low dry-stone wall marks a change in levels and also gives the gardener plenty of opportunity for creative planting. Crocosmia aurea and hardy native ferns have colonised the damp base of the wall, softening the impact of the stonework and making a bold contrast in foliage.

Dry-Stone Walls

Talking of walls, a dry-stone wall—that is, a
stone wall that is built without mortar—is most
appropriate as a terrace wall or low retaining wall in
a colonial-style garden. You have only to look at
some of the fine examples of such walling in the
Blue Mountains, the Dandenongs, in Tasmania or
in Auckland to see how good it looks and realise its
significance in colonial construction techniques.

To build a dry-stone wall, you need a strong
back, an ample supply of patience and at least one
willing worker. The largest stones will be needed
for the bottom course and should be laid on their
largest faces, with a slight slope backwards from the
open face of the wall. Pack the soil carefully behind
and between the rocks as each course is laid. The
work will be accomplished slowly but with a feeling
of satisfaction for the workers. It is possible to plant
such a wall with thymes, campanulas and small
succulents as you go, but deft footwork is required
to avoid crushing the small plants as the stones for
the higher courses are carried over them. Not an
easy feat when heavy stones are being lumped
about.

ABOVE
*Swagged with roses and planted along the base, dry-stone walls
can be marvellous garden features.*
TOP
A stroll garden defined by a dry-stone wall.
OPPOSITE PAGE
*Dry-stone walls hold up a terrace and act as a comfortable
home to a variety of plants.*

Espaliered Fruit Trees

Growing things in narrow side gardens along fence lines is always a problem, mainly because there are so few plants that will achieve the height needed to maintain privacy and at the same time not get so big that they eventually become a problem in themselves. Espaliered fruit trees take up very little space and can produce quick results, though not so quick as a fast-growing vine like a passionfruit—black passionfruit (*Passiflora edulis*), banana passionfruit (*P. mollissima*), blue-flowered passionfruit (*P. caerulea*)—Chinese gooseberry or Kiwi fruit (*Actinidia chinensis*), black coral pea (*Kennedya nigricans*), Russian vine (*Polygonum baldschuanicum*) or a grape vine. Fruit trees have the advantage of being longer lived than many of these vines, and they can be kept firmly in place by pruning without their developing the sulks, as may the more vigorous free-ranging vines.

While many deciduous fruit trees can be trained as espaliers, the most adaptable are apple trees, which readily develop fruiting spurs and require only basic pruning skills to achieve results. New varieties such as Fuji can be used for espalier work, but also think about using some of the antique cultivars that are once again becoming available. Dessert apples such as 'Brabant Bellefleur' (1700s),

'Cellini' (1832), 'Court Pendu Plat' (pre-1500), 'Golden Harvey' (1600s), 'King of the Pippins' (1800), 'Pitmaston Pineapple' (1785), 'Sturmer Pippin' (1831) and 'Worcester Pearmain' (1874) could add beauty and productivity to any narrow side garden. Apples for training as espalier trees should be bought as single-growth 'whips', that is, one straight growth coming from the understock on which the tree is grafted. This will allow you to prune the young tree to the height at which you require the branching to begin.

Summer pruning is as important as winter pruning; cut back or rub out completely sappy new growths and tie leaders into position. The training and removal of unwanted new growths need to be attended to regularly throughout the growing season. Ties need to be frequently checked and renewed as required. Expertise in training espalier trees comes with experience, but you should also seek out and talk to the gardeners at historic homes, display gardens and botanic gardens where espalier trees are grown.

Trellis Climbers

Narrow lanes and side gardens that face the afternoon sun may need overhead shade to keep the

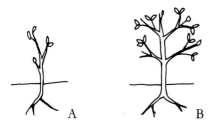

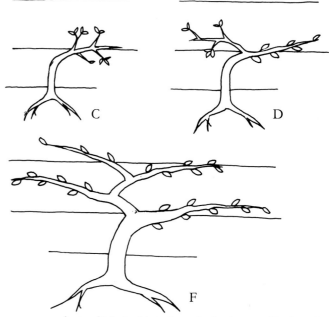

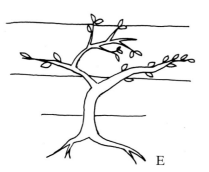

HOW AN EASY ESPALIER IS MADE

(A) Start with a simple whip-stick (young tree with a strong central growth or 'lead').

(B) Plant the young tree in well-prepared soil and make ready the training framework of wires strung between well-set posts.

(C) In midsummer, as the growth begins to ripen and harden (i.e., when it begins to turn from green to reddish brown), tie the lead growth to the lowest wire and cut off all the side shoots but the one needed to make the lead for the next stage.

(D) The side growths pruned in summer will make secondary

shoots which should, in the main, be short, stubby flowering and fruiting growths called 'spurs'.

(E) The training and pruning process is repeated summer and winter until the espalier reaches the desired dimensions. The branches will need to be tied in place, firstly to direct the growth and later to support the weight of fruit. Ties need to be checked regularly to make certain they are not damaging the branches and that they are not about to break.

(F) Summer pruning must be attended to in order to keep the tree shapely. Careful watering, feeding, pest control and mulching will keep espaliers healthy and productive for years.

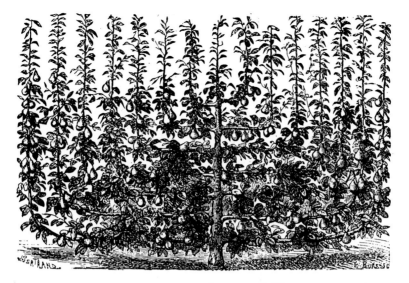

Building a Summer-house.—I have built a very pretty rustic summer-house in this way : Mark out an octagon, each side 4 ft. long : plant at each corner a rough straight pole 4 in. thick and 9 ft. long. Char or double tar 3 ft. of the thickest end and put 2 ft. in the ground. Level the tops, and connect them all round with crosspieces of similar timber, a few inches of each end sticking out. Take another piece 3 ft. long and saw one end to a point ; from it, as a centre, nail all round it, like spokes in a wheel, eight straight clothes-props slanting down at an angle of 40.° Put this on the top of the upright poles, and nail each loose prop end to the top of a pole, letting 6 in. or 12 in. extend beyond. This makes the roof. Now fill up with rustic lattice-work (1 in. or 2 in. thick) eight of the sides, leaving one for the entrance : then lattice the roof, or, better still, thatch it. Use strong French nails and the gimlet when

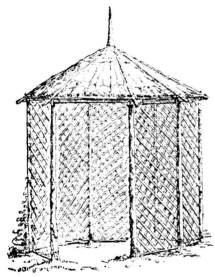

A Home-made Summer-house.

necessary. Fix the crosspieces into the tops of the poles by boring with a centre-bit through the whole, and hammer in an iron peg, 6 in. long. Leave the bark on the wood, which may be sized and varnished. Use throughout the hardest wood possible ; Oak or Beech for the poles, and Beech or Hazel for the lattice. Plant a good climber, for instance, scented Clematis, C. Jackmanni, Wistaria, Ampelopsis, Veitchi, scented Jasmine, Honeysuckle, climbing Rose, against each pole : well fill the outside borders with hardy Ferns. In two years you have a floral paradise. My house cost me under £1 without the thatch, but I did all the work myself.—W. L.

house cool. Or you may need to screen out the view into the next door bathroom window. In such cases stronger-growing vines can be most effective in achieving a pretty solid cover-up. The Chinese gooseberry can be very good in these situations. It is a vigorous grower and produces good leaf coverage but not so dense as to make the space underneath dismal. Two plants, male and female, are required to produce the luscious fruits; but even if there is room for only one, the foliage alone makes this plant worth while. Grapes would be a good choice too, and there are many delicious new table varieties to choose from as well as the traditional sultana, black Hamburg, Waltham and black Muscat. And there is always the crimson glory vine (see 'Covering the Woodshed' in chapter 4). The almost round, dinner-plate-sized leaves of *Vitis coignetiae* make a marvellous shady walk, and they turn a brilliant colour in autumn; this vine does, however need more water than other grapes to perform well. Rather different are the dusky plum-coloured leaves of *Vitis vinifera* 'Purpurea'— the purple-leaved grape which has deeply lobed leaves rather like a fig-leaf though with jagged edges instead of the fig's rounded rim.

Completely able as a strong climber and still something of a rarity is the giant Burmese honeysuckle (*Lonicera hildebrandiana*). Large glossy semi-evergreen leaves and vigorous twining growth enable this honeysuckle to clamber up and over any pergola or high chain-wire fence. It casts a dense shade and revels in a hot situation so long as the soil remains damp. At midsummer, small bunches of enormously long, curving, tubular flowers appear. Well scented with a sweet perfume, the flowers at first open almost white but deepen day by day until, near falling, they are a golden yellow. The plant is rather frost tender, especially as a youngster with no hard wood; once established it seems pretty hardy in areas where frosts are mild and infrequent.

ANTIQUE APPLE ORCHARD

Dunn's Seedling

Forge

Court Pendu Plat

Cox's Orange Pippin

Rokewood

Cox's Orange Pippin

Newtown Pippin

Pitmaston Pineapple

King of Pippins

A selection of antique apple varieties set out in a simple orchard would add variety to a garden and to the table. The orchard has roughly mown grass paths between the trees. While the trees are young the rectangles in which they are planted should be kept clear of growth. Once the trees are well established, a variety of small bulbs—freesias, babianas, sparaxis, grape hyacinths and jonquils—could be introduced for springtime pleasure. The only maintenance needed, apart from tree care, would be to trim away the dead foliage of the bulbs in early summer.

Specialist growers will be able to advise on suitable varieties for your particular area and suggest a mixture of cooking and eating varieties which will pollinate each other. Some of the most flavoursome and more interesting kinds are shown on the diagram. 'Cox's Orange Pippin' does best in cool areas and could be replaced by any number of other ancient (and tasty) varieties, among them 'Winesap', 'Pomme de Neige', 'American Mother', 'Rome Beauty', 'Ballarat Seedling', 'King Cole', 'Sturmer' and 'Catshead'.

Equally delightful orchards could be made by planting a grove of silver-leaved olives or black-green loquats, toothsome greengages and other plums, or crisp fruited Nashi pears. As well as bulbs, self-sowing annuals could be introduced to add seasonal colour. It is important to maintain such a garden as an orchard. The grass should never be fine turf. It should not be mown close, nor should it be immaculately free of broad-leaved plants. The borders between paths and tree plots should be blurred by the undergrowth of bulbs, annuals and grasses.

Larger Side Gardens

The wider spaces that were available to home-owners were frequently converted on at least one side into a shade house or a grape cage. These structures ranged from simple constructions of cheap timber, laths and chicken wire to elaborate confections of fretted timber and turned finials.

The other side of the garden, most often the sunnier side, was frequently developed as a shrubbery or even a small orchard; more energetic households used the space for a bowling green, croquet lawn, badminton or tennis court. In a modern restoration, the wider spaces may be authentically developed in any of these roles, at the same time serving the needs of a family. Some care needs to be taken, though, not to allow all the modern paraphernalia of tennis to intrude into the nineteenth-century feeling of the place.

THE GARDENER'S ORCHARD

If an orchard is settled on as the object of restoration, you might consider choosing trees beyond the cultivars commonly available through garden centres. Fortunately, comprehensive collections of old fruit trees are still held by some agricultural research stations, particularly of apples and pears. Some keen commercial orchardists also keep 'odd lines', favourite old varieties of dessert and cooking fruits, survivors of the hundreds of cultivars which were offered to the garden makers late last century. In cool and moderate areas, apples, pears, cherries and soft fruits could be the major plantings, with plums, persimmons and even medlars to add variety.

Peaches, nectarines and apricots would also be appropriate, but since some trouble will need to be taken over cultivating these trees anyway, a choice in favour of some of the toothsome varieties of bygone days could be made.

In warmer areas, citrus trees planted in a small grove might appeal as a restoration project. Blood oranges, pomeloes, citrons, shaddocks and limes could be attractive alternatives to the usual oranges and lemons, especially if you remember the flavour of blood oranges or enjoy making marmalades. For drier gardens, a grove of almonds, loquats or even olives could create the feeling of an orchard. To make it especially romantic, you could put in a dense underplanting of jonquils and Cape bulbs within the overall rectangular pattern of tree planting. Paths mown through the grassy orchard floors could strenghen the planting pattern.

RIGHT

Dwarf conifers set in random stone paving soften the hardness of the stone, and their dense, spreading growth blurs the boundaries of garden and pavement.

ABOVE

Near to the house a sitting-out area for taking meals alfresco is a great attraction in a warm, dry climate. Although the idea seems fairly modern, outdoor eating under grape-covered pergolas was not uncommon in the nineteenth century. Interpreted with appropriate old-fashioned style, the idea comes into its own.

ABOVE LEFT

An expansive mood is created by this orchard of young fruit trees. A continual display of flowers would spoil such a sylvan setting, but maybe a mille fiori *carpet of small spring bulbs could liven up the scene when the trees are bare of leaves in winter and early spring.*

LEFT

Orchards of fruit trees were often a feature of side gardens where space allowed. Pears and apples in particular are quite long-lived and can grow into large trees. A seat placed underneath such a friendly tree makes an instant garden.

OPPOSITE PAGE

An informal hedge of evergreen shrubs under high pruned deciduous trees makes a quiet bower for a garden seat and low, shade-loving flowers as well as visual interest at a third level.

Shrubberies

Shrubberies were a popular method of making gardens in the areas to the side of the house. They had the added advantage of being considered very fashionable and needing much less labour than orchards. As in previous cases, the choice was very wide, with a much greater selection of hardy shrubs from the temperate zones than is generally available today. Victorian gardeners did not subscribe to the modern idea that a good garden can be achieved with a minimum of maintenance—people who wanted good gardens expected to have to do some work! So pruning, trimming, training and disease-control activities were seen as part of the gardener's calendar and not as avoidable chores.

It was usual to arrange shrubberies as part of a walk around the garden, usually strategically placed to screen one part of the garden from another or the house from direct view from the street. Thus a shrubbery may have been aligned with the curve of a carriage drive but be broad enough to have an internal pathway so that strollers walked between banks of shrubs. Another popular style of making a shrubbery was called a serpentine. In this case the pathway wound snakelike from one section of the garden to another with deep plantings of shrubs on either side that hid from view the end points of the walk and those parts of the garden beyond the shrubbery. Large gardens sometimes had shrubberies that were made by densely planting around a series of small interconnecting winding paths. The 'wilderness' that was created as the shrubs grew to maturity was a novel idea that provided relief and contrast to the more formal gardens elsewhere in the grounds. According to the owner's interest, a wilderness could have been planted up with a collection of special shrubs—for example, those from north-eastern America, in which case it would have been called an American garden—or with plants from Japan and China and named accordingly. Even in gardens where the owners had no particular interest, the shrubbery may have been made more interesting by having at its centre a secret flower garden or a rockery, possibly with pools, grottoes and subterranean cave rooms.

OLD-FASHIONED SHRUBS

In smaller gardens the old-fashioned shrubs from England were popular choices. Foremost among these were the evergreen favourites, the lilacs, philadelphus, forsythia, deutzia and spiraea. Fortunately for garden restorers, many of the varieties available today were bred towards the end of the last century, so obtaining these plants is not a difficult task. However, some other shrubs grown during the reign of Queen Victoria are less easily

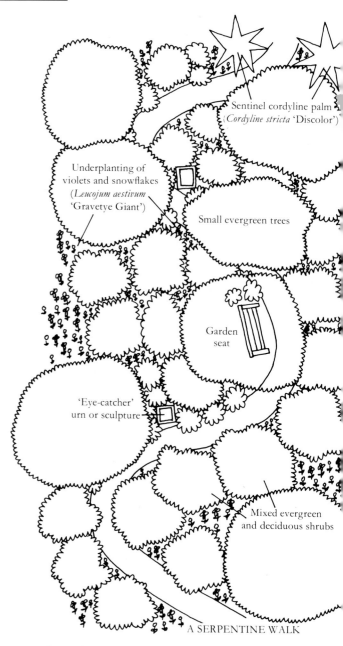

Typical of early gardens of the Victorian era is the serpentine walk. In the form of a shrubbery it can screen one part of a garden from another, act to screen a house from the street or to hide some of the ugly necessities like compost heaps. To function well, a good proportion of the shrubs must be evergreen. A quiet part of the garden, a serpentine could be made more interesting by the careful placing of an urn on a pedestal or a piece of old-fashioned statuary. Riotous colours and masses of flowering plants would be out of character.

Suited only for large gardens, the serpentine walk is for quiet strolls. Traditionally the path would be surfaced with fine gravel, but in wilder parts of the garden a deep layer of sawdust would serve perfectly well.

obtained; the spectacularly beautiful sacred flower of the Incas (*Cantua buxifolia*) with great clusters of pendant silky carmine flowers, the exotic orange-trumpeted *Datura sanguinea*, the matilija poppy (*Romneya coulteri*) with its huge crimped white blooms with golden central bosses, and the majestic plume poppy (*Macleaya cordata*) with huge silvered fig-like leaves and tall spires of rusty pink flowers, are among the best. This last plant was named in honour of the Australian naturalist Alexander Macleay and so is doubly appropriate for Australian gardens.

Semitropical plants flourished in most parts of the Antipodean colonies, and consequently plants that had been regarded as greenhouse subjects in Europe were used here in the open ground. Principal among these were oleanders, lantana and bouvardias.

True European evergreens had great sentimental attractions, especially for the traditions attached to Christmas, so box, yew and holly were much cultivated. Among the hollies were several that are worth seeking out: the hedgehog holly, with strange crests of spines on the upper leaf surfaces—the variegated form (*Ilex aquifolium horrida* 'Variegata') is especially good—and the plain variegated sorts 'Milk Maid' (yellow centre and curled green edges), 'Silver Queen' (silvery edges) and 'Golden Queen' (yellow edges). These will all make quite large shrubs; so unless you have plenty of room, care will be needed in placing them.

SCENTED SHRUBS

No garden restoration would be complete without scented shrubs. After colour, perfume is what most of us would call to mind as typical of a cottage garden. Lemon-scented verbena (*Aloysia triphylla*) is a powerfully scented small tree which is especially useful as it casts light shade and has an easy temperament (though it is frost tender). Rarer, but worth asking after, is *Azara microphylla*, which has minute yellow blooms under the leaves and a rich vanilla perfume. Quite different are Carolina allspice (*Calycanthus florida*), wintersweet (*Chimonanthus fragrans*) and the witch-hazels (*Hamamelis mollis*). The Bull Bay magnolia (*Magnolia grandiflora*) is a well-known small tree with delightfully perfumed flowers (usually around Christmas), which could be used with any of the above to create the scented atmosphere so necessary for a cottage or villa garden.

At lower levels, the many varieties of scented-leaf geraniums can fulfil the multiple roles of providing varied foliage, rich scents and easy culture. A selection from the thirty or so varieties available from specialist nurseries will satisfy even the most discerning gardener. Among the best are *Pelargonium tomentosum* and *P.* × 'Mabel Grey' (rich lemon scent) with large leaves. Contrasting leaf forms still with powerful perfumes can be had from varieties such as *P. crispum, P. abrotanifolium* and *P.* × 'Countess of Stradbroke' (citronella perfume).

Less well scented are varieties such as *P.* × 'Scarlet-Pet', *P.* × 'Pink Pet', *P.* × 'White Unique' and *P.* × 'Rollison's Unique' (brilliant red), but they are nonetheless very attractive survivors from the last century.

Butterfly bushes are less common than they used to be and should be more widely planted for their plentiful scented flowers and ease of culture. *Buddleia asiaticus* is still fairly common, though often grossly overgrown and in need of a hard pruning. *B. alternifolia*, with graceful wands dotted with small clusters of lilac flowers, and *B. globosa*, with large round heads of orange flowers dotted along the branches, are equally attractive and less common. *B. salvifolia* has a heavier look than the others, having dense foliage which hangs down on branches already weighed down by the large panicles of tiny lilac flowers.

TREE PEONIES

Most treasured of flowers following their introduction from Shanghai in the 1780s on behalf of Sir Joseph Banks, tree peonies were available through big nurseries which usually advertised them coyly as 'various varieties'. The colours were usually deep maroon (semi-double), lilac (fully double), pale lilac with a deep basal blotch (almost single) and white. The really sumptuous colours came early in the twentieth century at the hands of French breeders, so they don't strictly fit here, but I would bet any nineteenth-century gardener would have jumped at the chance to have one. Such rare beauties are mighty rich stuff for any garden, so tree peonies should be placed with great care and planted sparingly. If the cost of such treasures puts you off, you can raise them from seed. The disadvantage here is that they take from five to seven years to flower and may well turn out to be fairly ordinary—if any tree peony can be said to be ordinary!

By way of contrast, three much quieter shrubs which still attract attention in their due season are *Cedronella triphylla*, with its very pungent leaves and compact terminal leads of pale lavender flowers, and *Lonicera ciliata*, in either pink or white forms. All three have simple, plain features—none of the flamboyance of peonies—and fit well into any sunny corner of a cottage garden. The *Cedronella* is frost tender, so in areas where it gets badly cut back it will perform more like a herbaceous perennial than a shrub. In warm areas, it will easily make two to three metres.

In the Shade House

Passing from the sunny side garden to one on the shady side, we will almost certainly find some sort of shade house. Built rustic style of rough-hewn

LEFT ABOVE
This narrow garden opens into a larger, sunnier space beyond the pergola, but there is much to see along the way.

LEFT
Side gardens are not the only places where long, narrow passageways are found in gardens. Provided such paths are not major thoroughfares, they can be planted with only enough room for one person to get past.

ABOVE
Shrubberies under tall trees carry the eye deeper and deeper into the garden. The narrow, enclosed space focuses the viewer's gaze on the distance.

branches and brush, or more properly of sawn timbers and laths, it created a small haven of shade and coolness where ferns, palms and such treasured plants as coleus, begonias, gardenias and maybe some epiphytic cacti or hardy orchids were grown.

On the damp floor of the bush house grew such old favorites as baby's tears (*Helxine soleirolli*), Kenilworth ivy (*Linaria cymbalaria*) or perhaps *Mentha requenii*. Sometimes large pots stood directly on the floor with palms, camellias, hydrangeas, gardenias or other plants which required shelter from scorching sun and drying winds, in special soil. In a dark corner, that epitome of Victoriana, the aspidistra, might well be found. Known everywhere as the cast-iron plant, the aspidistra could be relied on to grow almost anywhere so long as it wasn't bone dry! Whether plain or variegated, it was a most obliging plant, at home in parlour or palm house. I have no doubt its curious bobble flowers, produced at ground level, excited many amateur naturalists and plant spotters. Local ingenuity often showed itself in pots devised from hollow gum logs and crammed with sword ferns, native dendrobium orchids (*Dendrobium speciosum, D. kingianum, D. delicatum*), native cymbidium orchids (*Cymbidium canaliculatum, C. madidum, C. suave*) or asparagus ferns such as *Asparagus falcatum, Asparagus densiflorus* 'Sprengeri' and *Asparagus plumosus*.

FERNS

Hanging baskets carved out of tree-fern logs or hollow gum logs by home handymen housed the real treasures of the fernery—the Boston ferns (*Nephrolepis* spp.), the caterpillar fern (*Polypodium glaucum*), the fabled Mander's golden polypody (*Polypodium aureum* 'Mandianum') or the huge weeping mass of a jointed polypody (*Polypodium subauriculatum*).

Among fern fanciers, a vast range of novelties and rarities were circulated and grown with exacting skill. The maidenhair ferns (*Adiantum* spp.) were extremely popular. Club moss (*Selaginella*), hen and chickens fern (*Asplenium bulbiferum*) and many other curiosities were well known. Native ferns had their advantages, too, especially when many wood-getters and bullockies could hawk them door to door in the towns. Hardy and still beautiful tree ferns, shield ferns (*Polystichum* spp.), wild maidenhair ferns, fishbone ferns (*Blechnum* spp.), bird's nest fern (*Asplenium nidus*) and the glorious elkhorn were brought in from the rainforests and eagerly sought by colonial gardeners.

The current fern revival has seen many ferns considered highly desirable in colonial times brought back into high favour, not only rarities such as the crested hart's tongues (*Polypodium scolopendrifolium* 'Cristata', et al.) but distinctive commoners like the sensible fern (*Onoclea sensibilis*) and the Japanese painted fern (*Athyrium goeringianum* 'Pictum').

Gardeners intent on reconstructing any sort of fernery should have little difficulty in obtaining suitable materials—brush, laths, tree-fern logs, etc. —for the job and should be able, with only a little searching, to locate a suitable diversity of hardy ferns. Some care should be taken over the use of some modern materials such as nylon shade cloth and trickle irrigation schemes; for, marvellous as they are, their thoughtless deployment in an old-time structure can totally destroy the illusion you want to create. This is not to say they shouldn't be used, just that they shouldn't be allowed to intrude. This is where ingenuity will be put to the test.

SEMI-TROPICAL EXOTICA

After the fern fad, a host of other pot plants were loved and grown by colonial gardeners. One of the least common and most surprising was *Hibiscus schizopetalus*, with finely cut pendant rose-red flowers. Why it's not more in demand I cannot tell, for it makes a unique plant for a tub in a sheltered corner.

Other highly regarded plants were bromeliads, a seemingly endless variety of the pineapple family, which were introduced from tropical America. Almost everyone had queen's tears (*Billbergia nutans*), and the purple zebra plant (*Billbergia zebrina*) was widely grown. Even Spanish moss (*Tillandsia* spp.), that curious grey wispy stuff (also known as air plant) was fondly treasured in many a shade house. There are many variegated and highly coloured members of this family, including *Neoregelia, Nidularium, Aechmia, Ananas* and *Dyckia*, which would have been known to enthusiasts and desired by many.

The wax flower (*Hoya carnosa*) was another pot plant whose scented bunches of white waxy blooms made it an attraction for every pot-gardener. There were rose-pink forms as well, and at least one with variegated leaves. Much smaller in all respects is *Hoya bella*, as popular then as it is now. There is also *Hoya australis*, which would have been brought from its rainforest habitat by plant collectors and sold to nurseries for resale. Its sharply reflexed blooms gave it the popular name of starry wax flower. All these and many more are still to be found in succulent collections and appear from time to time at plant sales. Every colonial dame knew that hoyas need very little root room and that flowers come on the same stubby spurs year after year—cultural facts that have been passed down to this day.

BEGONIAS

Angel-wing begonias enjoyed considerable popularity too, the very tall ones being grown in tubs, the smaller ones as pot plants; some, being pendant in growth, were suited to hanging baskets. Foliage varies from light apple-green to plum colour, some being spangled with silver spots and others having wavy or jagged, cut edges. Other popular begonias were the varieties with very succulent, stumpy stems and very showy large leaves. Two from this group which are still grown as porch plants are *Begonia ricinifolia* 'Maculata', with large green leaves like those of the castor-oil plant (*Ricinus*) and marked underneath by conspicuous red feathery bracts, and beefsteak begonia (*B. erythrophylla*) with large, rounded, deep green leaves. Varieties with marbled, speckled and streaked leaves and ones with feathery 'eyelashes' were thought very elegant and within the scope of home gardeners. Much more demanding were the tuberous begonias and rex begonias; though grown by keen exhibitors for showing, they were mostly the province of professional gardeners with heated 'stoves' (hothouses) at their disposal.

Begonia credneri

SUCCULENTS

Alongside these universal favourites (ferns, begonias, palms, etc.) a host of other plants made attractive companions. Chain of hearts (*Ceropegia barkleyii*) was a firm favourite. With its fine trailing stems and heart-shaped purple leaves veined with silver it makes an easy hanging-basket subject, one that is not sensitive to heat or drying winds. Its very curious tubular flowers and habit of forming small tubers along the stems only add appeal. Happy in similar situations to the chain of hearts is the necklace plant (*Senecio rowleyanus*) which has perfectly round, greyish leaves on thin, trailing stems. It has white flowers, rather like miniature thistles, but they are hardly exciting. A small hanging basket overflowing with a mass of poppet-beaded stems would have delighted any

child visiting a nineteenth-century garden, just as it does today.

To complete a trio of succulent gems found in colonial shade houses, we could not find a plant more suitable than the burro's tail plant (*Sedum morganianum*), still popular today and cultivated keenly by succulent collectors and hanging-basket experts. Its long stems, covered with silvery-grey leaves, need careful attention to keep all the leaves intact, but it is worth the effort.

Completely different are the leaf cacti, generally called epiphyllums. Popular in the nineteenth century and still attracting collectors today, the original plants from the Caribbean and Central America were extensively hybridised by German horticulturalists. Varieties from those days are still to be found—'Deutsche Kaiserin', which is a small grower with pale pink flowers, is still very common. Modern hybrids haven't altered much since the 1880s, though colours may be more varied these days, the flowers still showing an open funnel shape with three to five rows of silky petals. These leaf cacti can be grown in large clumps in pots or hanging baskets.

Similar in habit, with smaller flowers and round succulent stems instead of the flattened leaf form of the epiphyllums, are the rat's tail cactus (*Aporocactus flagelliformis*), with flowers in varying shades of pink, and the mistletoe cacti (*Rhipsalidopsis* spp.) which have tiny, waxy flowers followed by round berries.

Belonging to the same family, but much larger in every respect, is the tree-climbing empress of the night (*Hylocereus triangularis* syn. *H. undatus*) with its huge scented white flowers which open in the evening and close at dawn. Curiosities such as these were popular with colonial gardeners not only because of their unique beauty and novelty but also because they were rare, tender and too difficult for European gardens, although they proved to be easy and tough in many parts of Australia.

Fancy varieties of fuchsia were also very popular among shade-house gardeners of the 1880s. By and large, these finer varieties were susceptible to sun, wind, dry heat and frosts and so might be regarded as delicate in the harsh climate of much of the Antipodes. Nevertheless, many a keen gardener managed to obtain and grow as pot plants in hanging baskets at least a few of the larger flowered kinds of hybrid fuschia. (See chapter 10.)

Whatever its construction and whatever might have been grown in it, the bush house, shade house or fernery was a typical feature of the nineteenth-century garden and is a vital part of any reconstruction. By its very existence, it sets the tone of a garden in period.

ABOVE

Begonias come in many forms, from slender leafy shrubs to low rosettes of colourful leaves. The lax growth of many varieties is suited to hanging basket culture in shady spots.

OPPOSITE PAGE, TOP LEFT

Agaves are hardy and tolerant of a wide variety of soils. Their bold, exotic foliage makes them ideal for contrasting with smaller-leaved succulents.

OPPOSITE PAGE, TOP RIGHT

Clump-forming cacti such as echinopsis and lobivias will slowly make a solid mat of plant bodies. Their large, colourful flowers are an added bonus in dry gardens.

OPPOSITE PAGE, CENTRE LEFT

Crassulas are a varied family of succulent plants. Many have attractive coloured foliage and interesting 'bonsai' forms.

OPPOSITE PAGE, CENTRE RIGHT

The tones of red, orange and yellow in the leaves of this crassula make a colourful ground cover in frost-free areas.

OPPOSITE PAGE, BOTTOM LEFT

Dyckias make tight clumps of green or silver rosettes. Tall spires of orange or yellow flowers add height and colour.

OPPOSITE PAGE, BOTTOM RIGHT

Agave attenuata is a popular large succulent equally at home in a rockery, tub or garden of semi-tropical foliage.

4   The Back Yard

Can you cast your mind back to a back garden of your childhood? Not one of the new-fangled designer gardens of a new house in a fancy residential estate, but one of those gardens that just grew around a plain cottage on a quarter-acre block. Remember the grape vine on a trellis at the back joining up the house with the laundry, woodshed and storeroom? In pre-1900 houses, even the kitchen and bath-house were usually located near to, but separate from, the house proper and were joined to it by sheltered pathways. From the back door a gravelled path led straight past the laundry to the clothes line—a rather ramshackle construction of galvanised wire and tall forked struts to hold the washing off the ground—which occupied an open space about halfway down the yard. Perhaps you recall a stable and tiny horse yard, a cart shed, pigeon house and fowl house. And everyone will remember the 'little house' standing by itself down the back.

To re-create all or some of these structures would be a mighty undertaking, especially if it were done as a comprehensive exercise portraying all aspects of a colonial home. You would need to add to our short list an underground cellar, bee hives, an airing and ironing room, a separating (or still) room for milk, a chaff and grain store for keeping animal fodder and a tack room. And there should still be room left for a generous kitchen garden—but this would be more like a museum than a home garden. I should prefer to have more garden and fewer out-buildings if I were undertaking such a task, weeding and digging being infinitely more pleasurable than railing and painting. Having now admitted that I'm no handyman, I shall set out to put you in the picture about the kitchen garden.

The Kitchen Garden

Firstly, the kitchen garden must be taken seriously. It was the most important part of most cottage gardens of the time, as its produce frequently meant the difference between a satisfying diet and one of very meager rations. Secondly, the vegetable patch, however large or small, must be a business-like set-up; so unless you have plenty of time to put into it, it is perhaps best to keep it on the small and manageable side.

The form of the back garden was usually strictly utilitarian, the area being divided by narrow footpaths into beds which could be worked conveniently from both sides. Around the perimeter and across the back, grape vines and fruit trees screened the garden and provided small luxuries for the summer table or for jam and preserves. In cooler areas a demi-wilderness of raspberries or other soft cane fruits often occupied a remote corner, while in drier areas the ground was more often uncultivated, sparsely grassed and planted with figs or almonds. More adventurous gardeners may have tried novelties such as the prickly pear (*Opuntia ficus-indica* or *O. tuna*) or the tree tomato (*Cyphomandra betacea*). Those who kept poultry (and just about everyone did) would have kept a small patch of lucerne as green feed for the birds.

Closer to the house, on the perimeter of the intensively cultivated plots, perennial vegetables such as horseradish, rhubarb and asparagus were grown. An old tin or bucket buried up to soil level and planted with some sort of mint usually occupied some space in this part of the garden, close enough to get a good watering now and again but at a safe distance from the garden proper.

Home gardeners last century would have devoted a fair proportion of their garden space to basic commodities such as potatoes, onions, various

LEFT
A moment's rest from raking the paths of her back garden gave the photographer his chance to capture a charming garden of fruit trees livened up with a border of sunflowers.

BELOW
A large orchard such as this back garden contains would have provided much fruit for bottling. Why not try making an orchard of the best antique eating apples?

ABOVE
Gateways like this welcome visitors to an old-fashioned garden.
TOP
With a little work to keep the grass down, this old orchard could be easily transformed into a low-maintenance garden.

ABOVE
Silvered mallee branches bleached almost white by the sun form an old-fashioned tripod for a climbing rose.
RIGHT
A quince tree provides dappled shade for tea in the orchard.

members of the pumpkin tribe and a host of beans and peas. While antique strains of vegetables have their populists, many gardeners today would not wish to devote much of their time to the care of such things as 'Blood Red Italian' and 'Zittau Giant' onions, 'Hair's Dwarf Mammoth' peas, 'Magnum Bonum' potatoes or the 'Hundred-Weight Netted' pumpkin. A few things like the 'Turk's Turban' pumpkin or the 'White American Custard' squash could be grown for their novel appearance and their value as gourmet vegetables.

When it comes to planting the vegetable garden proper, the choice is very wide, wide enough in fact to satisfy the most fastidious vegetable gourmet.

New Zealand's Maoris already had well-established vegetable gardens when the white settlers arrived. These included many exotics such as sweet corn, turnips, cabbages and potatoes, which had been introduced by explorers and traders.

Almost any vegetable available today had its equivalent in the nineteenth century, the difference being that whereas many modern varieties are complex hybrids, the rarities of yesteryear were selected seed strains.

For extensive varietal and cultural notes you could not do better than consult Henry Vilmorin's *The Vegetable Garden* (1885) which has been reissued as a paperback. It is the classic vegetable gardening book and was written by the leading vegetable expert of the late 1800s. Herein the enthusiastic vegetable gardener will find all the good stuff about triple-trenched asparagus beds, the advantages of the different sorts of natural and chemical fertilisers and the combinations of each best suited to the edible members of the vegetable kingdom. It's not a new suggestion that the home vegetable grower should concentrate his energies on the production of early and late crops and on varieties not usually

grown by market gardeners. It is, however, sound advice by which a garden restorer can have both a faithful back garden and a productive one. Vegetable experts will need to be consulted about sowing times, harvest times and the daily operations in vegetable culture.

Among what are now popularly known as gourmet vegetables, the following were available to colonial gardeners as well as other more common vegetables: Jerusalem artichoke, asparagus bean (snake bean), kale, broccoli, Chinese cabbage, Cape gooseberry, capers, cardoon (the edible thistle or artichoke), red and pink celery, celeriac, corn salad, endive, kohl rabi, leeks, cos lettuce, okra (gumbo), purple salad onions, sugar peas, parsley (flat-leaved, fern-leaved, moss-leaved, triple curled), Chinese white radish, black Spanish radish, rosella, salsify (vegetable oyster), scorzonera, sea kale, sorrel, squash, cherry tomatoes, greengage tomatoes (yellow) and pear tomatoes.

Following the French: a Grand Design

Let me describe to you a new vegetable garden which encapsulates the traditions of old-fashioned back gardens but also takes into account the change in use that has occurred in the past hundred years. Picture a shallow valley with a broad flattened area made by cutting into a hillside and spreading the soil to partially fill the valley floor. The exposed banks on the low side and the high side have been carefully set with large rocks roughly fitted together and constructed with a slight slope to properly support and hold the earth behind. The shape of the level space created is roughly rectangular, but this is hidden by a perimeter planting of shrubby wild roses, such as *Rosa foetida* 'Persiana', *Rosa ecae*, *Rosa hugonis* and *Rosa cantabrigiensis*, and of almost wild roses like 'Frühlingsgold', 'Golden Chersonese', 'Schneewitchen', 'Blanc Double de Coubert' and 'Frühlingsanfang'. Here and there espalier fruit trees in their first years fill up spaces in the rough hedge that screens the garden from the bushland beyond the rabbit-proof fence.

Inside, the garden is made up of two sections. At the far end, built up with massive blocks of shale, a narrow platform holds four olive trees, behind them a low stone wall; still further back, a semi-circular wall of poplars stands outside the garden. The foreground is taken up by a large circular garden of raised stone-edged beds. Broad paths divide the garden into quadrants, and narrow curved paths lead off these following the circular line of the overall plan. Each bed is about a metre wide and can be gardened from either side. The stone work

The rich virgin soils of many colonial settlements grew prodigious crops—at least for a while. The New Zealand bushman should have been able to feed for a week on this gigantic cabbage.

raises each bed about 60 cm; a convenient height for weeding, cultivating, watering and harvesting, high enough to sit on comfortably and high enough to discourage jumpsome dogs. All of the pathways are made of a thick layer of crunchy quartz river gravel.

Obviously the design has been inspired by the great kitchen gardens of Europe. Circular designs such as those at Gravetye Manor, Sussex, home of horticultural publisher William Robinson, may well have inspired the design, while the combination of vegetables and flowers is surely drawn from the formal French *potager* such as that at the Château de Villandry. Robinson greatly admired the skill of French vegetable and fruit growers and may have developed his garden from the advice of his friend Henry Vilmorin, whose book *Plantes Potagères* Robinson translated and published as *The Vegetable Garden*.

PRODUCTIVITY, VARIETY, FORM AND COLOUR

In the golden light of the late afternoon sun the tall heads and massive arching leaves of artichokes stand silhouetted, brushed silver gilt and ready to pick; planted singly at the ends of rows or clustered centrally in fours, they supply the household for many weeks. Feathery fennel in bronze and green bolts skyward to flower. Thymes of all sorts tumble over the rockwork and spread across the gravelled paths, making a carpet of purple, pink and white. Many more plants can be found growing here ready to harvest, some as recently planted seedlings and others showing signs of flowering.

The variety would have pleased John Evelyn, whose book on salad vegetables, *Acetaria, a discourse of sallets* was published in 1699. He would recognise chicory (flowering in blue, white and pink), pot marigolds, nasturtiums, borage, dill, tarragon, oregano, basil, chervil, salad burnet, all manner of mints, sages (grey-green, silver tricolor and golden variegated), parsley (curled and flat-leaved Italian), and lovage. Unlike many of us, he would also be able to pick out ground-hugging silver-leaved costmary, the starry purple skyrockets of flowering salsify and the tangy-leaved lemon balm. Standing ready to pluck are endives, cos, romaine and radicchio with exotic names: 'Sottomarina Variegata', 'Verona Flamba', 'Treviso Rossa', 'Castelfranco Variegata', 'Rouge d'Hiver', 'Rossa Friulana' and 'Lollo Verdi'. With green, red and striped leaves, plain leaved, oak-leaved, curled, ruffled and frizzed, their neat patches show all the colour of a market stall. And they look so succulent. Alongside them young sweet-corn sprouts show in neatly planted blocks; eggplants, capsicums and celery march rank on rank with white, golden brown and purple onions. Files of

ABOVE

An old smokehouse has been rescued from dereliction and made the centrepiece of a garden restoration project. Although only a few years old, the garden has already begun to develop an atmosphere of its own.

LEFT

A pathway through a garden of culinary herbs to an outdoor dining area hints at a family that enjoys preparing interesting meals and sharing them with friends over a glass of wine. Gardens are for living in, and arrangements such as this show how flexibly gardens can be adapted to reflect our own lifestyles.

OPPOSITE PAGE

A rustic seat awash with the perfume of sweet peas. What more perfect spot from which to admire the beauty and utility of a well-tended and productive potager?

carrots and radishes stand under the towering purple drumsticks of garlic, and strawberries scramble footloose and fancy free.

Further towards the outer circles raspberries are neatly tied-in with strings and stakes; mange tout, runner beans and telegraph peas clamber up poles, gooseberries and redcurrants promise ripe goodies for high summer, and tomatoes (sheltered under wine-flagon cloches) indicate red-ripe ribbed 'Rouge de Marmande', Roman pear, cherry and Beef-hearts for January feasting. Bushes of rosemary sprawl here and there, but young bushes of bay show signs of early military training. Banished to the outermost quadrants, cucumbers, zucchini, squash and pumpkins ramble hither and yon like camp followers heedless of the comings and goings on the vegetable parade ground.

All this doesn't come about as the result of one frenetic weekend; it takes long-term planning (a year in this case) and a great deal of hard work, but it can be done. Jane and James Evans of Golden Point, Chewton, near Castlemaine in Victoria, have done it. Vegetable gardens don't have to be so splendid as theirs, but we all need the example of a visionary *potager* to inspire our planning. Closer to Melbourne, smaller and equally well maintained; is the *potager* at Heronswood, Dromona.

Simpler Arrangements

Maybe you won't want to go all the way with the restoration of your back garden; if a *potager* is not for you, you will be in good company—at least a hundred year's worth of fellow-travellers! No need to abandon your garden restoration project though, for a much simplified arrangement can be developed which reflects old-fashioned style but involves much less labour. This approach is particularly attractive for owners of cottages that are not permanently occupied. It is equally applicable to villa gardens, combining formal elements with plants that can be managed formally or informally. The general idea is to create the formal layout by setting out a rectangular grid of beds and pathways, which for ease of maintenance would be wide enough to let a lawnmower pass, and to line the bed edges with a permanent border of agapanthus (I prefer the miniature form) or belladonnas. Once these have been established a few years, they will fill out into hedges of foliage. The beds should be large enough to have a good clear space in the middle when the edging plants have grown.

Beds at least two metres by two and a half would be about right. In the centre of each bed could be planted cottage garden shrubs such as honeysuckle, lilacs, forsythia, *Hibiscus syriacus*, old-fashioned shrub roses, mock orange, Chinese beauty bush

(*Kolkwitzia*), St John's wort (*Hypericum*), weigela or some other old favourites. These should be allowed to grow naturally with little trimming. An underplanting of tough, colourful South African bulbs makes a colourful spring carpet and needs no care other than a quick tidy-up with an electric nylon-cord weed trimmer in late October. With a little extra work at the outset putting a barrier about 20 cm deep into the soil inside the edging of agapanthus, all the hassles of annual root pruning can be avoided.

A LITTLE MORE WORK—BEAUTIFUL POSSIBILITIES

Similar simple beds could be set out with lavender, rosemary, or lavender cotton (*Santolina pectinata*) as the edging or even used to create whole blocks of foliage, but these require more attention and trimming. If you have the time and inclination, the effects of the more varied planting could be striking. Within such a formal framework a serene composition of greys could be built up using lavenders, santolina, wormwood (*Artemisia*) and common sage with a filling of lamb's tongue (*Stachys lanata*), silver-leaved gazania, *Cerastium tomentosum*, *Veronica cineraria*, *Sedum spectabile*, *Artemisia stelleriana*, *Iris florentina*, *Thymus languinosus*, *Dianthus* spp., *Senecio cineraria*, gypsophila, *Convolvulus cneorum*, *Onopordon acanthium*, *Verbascum olympicum*, rose champion (*Lychnis coronaria*), *Chrysanthemum haradjanii*, *Senecio maritima* or *Ruta graveolens*. Such a setting would be the one place where I would avoid the usual conglomeration of plants found in a cottage garden. I should prefer to use only one or two plants in each bed, say spikey *Iris florentina* with trailing *Artemisia stelleriana* or *Stachys lanata* with *Chrysanthemum haradjanii*. This idea would be a real feature if some of the shrubs were displaced by a regular pattern of standard roses. Such formalism would suit the altogether grander style of a villa garden better than a simple cottage and could be supplemented with a simple arrangement of big tubs to heighten the Mediterranean feeling of a villa garden. Again, such a garden is both more labour-intensive and suited to a town garden than the original concept, though still retaining the nineteenth-century feeling.

My choice of roses for this garden would be 'Lady Hillingdon', 'Buff Beauty', 'Perle d'Or', 'Souvenir de Mme Boullett' and 'Crepuscule'—all lovely old-gold colours—but you could be happier with pinks such as 'Mme Lambard', 'Monsieur Tillier', 'Souvenir d'Un Ami', 'Papa Gontier', 'Mme Charles' and 'Noella Nabonand'.

We seem to have come a long way from the vegetable garden, if not the back yard, so while we are this far afield from a vegetable patch in the nineteenth century we might as well take a look at the effects of modern life on the back yard.

The Modern Back Yard

In a more affluent and leisured society with few pressing needs to grow enough to feed ourselves, the back yard, more than other parts of the garden, has changed its role quite radically. Instead of chicken runs, outhouses, wells and stables, you are far more likely to find basketball hoops, barbecues, patios and swimming pools—the problem is to meld these into the overall colonial feel of the place. Fortunately, all that goes before—the front garden and the side gardens—has served to create the impression of a cottage or villa garden, so a slight deception may find acceptance in a modern eye. The important thing is to continue the impression by the use of a suitable variety of plants arrayed in similar fashion to what has gone before, and to admit the modern intrusions without trying to hide them. If it is possible to plan the features before the garden is made, I should advise the use of simple formal shapes for swimming pools and paving areas. The hard edges can easily be softened by a profusion of overflowing plants, but the basic shapes of square, rectangle and circle are always in keeping. The kidney-shaped swimming pool and free-form paving areas are strictly modern concepts, and no matter how they are planted they always look wrong in a nineteenth-century garden. If you find your newly purchased garden blessed with such ill-fitting structures, then, unless you are very wealthy, you are stuck with them. If, on the other hand, you contemplate building such things, then choose simple formal shapes every time and eschew modern curlicues and staccato angles.

COMBINING OLD AND NEW
Should you attempt to disguise these free-form modernistic features? I should say no. Old-fashioned additions to modern structures generally don't do anything to blend them in. Instead, the violent contrasts between, say, a modern brick barbecue and an old-style gazebo only serve to heighten the sense of alienation. The best course would be simply to tie the whole outdoor living area together with lawn or paving and screen it from the rest of the garden by some sort of light fencing, preferably well clothed with climbers and shrubs—old-fashioned ones, of course! A semi-hedge made this way should be about two metres high. Useful plants for such a screen are any of the jasmines or clematis such as *Clematis cirrhosa* 'Balaerica', *C. napaulensis*, *C. tangutica*, *C. viticella* or *C. flammula*. Some of the newly introduced

honeysuckles would be well suited too—especially *Lonicera hildebrandiana* with its large evergreen leaves and golden flowers, and *L. serotina* 'Magnifica' with silver-grey leaves and brilliant orange-scarlet tabular flowers.

Useful light shrubs for such a project would be *Cedronella triphylla*, *Salvia rutilans* (pineapple sage), or scented-leaved pelargoniums such as *Pelargonium graveolens*, *P.* × 'Lady Plymouth'. *P.* × 'Mable Gray'. *P. papillionaceum* and *P. vitifolium* (see chapter 9: 'Simply Geraniums').

If space permits, and you have the energy, a simple structure of upright rustic logs spaced 2½ to 3½ metres apart and about the same height, linked at the top by very loosely strung wire or heavy rope, could increase the amount of screening, give visual interest, and add to the nineteenth-century feeling of a secret garden once vines and climbers had been trained over it. On such a structure, planting should still be light—it's the impression of *separateness* created by the structure and planting that is wanted, not a heavy planting which completely hides the area. Perhaps one or two more substantial climbers could be admitted, but only one or two!

Three less commonly found climbers which I would prefer over the more obvious choices of glory vine, Lady Banks rose and rambler roses are *Vitis coignetiae*, with huge round leaves and brilliant purple-red autumn colours, the rose 'Mme Gregoire Staechelin' with masses of blowsy two-tone pink flowers, and *Wistaria sinensis alba* or the double blue form. All these are variations on the more obvious choices but sufficiently distinct to impart that feeling of richness and diversity which touched the old cottage and villa gardens.

The Small Back Yard

If a little terrace house is being restored, almost the whole of the back garden would be occupied by outdoor living areas and garaging, so cottage garden colour would be limited to a changing display of annuals in large tubs. The tubs could be permanently planted with your special favourites—a rose or camellia, say. High boundary walls need some veil of greenery and flowers but nothing that will become a pest or a chore. For sunny walls, I would use climbers of moderate habits such as the large-flowered clematis, jasmine or maybe a rose—'Paul's Scarlet Climber' or 'Sombreuil' would be about right for size. For shaded walls, the choice could be *Trachelospermum jasminoides* (star jasmine) or one of the very slow ivies—*Hedera canariensis* 'Albo-maculata' (white leaves speckled green) or *H. helix* 'Deltoidea' with leaves like arrowheads—the climbing hydrangea (*Hydrangea petiolaris*) or even the

ABOVE
Being able to look over a garden from above brings a new perspective into play. More is revealed than can be seen at ground level, but mystery is retained by shrubs and trees which curtain off parts of the garden from direct lines of sight.

LEFT
Herbs and low flowers revel in the warmth and good drainage along this gravel path. Allowing plants to sprawl and self-sow among the pebbles is one way to achieve an old-fashioned effect in gardens.

FAR LEFT
An old wheelbarrow serves as a planter for colourful annuals.

TOP FAR LEFT
Pigeons—white tumblers, nuns and fantails—and old-fashioned gardens seem to go together.

exquisite Chilean waxflower (*Lapageria rosea*) if you can get one! Room being at a premium, the choice of the one or two trees that might be fitted in must be limited to those that give at least two tangible pleasures and let in the sun in the winter. *Magnolia salicifolia*, with lemon-scented starry white flowers and taller growth than *M. stellata*, could be a possibility; *Paulownia imperialis*, with blue jacaranda-type flowers and round furry leaves, might be another. The first is slow growing and the last can be pollarded (cut right back to the trunks) if necessary. Of course, you might wish to indulge in the pleasures of a walnut, pecan or fruit tree, any of which would be acceptable and attractive.

In small gardens such as these it's very difficult to recreate accurately a cottage garden. The right atmosphere can be created by the careful choice of plants, construction materials and fittings. The same applies to those whose back gardens must accommodate the activities of a young family. The feeling of cottage-garden cosiness can be brought about by an awareness of the basic essentials: variety and profusion and a maximum of informality within a regularised setting.

Covering the Woodshed

The number of sheds and out-buildings in the back yard of a colonial home must have driven the home gardener to establish vines and other climbing plants over them. In many cases the planting of climbers was a practical solution to the problems of how to keep corrugated-iron buildings cool and how to cover up buildings that were strictly utilitarian and basic in appearance and finish. A building wall was also a convenient place to grow vine crops.

For big sheds such as cart sheds (or in modern times carports and garages), there were some really vigorous climbers that could be relied on to smother the biggest shed in a few years. Among them were several plants with strong sentimental appeal. The Lady Banks rose (see chapter 8) is one big climber that is frequently seen on old buildings. Wistaria is another cover-all that really grew in popularity during the nineteenth century. Apart from the usual lilac form (*Wistaria floribunda*), other cultivars were collected from gardens in China and introduced in Europe—the white, pink and double blue forms. If you want to plant a wistaria, why not try to get one of these less common varieties? You may have to search around a bit to get one, but the result after a few years' growth would be a specimen plant that would have appealed to any keen gardener during the reign of Queen Victoria. China was not the only place to give wistarias to the plant collector; from Japan came *W. multijuga*, with

D.	**Medeola asparagoides** (*Myrsiphyllum*)	...		...	1 6
E.	**Muehlenbeckia Australis**, yellowish		...	...	1 6
E.	**Passiflora alba**, white ...	...	...	...	1 6
E.	**alata**, green, blue, red, very sweet-scented			...	2 6
E.	**cœrulea** (*Passion Flower*)	...	...	...	1 6
E.	**Constance Elliott**, pure ivory-white, flowers profusely ...	...	...	...	1 6

PASSIFLORA CONSTANCE ELLIOTT.

E.	**Passiflora edulis** (*Passion Fruit*), white ...		...	1 0
E.	**Imperatrice Eugenie**, blue and white, large			1 6
E.	**macrocarpa**, white and purple	...		...	2 6
E.	**quadrangularis** ...	...	...	...	2 6
E.	**racemosa (Princeps)**, scarlet	...		...	2 6
E.	**vespertilio**	...	...	...	...	1 6

From a nineteenth-century catalogue

flowering stems well over a metre in length—sufficiently impressive to satisfy even the most particular gardener.

Also from Japan came *Akebia trifoliata*, a vigorous twining plant with graceful leaves resembling a clover-leaf. In late spring, masses of smoky maroon-purple 'bobble' flowers give off a light but far-reaching perfume.

More spectacular in foliage, though without any blossom to speak of, are the true vines, the *Vitis* family. Many of us can call to mind hoary old specimens of the crimson glory vine with massive gnarled butts and arm-thick branches spreading far and wide. This ornamental grape is sold in southern Australia under a variety of names—'Alicante Bouchet', 'Teinturier' and 'Teinturier Male' as well as glory vine and crimson glory vine; however, the name 'Ganzin Glory' (*Vitis* × 'Ganzin Glory') has been proposed by researchers in South Australia. There were fruiting grapes too, for the table, for jam making and for drying.

Two rampant creepers from the south introduced to Europe as fine-flowered glasshouse plants were the trumpet vines, once known as *Bignonia* but now split off by botanists into a legion of relatives and leaving *Bignonia* almost bereft of family—in fact only two remain. Gardeners in Australia found only the frost deterred trumpet vines' rampaging growth. Possibly the most stunning of them is *Campsis radicans* from the south-east United States, which has flowers similar in shape to a gloxinia, brick-red with an orange throat. Such brilliant flowers teamed with lush, dark green leaves and supreme vigour added a touch of tropical luxuriance to many a shed and fence. The other rampager is *Pandorea ricasoliana*, with leaves and flowers similar but for their colouring, which is pale pink with deeper veining leading to a rose-pink patch in the throat of each flowery trumpet. Each is strong enough to cover a cow-shed—and the cow too if she stood still for only a week or two!

Another member of the family Bignoniaceae, *Tecomaria capensis* from South Africa, is only slightly less vigorous, though it seems to have been used more as a hedge than a climber. It has metallic green foliage arranged in 7–11 leaflets and strident orange-red tubular flowers in small clusters. All three are determined 'doers' with a considerable degree of wilfulness. Be cautioned! Only the bravest should plant them; prune ruthlessly or the entire garden will be the subject of a botanical coup d'état!

Equally vigorous is the Algerian ivy (*Hedera canariensis*) and its varieties, 'Gloire de Marengo', the common large-leaved variegated ivy, and 'Paddy's Pride', the dark green form with a golden central blotch. These ivies have sufficient appeal in their brightly coloured leaves to make whatever trimming is needed worth while. But do remember that trimming is necessary. Can you imagine your disgust at the slow death of a host tree due to strangulation should these great ground covers get started up the trunks of trees? Or what of the expense involved should stems get under the eaves and inside the roof of your expensively restored villa, lifting the cladding and admitting possums, starlings and sparrows? Better perhaps to choose something less vigorous.

One ivy stands out as a look-alike for the larger *Hedera canariensis*, though it is less robust. It is *Hedera colchica* 'Dentata Variegata' with large leaves broadly banded outside with creamy gold.

CLEMATIS

Strong growers but definitely not in the massive class are *Clematis montana* (white), *C. montana* 'Rubens' (pink) and *C. chrysocoma* (pearly white). They are all magnificent performers and have been known since the late 1800s. Personally I dislike the pink of *C. montana* 'Rubens', finding the colour too murky and too mauve. But the white form (*C. montana*) is pure and pristine, and almost a must for covering a small shed or wall. *Clematis armandii* just scrapes in, being introduced in 1900, but it is such a splendid plant that I would not have left it out even if it had been introduced in 1910 (and you will find there are several others like this that are too good

to leave out and have been included because they are characteristic of the age even if not quite chronologically correct). At any season the foliage of *C. armandii* is a knockout: deep bronzy fingers up to 18 cm long which slowly deepen to a glossy rich green as they age. The new growth is almost red. In early spring or late winter it smothers itself with tumbling tresses of perfumed white flowers. Magnificent yet still cottagey. It's an evergreen too, so it would be perfect to cover an ugly shed. Like all clematis it must have shade and coolness at the roots. Either protect the roots with other low plants to create shade or use straw spread thickly to make a mulch. I like using straw myself; bought by the bale, it is easy to handle and convenient. When the binding twine is cut, the bales fall apart in handy, compressed wads ready to spread. It doesn't smell either. After a short time in the weather the pale yellow straw turns grey and is hardly noticeable. It will only last one season, but by the following year your foundation planting of lavenders, scented-leaf geraniums, etc., will be established and create the shade at the roots which clematis must have.

When thinking of cottage gardens and clematis, most people would conjure up visions of the large-flowered sorts. These began to appear in England and France in the 1850s, and in the next twenty years an extraordinary spate of breeding created the style of bloom still held up as the ideal of perfection today. Obtaining plants can be a problem. Nurserymen seem to have more bad years than good when it comes to propagating them; yet it all seems so easy in Christopher Lloyd's very readable monograph *Clematis*, so maybe his advice needs some local interpretation. The outcome of all this is that gardeners can't always get the clematis they want and so snap up whichever are available. At least as far as appearance goes there is precious little difference between nineteenth- and twentieth-century cultivars. Genuine nineteenth-century varieties include 'W.E. Gladstone'—large silky lavender flowers with darker stamens (1881); 'Mrs Hope'—huge satin-finished light blue flowers with overlapping petals (1875); 'Durandii'—brilliant dark blue flowers with pale stamens, not a climber but a scrambler (1870), great planted with apricot shrub roses such as 'Period d'Or' or 'Buff Beauty'; 'Duchess of Edinburgh'—double, greenish-white flowers (1876); 'Belle of Woking'—double French-grey (silvery-white); 'Lady Londesborough' —silver-grey single blooms (1869); 'Fair Rosamond'—scented blush white (1873); 'Henryi' —large white with dark stamens (1855); 'Ville de Lyon'—brilliant beetroot-red, bright but not garish (1899); 'Star of India'—reddish-purple, starry petals (1867); 'Gypsy Queen'—very dark purple-red, starry petals (1877); 'Sir Garnet Wolseley'—deep lavender (1880); 'Miss Crawshay'—mauve-pink,

A place to eat outside is a great idea; however, it must be conveniently close for food, drink and dishes to be carried from the house without trekking across the entire garden.

LEFT

The impact of special feature plants such as espaliered trees immediately identifies a garden as having a certain style; whether that is classical French formal or English cottage garden, it is always old-fashioned.

ABOVE

This scene is remarkably satisfying; it looks so 'right'—the growth is mature; the foliage is varied in form and colour; the plants are layered one above the other; there are no jarring colours; the steps, paving and walls are well integrated and weathered. This is old-fashioned gardening at its best.

LEFT

Planning a garden means that we should consider not only the views looking out from the house but also those looking toward the house from the perimeter of the garden. Too often we forget to look back.

FAR LEFT

Seats, chairs and tables need to be sited so that they encourage use: they must be sheltered from prevailing winds and weather; they must be clustered together if intended for promoting conversations or set well apart if meant for solitary musing.

121

early blooms, double (1873); 'Comtesse de Bouchaud'—pink, vigorous and very prolific (1900); 'Nelly Moser'—almost white with a deeper pinkish bar in the centre of each petal (1897).

There are others too, but as I said most people are happy to take whatever they can get, and any of them will look right in a colonial garden. For pruning instructions I suggest you read Christopher Lloyd (see Bibliography). His book is the last word on this and other clematis matters.

Clematis viticella, C. flammula, C. alpina, C. × 'Venosa Violacea' and *C. campaniflora* are also good small climbers with small flowers which are in period and available from time to time. They are easily raised from seed, though they sometimes take their time about it (one to two years), and the Royal Horticultural Society seed list usually contains several species. *Clematis tangutica*, the lemon peel clematis (1898) and its similar cousin *C. orientalis* (1731) are two curious types with small flowers which have 'thick-skinned' petals in clear yellow and greenish-yellow.

Colonial gardeners in Australia and New Zealand also had some native species of clematis—old man's beard, traveller's joy or virgin's bower they were called. *Clematis aristata* from Australia is a common bushland climber which was brought early into settlers' gardens because of its similarities to the old man's beard (*C. vitalba*) of the homelands and for its perfumed flowers. *C. afoliata, C. forsteri, C. hookerana, C. parviflora* and *C. paniculata* are all New Zealand species which attracted the attention of garden-conscious settlers. Though frequently referred to as 'old-favourites' for sheltered walls, *C. napaulensis* and *C. cirrhosa* var. *balearica* are two whose dates of introduction elude me. I would include them anyhow, for their winter flowers are small and charming. Each bears pendant flowers of greenish-yellow. The former has protruding anthers of clear lavender, and the latter has maroon flecks on the petals. Neither are world-shattering, not yet great rarities, but both are welcome and just the sort of 'vegetable curiosity' so loved last century. *C. napaulensis* is deciduous from late summer until winter and *C. cirrhosa* var. *balearica* is evergreen with dark bronzy fern-like leaves.

BOUGAINVILLEAS, JASMINES AND HONEYSUCKLES

After clematis, what else? Not much for many gardeners (even in colonial times there were plenty of one-eyed gardeners), but other climbers have their charms and their devotees. In tropical climes bougainvilleas were *the* climbers, and even in temperate areas they were widely planted. Just how many varieties were in commerce a hundred years ago is uncertain. Lists with a dozen or so sorts seem to have the usual purple, red, pink, white and variegated types. The teaser is in the small print underneath: 'Other varieties on application, plus newer novelties in short supply'; and, 'Some other recent introductions' which tantalise and confound. Were there nineteenth-century equivalents of our modern dwarf, double and particoloured forms? It seems highly likely to me that such cultivars were in existence, bearing in mind the passion, leisure and wealth with which some colonial gardeners could pursue their hobby, and the extent and sophistication of the native nurseries of the Far East, near at hand and ready to satisfy the planters' whims and accept their patronage.

There yet remains a goodly selection of other climbers which produce a permanent framework, as well as perennial and annual climbers. Foremost among those which make a permanent growth are the jasmines, as popular today as they have ever been for their pervasive perfume, especially welcome on still summer evenings. Among the real jasmines (*Jasminum* spp.) known in the nineteenth century there were *J. sambac* and its double form, *J. gracilis, J. grandiflorum, J. officinale, J. poicoceum* and *J. ×* 'Maid of Orleans'—a double form I would like to meet. There was also *J. polyanthum*, so common these days it's almost ho-hum; yet it's anything but that. Despite its covering power, the fine foliage and delicate, graceful sprays of bloom lighten the dark green growth so that the effect is not overbearing. Apart from the real jasmines, there are quite a few plants known as jasmines that belong to other families: *Cestrum* spp. (day and night jasmines), *Trachelospermum* (star jasmine) and also the Confederate jasmine and the Carolina yellow jessamine, *Gelsemium*. Other possibilities, if you still have some room left on a wall somewhere, are *Stephanotis* (Madagascar jasmine) and *Mandevilla* (Chilean jasmine).

Honeysuckles too were a family of climbers well known in those times. Some are very exuberant, so be careful to select varieties that will suit the space you have available. Two commonly found in old nursery catalogues are the very well-known *Lonicera aureo-reticulata* and *L. confusa*, both evergreens and prodigious performers. The early Dutch honeysuckle (*L. periclymenum* var. *belgica*) and the late Dutch honeysuckle (*L. p. serotina*) are both well perfumed and have similar flowers, purple-red outside and creamy yellow within. The trumpet honeysuckle, *L. sempervirens* 'Superba' (also *magnifica*) has recently been introduced here and deserves inclusion. It has been known in English gardens since 1656 when it was introduced from the United States. It's odd that it isn't recorded in Australia in colonial times, as far as I can discern, for it certainly would have been well established in England by the nineteenth century. It has circular, paired leaves which are grey and often joined around the stem; the flowers are bright orange-red and tubular. Although there is no scent, it is still worth while.

TENDER TROPICALS, PERENNIALS AND OTHER CLIMBERS

Colonial gardeners were also fond of tender climbers which could be treated as annuals. In some seasons these might come through the winter and make good regrowth; in others new seedlings would be needed to start the plants again. Two such that are still moderately popular are the cup-and-saucer vine (*Cobea scandens*) and the moonflower (*Calonyction aculeatum*), but what has happened to the curious green cobea from San Salvador that appeared in seed lists at the turn of the century? Its strange pendant flowers with very long stamens and thin twisted petals would make it a talking point in any modern cottage garden. It is probably either *Cobea hookerana* or *C. penduliflora*. *Eccremoncarpus scaber*, in yellow, orange and red strains, was another fairly reliable tender climber. They are still available (Thompson Morgan have them) but are not much seen.

One reliable perennial climber is the hop plant, but who sells it these days—to gardeners anyway? There are golden and variegated varieties, but these seem quite lost as far as Australia goes. A pity, as both the foliage and fruits are attractive; it was grown for use in home brewing and home medicine.

The perennial peas have become naturalised in many parts of southern Australia, particularly the two-toned purple-red *Lathyrus tingitana*. The old-fashioned sweet peas, *Lathyrus odoratus*, grown before a certain Mr Spencer started breeding them into today's large ruffled brands, may still be found in many old gardens. Their perennial roots live many years and they seed moderately, too. They come in white, pale pink and rose and some intermediate forms with deeper coloured keels and lighter guard petals. The pure white form is particularly beautiful.

In favoured gardens where cool climate and acid soil are found, the flame creeper can be grown. It is a *Tropaeolum* and therefore a relative of the nasturtium. *T. tricolor* has small nodding red flowers with a single spur, and black and yellow markings at the mouth. The ferny leaves are trifoliate like miniature clover leaves. It grows from a dahlia-like tuber which demands damp, sandy, peaty soil in a cool place. In spring, fine wiry stems shoot up, entwining whatever is handy, and flowers appear in midsummer. It produces a very startling show

from very light growth. Grown among dark, slow conifers such as *Pinus mugo*, *Taxus baccata* 'Fastigiata' or *Picea abies* 'Maxwellii', it is especially brilliant.

Finally, we should mention the gourds, those members of the cucumber and pumpkin family whose variegated fruits in curious shapes and covered with warts have been objects of fascination for ages. Though not so decorative as to warrant a prominent site in a garden, a few vines planted over a henhouse or by the back fence will provide an ample supply of decorative fruits for indoors. The vines are annuals and need good soil preparation and ample water during early summer.

The range of climbers grown in modern gardens seems much smaller than those grown in colonial gardens. I would hazard a guess that a good many modern gardens have no climbers at all. I think it would be rare to find a nineteenth-century garden that did not contain a grapevine or even a lowly choko!

The Garden Creek

If you are lucky enough to have a natural stream in your back yard, one that runs all year, you are indeed blessed and should make the most of it with attractive plantings. If you have a stream that is dry by midsummer, don't despair and send out for tonnes of concrete, butyl rubber liners and a reticulation pump. A dry creek can be just as attractive as one running with water if it is planted with interesting plants and carefully maintained. The latter is easy; as the stream dries up, remove all the debris washed down in the winter rains and clean up as far as possible dead and decaying foliage, spent flower stalks and other vegetable trash. What is left should be boulders and rocks along the watercourse, a sandy or pebbly bottom and a fringe of growing plants. In effect, the result should look somewhat like a Japanese 'dry' garden without the obvious lanterns and sculptures.

What can you plant along a creek? Remembering that most streams remain damp all summer under the sand and gravel bottom, there are a good selection of interesting plants that can be grown, more if some additional water can be supplied by hoses or sprinklers. The following are good plants for the margins of creeks:

Amsonia tabernaemontana, Astilbe, Astrantia, Macleaya cordata, Eomecon chionantha, Hosta 'Krossa Regal', *H.* 'Frances Williams', *H.* 'Sum and Substance', *H. ventricosa* 'Aureo-marginata', *Hemerocallis, Heracleum giganteum, Hibiscus moscheutos* 'Southern Belle' *Iris siberica, I. laevigata, I. forrestii, I. bulleyana, I. pseudacorus* 'Aureo-

marginata', *I. foetidissima* 'Variegata', *I. delavayii*, *I. ensata*, *Kirengeshoma palmata*, *Lysimchia*, *Lythrum*, *Crocosmia*, *Ranunculus acris* 'Plenus', *Rodgersia*, *Primula*, *Caltha palustris plena*, *Brunnera macrophylla*, *Polygonatum multiflorum*, *Polemonium caeruleum*, *Polygonum reynoutria*, *Thalictrum speciosissimum*, *Crambe cordifolia*, *Houttuynia cordata* 'Chameleon', *Pulmonaria saccharata*.

Ferns: *Osmunda regalis*, *Onoclea sensibilis*, *Athyrium felix femina*, *Woodwardia radicans*, *Asplenium nidus*, *Blechnum gibbum*, *Pellaea rotundifolia*, *Polystichum setiferum*, *Rumohra adiantiformis*.

Grasses: *Arudinaria viridistriata*, *Miscanthus sinensis* 'Striata', *Miscanthus sinensis* 'Zebrinus', *Stipa gigantea*, *Pennisetum alopecuroides*, *Chasmanthium latifolium*, *Sasa veitchii* (with care to contain its roots).

Can you plant in the creek bed? This can be tempting, but the results are not always happy. Streams tend to rage and flood following winter downpours and summer thunderstorms. Plants growing in the stream bed can easily be dislodged by the rush of water and swept away downstream, where they will become someone else's garden assets. Even well-established plants can be scoured out of their positions. Snags tend to gather around plants growing in streams too, the dead weight of accumulating flotsam and jetsam eventually tearing the plants' roots out of the soil. If the creek is wide and shallow, these problems are less likely to occur and some planting could take place in the creek bed; however, bear in mind that half the beauty of a creek, flowing or dry, is the uninterrupted ribbon of water or sand that marks its course.

An almost wild garden surrounds and encloses a small pond. Great care has been taken to ensure that the reflective surface is framed by trees, shrubs and water plants but not obliterated by them. Sensitive trimming and pruning make this scene possible.

ABOVE
Overhanging trees and shrubs have cut out the possibility of this pool reflecting the sky. Even so, it can still be brought to life by the flash of goldfish and by growing some curiously formed floating water plants.

ABOVE LEFT
A variety of plants with iris-like leaves relate the garden around to a small artificial pond where poor soils would make it difficult to grow more luxuriant water-loving plants.

LEFT
Contrasting leaf forms of waterlilies and water irises do not completely hide the water of this pool.

5 On the Verandah

Having already passed through the fernery of our mind's eye's restoration we should return briefly to the front verandah to take in the collection of potted plants displayed there. Keen gardeners last century were no less acquisitive than their modern-day counterparts. Delicate plants were sheltered from the harsh elements in the shade house, small glasshouses or frames. Hardier specimens were housed, much as they are today, in places safe from the sun's scorching rays but where the free flow of air and intensity of light were sufficient to keep growth healthy and compact. The shelter provided by the overhang of a front verandah provided an almost ideal place for growing hardy pot plants.

Potted Plants

The first of these might be small palms, frequently a kentia palm, *Rhapis* or cycad, but just as likely a camellia or two in halved wine-barrels, half of a forty-four-gallon drum or a square kerosene tin (suitably painted, of course). In the drier areas, hydrangeas were very popular as porch plants, because by using imported mountain soil or chemical means the growing mixture could be made acid enough to produce blue flowers—desired so much more than the common pinks produced in the inland plains and alkaline soil areas.

Other subjects for big tubs were cliveas, pink tiger lilies (*Lilium speciosum*), the common orange tiger lily (*L. tigrinum*), the sacred lily of the Incas (*Ismene festalis*) or the eucharist lily (*Eurycles amazonica*). Hippeastrums, too, were enjoying their first big vogue and were a available in red and white and striped combinations of these two colours, only the refinements of the blooms separating them from the majestic blooms of today. German hybridisers were the main workers with these bulbs, possibly because of the concentration

of German explorers and botanists in their South American homelands.

In the really dry areas in the days before regular water supply systems were installed, such drought-hardy bulbs were valued pot plants, as they could be kept going with waste water from kitchen and bathroom without damage. Even today, there are many who swear by the drainings and dregs of the teapot—a demonstration of the staying power of this lore of colonial gardeners.

Florists' Flowers

In an earlier chapter, 'florists' flowers' were mentioned in passing as being not much used by cottage and villa gardeners as they required too much attention when grown as cool glasshouse subjects, what with damping down, ventilating and pest control to be attended to daily, as well as watering, feeding, pruning and tying up of each potted plant. But where growing by the dozen was entirely too much to manage, growing one or two specimens to perfection was a challenge. Among the most popular florists' flowers were calceolarias (purse flowers), cinerarias, cyclamen, schizanthus (poor man's orchid) and salpiglossis.

'Florists' were not flower sellers and providers of wreaths and floral gifts as we know them today but a class of gardening enthusiasts who specialised in collecting, breeding, growing and showing a restricted group of plants selected for their floral perfection according to the ideals of the day. Those ideals, put very generally, were flowers circular in outline, with clear and regular markings—stripes, edges, flakes, spots, eye zones, etc—and a uniform arrangement of petals. Amateur and professional gardeners have delighted in this solitary recreation since at least the eighteenth century.

Plants that have attracted florists at various times since then have been auriculas, pinks, tulips, ranunculi, anemones, camellias, pansies, violas, hyacinths, dahlias, roses and chrysanthemums, as well as those previously mentioned and others (see Roy Genders's *The Cottage Garden and Old-Fashioned Flowers*).

It's not hard to see how these basic ideals of perfection have influenced flowers and flower shows right up to the present. Contemporary developments in peonies, day lilies (*Hemerocallis*), gladioli, irises, liliums and roses all show the strong influence of the 'round and regular' school of thought. Fortunately for today's gardeners, there are some breeders sufficiently individualistic to persist in raising and introducing plants with a greater degree of variety than the old florists' rules would allow us. We would be foolish to throw away the plants that have come down to us from the florists of old, but neither should we let them dominate a garden restoration.

Other flowering small plants commonly found on the verandah were ordinary garden things chosen for the pleasures of close association—the colour and perfume of favourite flowers brought almost indoors. Freesias, lachenalias, geraniums, campernellas (*Narcissus campernella*), Regal pelargoniums and various primulas are just a few of the everyday plants put into pots and brought onto the verandah.

Succulents

Far less common, and most intriguing, were the varied assortments of succulent plants cultivated by many householders. All sorts of cacti and other succulents were grown in everything from half wine-barrels to jam tins. The 'cute' use of old boots as pots seems to have been a development of the 1950s, and perhaps this novel idea should be eschewed. If you are seeking to develop some sense of colonial rusticity, perhaps you could use one or two old cast-iron cooking pots as plant containers

—if you could keep them out of the hands of the antique collectors! Exotic specimens from South Africa, South America, the dry lands of Central America and the western United States were imported as mature field-collected plants in the days before Commonwealth quarantine laws. Seed-raising played its part too, as well as propagation by offsets, and succulent plants gained a wide popularity.

Aside from their desirability as potted plants, many succulents were advertised as being very useful for edging and bedding-out. The most popular plants for these purposes were some of the rosette-forming succulents known as echeverias. Ranging from 10 to 30 cm in diameter, these hardy Mexicans made colours such as silver, pink and olive green available for permanent plantings in garden colour schemes. The following are among the hardiest and most prolific: *Echeveria elegans*, silver foliage; *E. albicans*, white foliage; *E. metallica*, metallic grey foliage; *E.* × 'Huth's Pink', rose pink foliage; *E.* × 'Perle von Nürnberg', pink with purple edge; *E. gilva*, olive green foliage; *E. byrnesii*, bright green foliage; *E. secunda*, pointed silver leaves (see also chapter 12). All are frost tender and suffer badly in hailstorms. A single row of rosettes lined out in early spring will soon multiply into a solid edging that's proof against the hottest summer.

Should you be blessed with a dry-stone wall (see chapter 3), a few echeveria rosettes tucked into the crevices here and there will soon settle in and look as if they've been there for at least a hundred years. If you haven't such a wall, then the echeverias will look just as good in an array of squat pots on your verandah, multiplying happily while they wait for you to build them a wall for a home.

For small pots, the range of succulent plants is large. Aloes such as the partridge-breasted aloe (*Aloe variegata*) and *A. aristata* were well known, along with aeoniums, mesembryanthemums (pigface), crassulas, *Portulacaria* (jade plant) and especially sempervivums, the house leeks. Popular since the Middle Ages for their reputation as protectors of houses against thunderbolts, these tiny rosetted plants were given a fresh boost by the activities of alpinists during the Victorian era, and many outstanding varieties were introduced at that time. They are ideal subjects for pots, being hardy, colourful and prolific multipliers. There are at least a hundred varieties in the hands of private collectors, a few of the best being *Sempervivum arachnoideum* and the hybrids 'Malby Hybrid', 'Sir Trevor Lawrence', 'Triste', 'Olivette', 'Omicron', 'Cleveland Morgan', 'Old Copper', 'Flamingo', 'Grigg's Surprise', 'Ohio Burgundy', 'Raspberry Ice', 'Jungle Shadows' and 'Blue Moon'. These are not all nineteenth-century varieties, but it's very

FAR RIGHT

This small garden is necessarily fairly low key because of the dominant influence of the brightly painted house. A light climber scrambles around the doorway, and a foundation planting of potted herbs and small plants occupy the narrow garden.

RIGHT

Pots beside steps draw attention to plants of special interest and help soften the hard lines of the pavement.

BELOW

A collection of old pots and makeshift planters on a low stone wall provide a variety of colour as the seasons pass.

ABOVE

A well-chosen pot filled with a selection of colourful succulents (Sempervivum spp.) *makes a welcome sight in an otherwise dull corner and needs much less care than most other pot plants.*

ABOVE

While pots are available from many sources, the best-looking kinds for old-fashioned gardens are hand-made. Always check that the pots are large enough to allow healthy plant growth.

RIGHT

Small rare bulbs are best displayed in pots where their beautiful flowers can be enjoyed at close range. Crocuses, dwarf daffodils and the like are too easily lost in garden beds.

hard to determine just which varieties were grown then, so great is the confusion of species, cultivars and hybrids.

Sempervivums are natives of Europe and quite naturally were objects of sentimental attachment for many settlers, but the gardeners of the period were equally enthusiastic about the latest succulent novelties from South Africa. Haworthias were one such group that found early favour as attractive pot plants. There are two distinct groups in this family: one has green succulent leaves with 'see-through' tips; the other has grey-green leaves with pearly white spots. A visit to the garden of any collector of succulents would almost certainly enable you to obtain a few specimens.

During the nineteenth century the flow of plants from the New World to Europe included many cacti. As pot plants they were especially attractive because of their unique form and often brilliant flowers. As in many other plant families, the cactus tribe is still the subject of much name changing and revision by botanists, so making a comprehensive list could easily turn into a nightmare. I will list a few that should be recognised by the cactus buff, even if they do preface their sales with the comment, 'Of course, you know the name's been changed to. . . .' 'For pot culture the *Mammillarias* are both easy and very pretty, *Rebutias* and *Echinopsis* too. For a big impact the golden ball cactus (*Echinocactus grusonii*) can't be beaten, though the *Ferocactus*, heavily armed with hooked thorns in black, red or tan, are almost as stunning. The peanut cactus (*Chamaecereus silvestrii*) is an old familiar well suited to pot culture; its cheery tomato-red blooms are produced in profusion on a no-fuss plant. These few are but a small number from an amazing procession of succulent plants which first came to our gardens last century. They are not especially significant; just a sample of the range of plants available to colonial gardeners for use as front verandah pot plants.

Potting Soils

Horticultural research has declared that soil—real dirt, that is—is not adequate for the growing of plants in containers. The problems with common garden dirt are simply that when used for potting plants it does not have the best drainage and water-holding qualities; nor does it have enough air between the grains of soil. It also has some disadvantages in that it is very heavy, it is difficult and expensive to rid of pests and plant diseases, and it uses up a precious resource—the soil in your garden. The best answer to the problems has been to develop soilless soils. Various universities, horticultural research organisations and commercial

interests have invented blends of materials such as sand, pine park, sawdust, rice hulls, peanut shells and peat moss which are designed to meet the required growing conditions of a variety of container-grown plants. These mixtures usually need to be supplemented with slow-release fertiliser granules or a liquid fertiliser on a regular basis to keep plants growing happily. For most potted plants an acidic or regular (slightly alkaline) potting mixture will be perfectly suitable. Orchids need very well-drained potting mixtures; as many do not grow in soil in their natural state, they are best planted in a mixture specially developed for orchids.

CAN I MAKE MY OWN?

Making up a soil mixture for potting plants is very time consuming and is also hard work. To begin with, at least three compost heaps are needed: one ready to use, one completed and in the final stages of rotting down, and one that is being made with fresh materials. Also needed are neatly stored dry supplies of very gritty sand, leaf mould and/or well-rotted animal manures, charcoal, small gravel screenings, supplies of a slow-acting 'acidifier' such as flowers of sulphur (dusting sulphur) and a slow-acting fertiliser such as hoof and horn meal or bone meal. A supply of soil will also be needed that is free of weed seeds and has been sterilised by heat—chemical sterilising treatments are too dangerous for home gardeners to use. This all needs to be stored in a convenient work space along with pots, sieves and other gardening necessities. A proper potting shed is the answer, but how many have room in their gardens or the time to do all this. Even those who do have a potting shed often find that buying a basic potting mixture and 'doctoring' it with extra leaf mould, compost or grit is the most convenient way of potting their plants.

Watering

Clever old gardeners can tell by listening whether or not a pot plant needs watering. When tapped with a small wooden hammer a wet pot has a distinctive ring. Those not adept at telling a *clunk* from a *clink* will have to rely on other methods. The simplest is to poke a finger into the soil of a pot plant and feel if it is damp about 3 cm (up to the first knuckle) deep. More plants die from over-watering than anything else; so if the soil feels damp, leave it a few more days. Pots in exposed, hot places need to be watched carefully. In such sites large tubs and pots are best. Small pots are best suited to clustering in semi-shaded and cool settings.

Applying water is best done with a water breaker or watering can. A water breaker is a large watering rose that fits on the end of a hose and breaks the pressure of a flow of water to a gentle pace and sprinkles it evenly over a large area. This is fine for watering large pot plants and those that don't mind cold water. Pot plants from warm climates can be shocked by cold tap water and are best sprinkled with tepid water using a watering can. If a watering can is filled and allowed to stand overnight, the water temperature should be tepid by morning. Where more than one can is needed to do the rounds, water should be stored in a barrel or small tank.

While soilless potting mixtures have many advantages, they have one drawback: once the mixture dries out it is very hard to make wet again; water tends to run straight through without wetting the 'soil'. To fix this, the whole pot needs to be immersed in a large container filled with water and left to soak. Bubbles of air will at first burst up through the water at a furious rate. After a short time the flow of bubbles with subside and eventually become an occasional slow *plop, plop, plop* until none appear. Let it soak for an hour. Refreshed by this, the plant can be taken out and returned to its position. The pot will quickly drain of excess water, and things have been set right once more. Careful attention to watering can obviate the need for this; however, plants seem to appreciate an occasional soaking just for the refreshment it gives.

There are now available wetting agents which when added to the potting mixture, or when watered into it, improve its capacity to take up water and its water-holding capacity. Using these can be a real boon to busy (and forgetful) gardeners. The expense of purchasing wetting agents may prevent them being used in large pots or where large numbers of pots are involved. Bear in mind also that the agents do not last indefinitely and will need to be replaced whenever the potting mixture is replaced.

Potted plants should always look in tiptop condition; half-starved, dehydrated plants can never make the eye-catching contribution to a garden that they are designed to do. If tending for potted plants is not your strong point, and I speak from experience, it is best to have few of them and to concentrate on looking after them well. Remember also that large pots are, as a general rule, easier to look after, less susceptible to drying out and more eye-catching than a huddle of small pots.

Managing Large Shrubs and Trees

In recent years potted trees and shrubs grown as standards have become a feature of many gardens, particularly to bring emphasis and distinction to some important point such as a doorway, the beginning or end of a path, or beside garden steps. In problem areas large potted shrubs such as camellias are often used to provide flowers and greenery. Both categories of plants need special care when it comes to their management as pot plants. The watering and feeding of these plants, often regarded as expensive investments in garden decor, must be carefully attended to, so too must attention be paid to trimming and training and to exposure to the sun and wind. Least thought is usually given to re-potting and root pruning, which are also important to the good health of these plants.

Every four or five years potted trees and shrubs need to be given a thorough going over. This means removing them from their containers, trimming the roots and replacing the outermost 5 cm of the soil all round (including the top and underneath). Such an undertaking demands two people to perform safely. The tubbed plant should be carefully tipped on one side. With one person holding the tub and the other doing the work, the ball of soil is loosened by poking through the drainage holes with a broom handle until the whole thing will slip out of the container easily. Then while one person holds the plant and ball of soil steady, the other carefully shaves away the exposed roots and soil. Sometimes, if the soil has been allowed to dry out beforehand, more soil can be teased out from between the roots. This allows more new soil to be introduced, but it is also more risky and demands more time and care.

Once the desired amount of soil has been removed, the plant can be repotted. Place drainage —gravel or fly wire—over the drainage holes, and cover the bottom with a layer of potting mixture. Scatter a handful of slow-release fertiliser granules thinly over this, reset the plant in the tub. Carefully pack new soil between the roots and around the sides of the tub. Once the soil level is restored to its original level (there will be telltale marks on the bark of the plant) thoroughly saturate the whole thing with water. If the soil settles lower than it was before the repotting, add some more.

Finally, some top growth should be pruned away to compensate for the roots that have been severed. Roughly one-third of a plant such as a camellia can be pruned back. With standard trees such as bay trees, citrus, conifers and other evergreens, much more care must be taken to retain the balanced, formal look of the plant. Having safely repotted a standard, many people prefer to leave well enough alone and do not touch the top growth. If this course of action is taken, the plants must be very carefully nutured until they are re-established. This means protecting them against toppling in the wind and being dehydrated or scorched by heat and the sun.

There has been a great deal of use of *careful* in this section; it has not been overdone. Potted trees and large shrubs do need extra care; without it they can never be the lovely garden features they are meant to be.

Containers

Before closing this chapter on pot plants, we should take a look at the pots themselves. Passing mention has already been made to half wine-barrels, half forty-four-gallon drums and jam tins, which, though not always aesthetically pleasing, did serve their purpose well and demonstrate the commonsense approach of most colonial gardeners. There were real pots too, beautiful terracotta pots with rolled round rims and bands of herringbone decoration. They came in all sizes from tiny 2.5 cm thumb pots right up to huge palm pots. There were special-purpose pots too. Seed pans were shallow and wide mouthed; orchid pots had deep slits incised into the sides and often had holes pierced just below the rim to facilitate hanging. Some were even made with a flat surface so they could be hung against a wall. 'Long Toms' were very tall in comparison to the pots made to accommodate shallow, fibrous-rooted plants such as azaleas and tuberous begonias.

Pots such as these are still made by a few potteries, though not usually in continuous runs. Production is frequently limited to only one or two lots each year, as they are hand thrown and the decoration applied by hand as well. All this means that the pots cost more than the usual machine-made clay pots.

A note of warning: pots with narrow necks are not suitable as containers for plants, as it is difficult to avoid breaking the pot during repotting operations. If you must use a pot of this kind, grow the plant in a pliable plastic pot and slip it into the decorative narrow neck. A packing of loose gravel will support the pot plant and keep it steady inside its container.

If cost is an important consideration in the purchase of the dozen or so pots you may need, you could look to the purchase of seconds-quality pots. These have minor imperfections, usually hair-line cracks. From careful inspection you should be able to gauge the extent of the imperfection and the likely life span of the pot. Some variety in the pots chosen for display on the front verandah can be achieved by introducing one or two jardinieres of Oriental or European design, but restraint should be exercised lest the cottage porch be furnished in a manner too opulent and exotic. Some further variety could be added by using home-made pots

TOP

A handsome terracotta pot overflows with Echeveria elegans; *a subtle contrast with the lush foliage of* Acer palmatum.

ABOVE

The secret of good-looking hanging baskets is daily grooming and watering and the use of hardy trailing plants.

constructed from hollow logs cut to convenient lengths and with one end closed over with a sheet of perforated tin or wire mesh. A mixture of a few precious decorative pots, some clay pots and some home-made improvisations would be entirely appropriate housing for a collection of potted plants on a cottage verandah.

ABOVE

The lush, fleshy leaves of Euphorbia neriifolia *cover stout stems armed with thorns; the plant's habit is architectural.*

ABOVE LEFT

A split-rail fence and a simple foundation planting bespeak relaxation. 'American Pillar' rose adds a note of colour.

LEFT

*On a shady verandah sheltered from drying winds, ferns such as staghorn (*Platycerium bifurcatum*) will slowly grow into magnificent specimens.*

6 Gardens of Whimsy

There is a kind of garden that relies not on plants for the material from which it is made but on objects. I refer to gardens made of collected bits and pieces such as you can see when you least expect to in seaside towns, country hamlets and suburban byways. These gardens are not so much grown as constructed and, although the materials may have changed over the years, seem no less popular than they were in the last century.

Frequently the gardens comprise rockeries, grottoes, fishponds and rockwork constructed from pieces gathered by the folk of the household in the pursuit of their work and hobbies. Thus in mining areas extraordinary displays of various rock and mineral samples may be found displayed by being incorporated in cemented garden structures. In coastal towns flotsam and jetsam such as glass net floats, pieces of driftwood, whalebones, corals, shells and giant crab claws are utilised in garden decoration. In rural areas old farm wagons and ploughs or odds and ends welded into whimsical creations are employed. Everywhere, but particularly in the bigger towns and cities, the well-known cement statue battalions take over a few gardens; brigades of rabbits shelter in forests of mushrooms; and squads of flamingos stalk gnome armies amid a landscape of balustrades, urns, plinths, Japanese lanterns, assorted gods and goddesses and dozing Mexicans.

As far as nineteenth-century gardens are concerned, the important thing to remember about gardens of whimsy is that they did exist and were generally constructed from collected bits and pieces rather than made from bought manmade objects. Thus objects covered with a glittering collection of glass, china and mirror pieces could be appropriate in a Victorian era garden, but a collection of garden statuary would not; shell and crystal covered work would be suited to the spirit of the age, but Italianate fountains, waterfalls and Japanese pieces generally would not do; pebble work, cobbling, rustic woodwork or even tin windmills and whirligigs may well find a place in an exceptional restored garden, while decorations assembled from hubcaps and radiator grilles and bumper bars,

ABOVE

An elaborate scrollwork of low clipped plants adds a touch of distinction and whimsicality to a simple garden proudly displayed by an old-fashioned family.

however curious and inventive, would be completely wrong.

If you happen to have some bent towards making a whimsical garden, then a careful selection of appropriate material will need to be gathered for use. Some objects may be easily obtained, but the likes of whalebones, lumps of crystal and old farm wagons will be more difficult and may also now be regarded as more valuable by antique and bric-à-brac collectors than by you. I rather think the cost of such a project might be daunting—perhaps just as well, going by the attitudes of many 'refined' gardeners and restorers who gladly enough erect Cape Cod weather vanes atop sheds but think precious little of own home-grown devices created with our own motifs. The surprise created by gardens such as these, if gardens they be (more than often they seem like outdoor extensions of the owner's magpie proclivities), is a useful diversion from rural and urban sameness, but it is their rarity that makes them noteworthy, far less than the objects they contain or the manner of their composition. Generally speaking, the distribution of such displays is just about right to spice up our gardening lives; many more would be a freak show. There are, however, several other sorts of garden which are regarded as curious and related to our nineteenth-century theme: they are cactus gardens and topiary gardens.

Cactus Gardens

Cactus gardens seem to be almost peculiar to Australia, though they can be found in isolated instances in other temperate climates such as South Africa, the Mediterranean and California. But whereas in South Africa and California they were extensions of a general interest in plants native to those zones, and in the Riviera they were the sportive tricks of very wealthy gardeners, in

Thread-leaved pine, agaves and yucca in an old garden.

Australia they seem to have exerted a strange and compelling influence on small garden owners. Doubtless some of this influence was brought about by a generally harsh climate and a need for plants tough enough to survive it; perhaps, too, the migration of gold prospectors between the Cape, California and Australia played its part in familiarising home gardeners with these curious plants.

While almost every garden had one or two aloes and possibly several clumps of columnar and barrel cacti, and almost certainly one or two clusters of century plant (*Agave americana*), a great deal of interest in these plants was also displayed in the horticultural papers of the day. And just as there were a few people interested in making gardens from the curiosities of the marine and minerological worlds, there were a like-minded few interested in making gardens from the oddities of the plant world. As a result, gardeners acquired aeoniums from the Canary Islands, aloes, *Crassula*, *Mesembryanthemum*, *Euphorbia* and *Stapelia* from South Africa; *Echeveria*, *Melocactus*, *Cereus*, *Mammillaria*, *Echinopsis*, *Cephalocereus*, *Hamatocactus*, *Echinocereus* and half a hundred others from the Americas to adorn gardens with their gaunt, compelling forms and brilliant silken flowers—not to mention the much cursed prickly pear, which rapidly took over large areas of hot dry pasture land when it was introduced as a fodder substitute in the last years of the nineteenth century.

Planted up with all the formality of the biscuit-cutter beds—circles, stars and ovals outlined with rocks—these tough plants gave colour where ambitions must otherwise have been thwarted by lack of water. Within the beds rose columns taller than organ pipes; some naked, others fiercely spined and yet others covered in long hairs; great barrels of green laced over with a network of cast-iron fish-hooks and broad mats of close clustered fine-spined fat bodies creating marvels of symmetry —enough to satisfy the most enthusiastic whimsicologist.

RIGHT

A thick layer of fine gravel keeps weeds under control and provides an apt setting for a fine selection of varied succulents.

BELOW

The tall white-haired columns of Cleistocactus strausii *add a touch of drama to a rock garden.*

ABOVE

Fat round barrels of Mammilaria *sp. will be ringed with small purple-red bells in early spring; as with many cacti, the flowers are highly coloured.*

RIGHT

Crassula, three kinds of euphorbia and the silver-felted leaves of Kalanchoe beharensis *show the diversity of succulent plants.*

FAR RIGHT

The architectural qualities of succulent plants are shown to great advantage against a bed of gravel, a compostion of rocks and by a selection of contrasting plant forms.

A selection of elaborate knot-garden patterns from The English Husbandman *(1635) by Gervase Markham. Simpler designs are just as effective for most gardens.*

Topiary Gardens

Topiary, the art of cutting, pruning, and training trees and shrubs to grow in predetermined shapes, has interested gardeners since Roman times. The Romans produced both simple and complicated shapes, ranging from cubes, balls and pyramids to elaborate replicas of statuary. The Elizabethans, too, were enthusiastic topiarists. But topiary generally has been looked on as an antique fascination rather than a garden necessity and found few devotees in colonial Australia, if old records are anything to go by. Although we may find ample evidence for hedging and edging using trimmed plants, there seems to have been little time for more frivolous works. As a child I can recall the fascination of several places where hedges of cypress were embellished with the name of the house cut from the greenery, over-arched at the gateway and beset with a pair of vaguely bird-shaped pieces, but these gardens would not have been made until the very early 1900s. There were also a table and two armchairs cut from privet in one small garden, and a migrant scandalised the neighbourhood by trimming ivy trained over his mail-box into a female torso (but that was in the 1950s, too late by far to be of much importance here).

From photographic records the topiary that was made was usually of the simplest design and carried out in the houses where professional gardeners were employed. One may find examples of ivy trained up tree-ferns and palm trunks and cut into bottle and umbrella shapes, or in drier climes trained over wire baskets and umbrella forms and kept neatly cut. Ivy

seems to have been a very popular choice, probably because effects of great age could be achieved in a very short time and because the traditional materials, box and yew, were not always easy to grow and usually not available in quantity or advanced sizes. In tropical areas bougainvillea seems to have been a popular substitute; with its greater vigour it probably suited very well.

A photograph taken at Mount Bischoff in Tasmania at the turn of the century reveals trimmed edging plants cut into a kind of scrollwork, and we may presume from similar photographs taken in other parts that such things were not uncommon. The choice of plants to carry out such schemes was catholic, encompassing dianthus, thymes and ivy as well as the more usual rosemary, lavender, santolina, *Rosa chinensis* and a dwarf strain of *Rosa multiflora* (fairy rose). Sometimes an alternative treatment was followed that would today seem odd; that was to build little banks of earth along the desired shapes and to puddle over a clay slurry which was smoothed and allowed to dry.

In gardens where trimmed plants made up the whole creation, the ground was usually 'decorated' with coloured gravels, pebbles and shell-grit. I do not know if such 'knot gardens', as they were known, were decorated with crushed coloured glass and different colours of broken tile and brick, as advocated by some English writers, but I am sure that like their modern-day counterparts who go in for pine-bark, river stones and the like, they found the constant picking off of leaves and papers a tiresome and unrewarding chore.

TOPIARY PLANTS AND TECHNIQUES

At the moment there appears to be a renewed interest in topiary, though it is not so widespread as to be regarded as a revival. Ready-made topiaries can be bought, but it is more fun to grow them from scratch, and doing it from the beginning creates understanding about how to care for them properly. Growing topiary successfully begins with choosing the best plants. Box and ivy have long been favoured because they are hardy, long-lived and amenable to clipping, cutting and training into shape. Some other plants, such as daisies and a variety of conifers, are sometimes used, and while young they perform reasonably well; in old age they are less reliable and some are downright cantankerous, and some do not live long enough to achieve old age. If box will not thrive where you live, then ivy will do nicely, especially the small-leaved forms. The other plants that are used to make topiary pieces require much more care in training and especially in clipping.

Simple shapes are easiest to make and are a good way to get started. Compact shrubby evergreens, such as box, need simply to be regularly clipped and snipped into shape as balls, cones, cubes and cylinders. If a small plant is to be trained, the overall growth must be allowed to get a little larger each year until the full size required is attained. It is possible to gain time by purchasing larger plants and trimming them fairly drastically into shape. The immediate effect may be a little gappy; but within a year or two, short side growths should have filled in most of the holes.

You can make a shape atop a standard if you buy an advanced plant with a strong central stem. By cutting out all the other branches of the shrub and leaving the central growth, the framework of a standard can quickly be established. The standard should be stripped of all unwanted side shoots and sprigs until a topknot of greenery remains. This can be shaped exactly as if the standard is at the height needed; if more height is wanted, the top growth can be roughly trimmed to shape for neatness. As the plant-in-training grows taller with each passing year, remove some of the bottom twigs and branchlets and allow the height of the standard to measure until the right stature is achieved. Once this has happened, the top growth can be cut more formally into shape.

Ivies trained as topiaries are not naturally bushy and need more help to grow into shape. Usually a framework of gavanised wire is bent and spot-welded (or secured by tying with very thin wire) to make the desired shape. Fine wire netting is attached over the framework, and the body of the shape is packed with thoroughly dampened sphagnum moss. This structure is set firmly in the ground or pot where the topiary is to grow, and runners of ivy are trained over the shape, using hairpins and plastic-coated ties to keep the plant as close as possible to the framework. Well watered and fed, ivy will quickly give complete coverage to any framework and from then on needs only

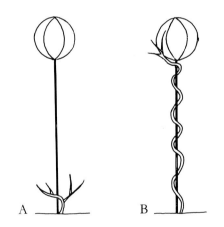

HOW AN IVY STANDARD IS MADE

(A) Choose the basic wire 'training' frame for an ivy standard from the range of such hardware available in all good garden centres, or make one from galvanised wire. Prepare the ground well and plant a small-leaved, dark green ivy near the base of the frame.

(B) Train one strong growth upwards using plastic-coated wire 'twistems'. Cut off all other shoots found on the original plant. Keep the plant well watered and feed occasionally with liquid fertiliser. As the plant grows upward, remove any side

growths by rubbing them between fingers and thumb.

(C) Once the ivy reaches the top structure of the training frame, fill the sphere with sphagnum moss and pin the trails of growth to it with bobby-pins or pieces of bent wire. Keep the moss damp by hosing it every day, and encourage the formation of short side growths by nipping back trails.

(D) When the ball of moss is well covered with short growths, the ivy can be clipped over to trim it into a tight ball of leaves. With careful watering and feeding, such a topiary will last many years.

LEFT
A trim hedge provides a neat visual point of separation between lawns and an area of paving around a small brick-walled pool. The architectural lines of the hedge pick up those of the built structure.

ABOVE
A peacock is not a job for a first-time topiarist.
BELOW
Simple treatments such as growing ivy on chains swung between posts and trimmed as swags can be most attractive.

snipping over to keep it in shape. This method is a relatively painless way of making more complex topiaries, including baskets, teddy bears, peacocks and kangaroos.

Commercially produced training frames are available in a wide variety of shapes, and to order, from many garden shops specialising in garden decor and old-fashioned garden design. While ivies can be trained and clipped to recreate fairly close detail, box and other evergreens can only be used to suggest the most broadly sketched features of any subject. A clipped topiary shape may roughly resemble a peacock or a squirrel, but it is difficult to cut with such finesse the differences between wings and paws, feathers and fur. Even small items like ears and beaks can be hard to produce unless a sprig appears in just the right position. Happily the sculpture itself can be just as magical whatever its real-life identity.

CUTTING CURLICUES

A pair of spirally trimmed box trees is a stunning addition to a cottage garden or to a more formal old-fashioned garden. Most often they appear overnight in gardens where costly items are commonplace, having been purchased from expert commercial growers. However, verdant sculptures such as these can be home-grown given time, thoughtful observation and careful (that word again!) clipping. The hard part is maintaining a three-dimensional mental picture of what the end product of four or five years training will be, being able to envisage that form growing out of the unshaped plant in the garden and having the confidence to give it a go. Mistakes with growing plants are rarely long lived, and the first steps are the most important.

To make a spiral in a box tree, you need a plant with one strong central growth; a well-established plant about a metre tall seems to be the best size to start training, at least for beginners. Start working from the bottom upwards by cutting selected branches right back to the trunk in a fairly loose spiral—this is where that mental picture comes into play. Having the spiral cut clean to the trunk gives a good line of sight to work to and helps later clipping to be done more confidently. It also looks best. When the top of the plant has been reached, the basic stripping is completed and work can begin on shaping the remaining side growths into the desired graceful swirl of growth.

Where to begin—top or bottom? Stand away from the plant and see how broad the base is; imagine the finished plant tapering neatly to the top point of the topiary. Carrying that image in your mind, begin clipping from the bottom. Step back frequently to check progress, and move around the plant to ensure a smooth, symmetrical outline. First efforts may appear less than perfect; but with another six months growth, small imperfections will have disappeared among new growth and will not show with the next trimming.

AFTERCARE

Like all plants, topiaries need adequate sunlight all round to grow evenly. They need to be carefully watered in summer to make sure they are not so stresed that they lose their leaves. They need to be well fed and mulched, and they need to be grown away from the roots of hungry trees.

Clipping is best done after the plants have made strong new growth. This often happens in early summer at a time when fresh leaves can easily be scorched by an unexpectedly hot day. Try to choose a time to do your trimming ahead of the arrival of a few days of cool, cloudy weather. Hose cut plants every few days for a week or so; this seems to have a good effect, and in doing so you will be keeping a watchful eye on things. In heatwaves, shadecloth draped loosely over newly clipped shapes will prevent leaf and bark scorch.

Most gardeners who regard themselves as sensitive to the beauties of foliage, flowers and form cannot take seriously those who make gardens out of curious objects and whimsical collection. However, these gardens have had some small place in the development of cottage and villa gardens and so cannot be omitted. As they are the unique creations of individuals with their own special perception of what their garden is about, it is perhaps as well that few such gardens long survive their makers. Not all gardeners of yesteryear were adept at throwing together a glorious display of mixed cottage plants. Some were simply entranced by the potential of flotsam and jetsam for creating items of whimsy.

Should you feel the urge to have a curious garden, make one only if you can do so wholeheartedly. It takes strength of character to create a whimsical garden. It must be done with a sense of style, even though it is not the style accepted by the general community. It may be better not to have read any gardening books if you wish to create such a highly individual garden; motor car spare parts manuals and builders catalogues may be more appropriate reading materials. Can you plan a curious garden? It seems that the best examples of gardens of whimsy, like Topsy, 'just growed'. Individual pieces of construction and planting are often intensely thought through, but the overall garden plan seems to develop organically as one part is finished and a new part takes shape in the mind of the maker.

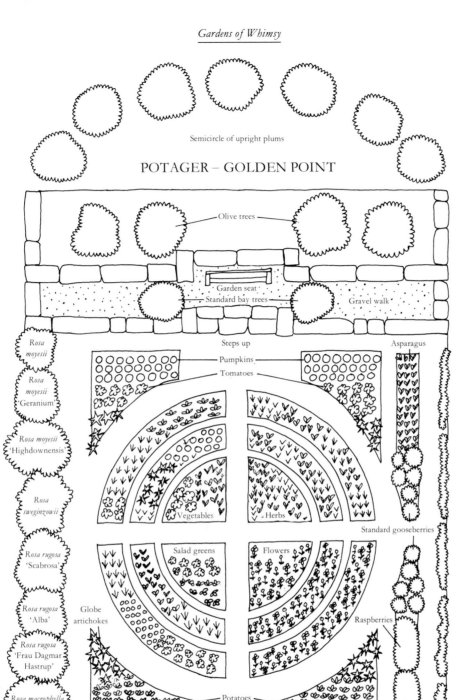

Semicircle of upright plums

POTAGER – GOLDEN POINT

Olive trees

Garden seat
Standard bay trees
Gravel walk

Rosa moyesii

Steps up

Rosa moyesii 'Geranium'

Pumpkins
Tomatoes

Asparagus

Rosa moyesii 'Highdownensis'

Rosa sweginzowii

Vegetables

Herbs

Rosa rugosa 'Scabrosa'

Standard gooseberries

Salad greens

Flowers

Rosa rugosa 'Alba'

Globe artichokes

Rosa rugosa 'Frau Dagmar Hastrup'

Raspberries

Rosa macrophylla 'Master Hugh'

Potatoes

Rosa virginiana

Rhubarb

Espaliered fruit trees: apples, pears, plums

Chestnut trees

Dry-stone retaining walls mark this potager for distinction. The garden is entered through a row of chestnut trees, and the raised beds strike the first note of the grand scheme. Gravelled pathways awash with spreading thymes and oregano lead past beds of potatoes and clumps of globe artichokes towards the central circular beds cut into manageable segments by radiating paths. Each bed is planted with blocks of vegetables, salad greens, flowers and herbs that change with each season. Side beds of asparagus, gooseberries and raspberries are planted apart from beds that need high levels of cultivation.

Part 2
Old-Fashioned Flowers

7   *The Lilies of the Field:*

Self-Sowing Annuals and Biennials

Those who have at some time reached the heights of Senior Sunday School or Bible Study class will surely recall the lines from the Sermon on the Mount (Matthew 6:28): 'Consider the lilies of the field, how they grow; they toil not, neither do they spin'. For the garden-minded biblical scholar the word lilies *is an interesting one, for it is not really clear just what flower Saint Matthew was writing about. From time to time erudite papers are published in learned journals asserting that some particular flower must have been 'the' one.* Lilium candidum, *the Madonna lily, has been a strong favourite, while colchicums, scarlet poppies, crocuses and white-bearded irises have all found champions. But there are those who think that the word was a general term that applied to all the flowers that grew in the hard, dry, stony fields of Palestine. And the plants that I want to talk about in this chapter are those that will grow and self-sow in your garden without worry, annuals and biennials that are tough, colourful and thoroughly carefree both in appearance and nature.*

John Codrington and Miriam de Rothschild, two English gardeners, have been among the vanguard who have championed wild flowers and grasses. Annuals in particular have excited their artistic talents, and a zany willingness to try un-gardening with their plants has led to the discovery that many annuals perform best in places where they would normally be disallowed—gravel paths and driveways! Now it happens that in a climate as warm and dry as ours the outer parts of our gardens tend to become parched and difficult to maintain during summer. Plants rapidly

dehydrate and succumb to heat and drought. Why fight nature? Why not let that part of the garden rest in the hottest months? Why not give it over to self-seeding annuals

ABOVE
Well-established fruit trees, an evergreen hedge and a splendid clump of Madonna lilies frame a proud gardener.

PREVIOUS PAGES
*A carpet of Spanish bluebells (*Hyacinthoides hispanica*) makes this perfect spring picture under deciduous trees.*

and some hardy bulbs which will become verdant with the rains of autumn, flower and form seed in early summer and then dry off with the onset of the heat? It takes a certain amount of bravery to do such a thing, and it would certainly not do over a large part of the garden, but in out-of-the-way corners it can be very effective. In my corner of the world, olive and almond groves are now becoming housing estates. How exciting it would be if one or two daring gardeners would retain as many of the trees as possible and make gardens under the groves of trees. They would necessarily be simple gardens such as are sometimes found on the hillsides of southern France and in Italy. A simple background of trees, some low stone walls, a vine-covered pergola and a sea of bright field flowers. How delightful! Once the seed pods had ripened and the seed been broadcast, the entire area could be mown neat and gardening left in favour of summer relaxation.

The flowers described here would all be suitable for such a bucolic garden, if there is anyone inclined to try the idea; otherwise they can be grown in a normal garden setting—but don't be surprised if the best flowers come from plants that come up where they want.

Annuals

Agrostemma githago   Long known as Corncockle, indicating that it dwells in corn fields and other cultivated places where the soil is tilled. A rather nondescript plant, it produces a crop of splendid, though rather subdued, lilac-pink flowers, flaring and trumpet-shaped. There are a number of colour strains ranging from almost white to ones with more lilac or rose-pink tones. To keep the strains coming true from seed, they must be kept well separated in the garden. A splendid addition to country-style flower arrangements; 45 cm.

Althea rosea (**Hollyhock**)   One of the most popular cottage flowers. While it can be treated as a short-lived perennial, the best display of flowers will always occur in the first year and it is best treated as an annual. Since its introduction from the Holy Land in 1573 it has been much improved by selective breeding. Besides the original rose-coloured flowers, cream, yellow, apricot and soft coral tones were developed, and some fine dark garnet shades as well as double, semi-double fringed and anemone-centred forms. They need rich soil to attain their full (3 m) majesty. Rust can be a cause of serious defoliation and needs checking by removal of diseased leaves—always burn them, or use a fungicidal spray. Some of the less common colours and forms are still grown in private gardens, so be watchful for them and don't be afraid to ask for seed. Most gardeners will be glad to help out.

Alyssum maritimum (**Sweet Alice**)   This is among the commonest of annuals and is a willing self-seeder in almost any situation. There are now many colour strains which are useful in creating ribbon borders, bedding-out schemes and gardens based on a colour scheme, but the plain white variety, though somewhat less compact than the others, is hardiest of all and ideal for sowing in arid spots where the soil is mean and the aspect hot. Once it is established and seeding freely, there will be a continuous succession of flowering plants throughout the year in all but the most inhospitable conditions. It mixes happily with other flowering plants such as bulbs, perennials and biennials and can act as a ground cover, though never so dense as to choke its neighbours; 10 cm.

Amaranthus caudatus (**Love Lies Bleeding**)   Once a very popular flower with floral artists (Constance Spry was very fond of it in the 1950s), this unusual flower has gone into eclipse in city gardens. It survives handsomely in country gardens, giving height and colour to the church flowers and to the garden. A rather coarse-looking plant with beetroot-red stems and leaves, it grows to a towering 2 m and sports long rope-like tassels of insignificant flowers in the same colour. The drooping flower stalks are quite special in a very curious, melancholy and old-fashioned way. There is a pale green coloured form too, in *Amaranthus caudatus* 'Viridis', which is a touch more refined than the bold red kind. Volunteer seedlings should be transplanted to places where they can grow without threatening passers-by.

Ammi majus (**Queen Anne's Lace**)   Another tall and willing grower which will grow almost anywhere. In cultivated soil it can easily reach 2 m. Rather slight palmate foliage that supports a many-branched stem of white lace-cap flowers. It is an annual, though there is a perennial look-alike about in *Daucus carrotus*, which has rounded, tightly clustered flower heads. Those of Queen Anne's lace are flat-topped, well spaced and airy in appearance. Seed is set prolifically, and excess seedlings must be weeded out carefully. Each plant needs about a square metre of space to develop properly. The plants do not stand wind well, especially if the flowers are weighed down with rain.

Asarina procumbens   Sometimes perennial and sometimes annual depending on the summer climate of your garden. In cool areas where summer rains provide constant moisture, it will last for several seasons, but in warm dry areas it is inclined to fade away in the hottest months. In its time it has also been known as *Antirrhinum asarina*. It is a small trailing plant with heart-shaped hairy leaves of light apple-green. Individual flowers are carried in the leaf axils. The snapdragon flowers are creamy-white with some small dark purple spots in the throat. An unusual flower which is charming for trailing over path edges and filling shady corners; 5 cm.

Borago officinalis (**Borage**)   A well-known herb whose flowers have a reputation for doing marvellous things to drinks. Blue star-like flowers drifting around in my G & T are not my taste, however. This herb can be very useful in the garden, for it has a happy knack of seeding itself into dry, gravelly spots where almost nothing else will grow. The young seedlings appear in winter, don't mind being transplanted and will rapidly re-establish to plug any gaps that may occur in garden beds. Coarse hairy leaves and stems hold up masses of blue starry flowers and carry on for a long early summer season. It is not unusual for these plants to ripen their seed and die and for a further crop of seedlings to appear and flower before winter arrives. There is an especially fine white-flowered form in *Borago officinalis* 'Alba'. Seed given me by Margaret Windmill of Badger's Keep has self-sown for several seasons and comes true year after year; 75 cm.

Briza maxima (**Quaking Grass**)   Also known to the local children as Chinese lanterns. As an annual grass it can be quite invasive, so is not allowed in my garden proper, but it is always encouraged in the gappy spaces between shrub roses along the laneway. We get a lot of Sunday strollers out with their dogs and children, and we like them to have something to pluck as they pass. With Shirley poppies, love-in-a-mist, corncockles and Queen Anne's lace they can make a pretty country-style posy. There is also a much smaller version of the same grass in *Briza minor*, we let that seed around too. Pulling up stray seedlings is easy, and for the simple pleasure of having such child-pleasing plants it is worth the slight trouble; 40 cm.

Clarkia elegans   A variable plant from which a number

ABOVE
Biennial foxgloves intermingle happily with annual Queen Anne's lace and perennials.

ABOVE RIGHT
A happy accident: annual grasses have self-sown among red and yellow geums.

RIGHT
Violas have been popular garden plants since Shakespeare's day.

OPPOSITE PAGE
California poppies come in a range of colours from cream to vibrant reds.

of coloured forms and varieties of differing heights have been developed. Many will be found in old catalogues, but the range today is much restricted. Plant what you can get, for they are hardly changed at all from the old types. David Crichton wrote of them in *The Australian Horticultural Magazine and Garden Guide* of September 1877:

Named in honour of Captain Clarke, who attained celebrity through making a journey across the Rocky Mountains. There are several species, all of which are natives of California and the north-western portion of the American continent. Most of them are elegant and showy, making a brilliant display for several weeks in succession during the spring and early summer months. They are moderately hardy and may be grown successfully in almost any soil or situation.

Growth is fairly upright and the greyish foliage sparse so that the brightly coloured silken flowers stand out well. There are semi-double and double forms which by reason of the delicacy of the petals are not as gross as many double flowers. The colour range is limited to shades of rose, lilac, mauve, pink and purple; 30–45 cm.

Convolvulus tricolor   One of those plants that move in and out of seed lists so often that it is frequently hard to find when you want it most. It is very rarely seen in the trays of seedlings available at nurseries. Why this is so is difficult to understand, for it has one of the most brilliant cobalt-blue flowers imaginable. The trailing growth covers itself in masses of short bright blue trumpets which have a clear white throat and a yellow central zone. The colours sparkle and set each other off to perfection. A delightful flower and one that is quite innocent of the reputation of its relatives for invasive behaviour. There are some pinkish coloured versions getting about, but they lack the clarity and sparkle of the blue forms; 30 cm in rich soil, less in hard conditions.

***Dipsacus fullonum* (Teasel)**   This plant is too often left at the roadside when it could with distinction be brought into our gardens. In midsummer it throws up tall candelabras of large, rather thistle-like flowers covered with short hooked spines. Their height and strong features are outstanding for adding quick height to an otherwise undistinguished garden, and the flower heads can be cut and dried for indoor decorations. Easy and much safer to grow than the equally statuesque Scotch thistle (*Onopordon arabicum*), which, despite its wonderful silver leaves, is a danger in any garden unless its wide-scattering seeds are dead-headed early to stop them scattering on the wind. Teasels grow to 2 m and more and are reliable self-seeders.

***Eschscholtzia californica* (California Poppy)**   My own preference is for the pale lemon and cream forms of this easy Californian. There are many other brighter colours, including all shades of yellow, orange, brick-reds and some rather mawkish terracotta-pinks. Such lovely simple poppies are not improved by doubling of the petals; doubles should be avoided in the interests of enjoying the wild natural form of the flower. Historically there have been all manner of mutations and variations, including striped forms, doubles, dwarf kinds, etc. All best left behind us; 30 cm.

Godetia   Hybrids of this plant once formed the backbone of many a good floral display. Then they suddenly lapsed from fashion, so much so that keen gardeners began to advertise for them in the 'Wanted' columns of gardening papers. Cultivation is easy, but there are a few simple rules to be observed if these colourful Californians, and other annuals from the same area, are to be grown well:

As with other hardy annuals, the most favourable time for sowing in mild districts is during the autumn months, but it may be done at any time successfully up to the middle of September . . . the plants will adopt themselves to a variety of soils and situations. They do not bear transplanting very well, though that practice may be followed successfully if extra care is taken not to break the roots, and to shift the plants when small. More satisfactory results can, however be generally obtained by sowing where the plants are to remain, and thinning out when two or three inches high (David Crichton, The Australian Horticultural Magazine and Garden Guide, *September 1877).*

Colours vary from white through all shades of pink and rose to crimson. Some kinds have contrasting white or purple blotches at the centre of the flowers; 30–60 cm.

Gomphrena globosa   This little annual, known to some as globe amaranth, has flowers very like tiny purple everlastings. It is sometimes seen in old gardens, where the seed is saved from year to year, and less often in parks and gardens bedding displays. It is small, bright and a delight to children. The colour can be hard-hitting to the eyes but is easily toned down in a mixed cottage border or when planted with white flowers such as sweet alice and plants with silvery leaves like the various forms of dusty miller (*Senecio bicolor* ssp. *cineraria*); 30 cm.

***Hesperis matronalis* (Sweet Rocket, Dames' Rocket)**   Another not-quite-reliable perennial that is best treated as an annual. It is a delightfully perfumed flower which grows about 75 cm tall and carries masses of mall mauve-lilac flowers in late spring and early summer. The perfume is most pronounced in the evening. There are white and striped forms, and a very rare double white which must be propagated by cuttings. The single-flowered kinds come freely from seed. No cottage garden should be without this lovely flower.

***Limnanthes douglasii* (Scrambled Egg Plant)**   A robust and sprawling annual introduced from California in 1833 and immediately popular as a low edging plant which produces an abundant display of small daisy flowers. Individual flowers are yellow paling to white at the centre. There is a slight perfume; 15 cm.

***Linum grandiflorum* 'Rubrum' (Scarlet Flax)**   A standard garden annual ever since it was introduced from its homeland in northern Africa. Popular as a potted plant and for general planting, its dark red flowers float in airy clusters over a plant that grows to about 60 cm. In Australia it is most often seen as a flowering pot plant, though some older gardeners sow their own need and dot the plants through their gardens in small colonies. If started early in autumn it will be in flower for six months provided there is no lack of water.

***Lunaria annua* (Honesty)**   Beloved of floral artists for its curious flat and circular pearly-white seed pods which can be dried and used indoors for months, this annual is widely grown commercially but hardly at all by home gardeners. It sometimes acts more like a biennial than an annual, particularly if the seed is not sown until late winter. The leaves are large, broad and come to a point; they make a good-sized clump about 30 cm across, so good spacing between plants is needed. In late winter the much-branched flower stem carries many small lilac-purple flowers and from these the fantastic seed pods develop. Once the seeds are ripe, the stems wanted for drying can be cut and taken indoors, where they should be hung to dry completely. Once this is done the outer skin of each seed case can be carefully cleaned off by gentle rubbing; the two seeds will fall out leaving behind the satiny white 'moons' that we see in florists' shops when fresh flowers are scarce. There is a lovely white-flowered form which is more useful in the garden than the dull purple form. A variegated form mottled with cream is also grown, but its only garden value is as a curiosity; 60 cm.

***Molucella laevis* (Bells of Ireland)**   Do you remember this plant? It was one of the great stand-bys for ladies who arranged the church flowers. Its long, slightly curved stems are covered with scattered whorls of flaring green bells. They are quite sturdy and long-lasting, eventually fading to a papery cream colour as they dry out. They can be dried for use indoors, though once they lose their fresh green colour they become rather lifeless and dull. Best sown where they are to flower, as they seem to make sturdier plants than those that are transplanted. Fortunately florists seem not to have yet discovered how to dye it or spray it with fluorescent colours. It has been called Molucca balm in some parts of the country; 1 m.

***Myosotis* hybrids (Forget-Me-Not)**   It seems nowadays that no gardener or his dog can be satisfied unless the old flowers are made more novel by being grown in 'rare' varieties. Thus it is that where once we made do quite happily with the lovely sky-blue forget-me-not, 'everyone' is growing white or pink forget-me-nots. Where once we could enjoy great carpets of the sky-blue kind as it romped away under trees and shrubs, we must now weed out such invasive pests and be content with a small pot of white or pink kinds bought at great expense from the garden boutique in the shopping village. Although the blue kinds do need careful watching in small gardens to make sure they do not smother other plants, never imagine that a potful can ever match the beauty of a spreading sheet of blue in some out-of-the-way corner. The pink variety seems something of a fake; it is never quite convincing, as there is always enough blue in the colour to spoil the effect at a distance. The white kind is good in confined gardens where its pure white flowers can be appreciated close up; at a distance the effect is lost, as the flowers are lost amid a sea of green foliage.

***Nigella damascena* (Love-in-a-Mist)**   This needs no introduction, for almost everyone will remember it even though it is not so much grown now. The fennel-fine foliage on upright stems encloses pale lavender-blue flowers which, in the best kinds, have several rows of petals. Once the flowers have finished, the balloon-shaped seed pods swell until they are about 2 cm across and 3 cm tall. There are white and mauve-pink forms and a very nice darker blue form. It will seed freely and sprout in masses; thinning out is necessary to encourage strong flower plants and a good display; 45 cm.

Papaver rhoeas   The Shirley poppies are a selected strain of this wild poppy from the common corn poppy of the wheatfields of England and Europe. This particular strain was isolated in 1880 by the Reverend William Wilks, who once occupied the vicarage of Shirley in Croydon near London. There are other strains too, including those with fringed edges (called carnation poppies), ranunculus-flowered and picotees, which have flowers edged with white, pink or red. The colours range from white to pale pink, salmon, rose and crimson, and may have a different-coloured edging as in the picotee-flowered forms. The original Shirley poppies had only single flowers, but the strain seems now to include doubles and semi-doubles as well. Like all poppies, the petals are silken and crinkled. Given good soil, the flowers can be about 8 cm across and the plants up to 75 cm tall.

***Papaver somniferum* (Peony-Flowered Poppy)**   This plant is illegal in Australia, as it is a garden form of the notorious opium poppy. Even so, it is occasionally seen in gardens where the owners, ignorant of the facts, grow it for its lush glaucous foliage and huge fully double flowers which verge on being gaudy, so rich are their colours. It is probably illegal in England and America too, but in those countries, as here, some plants in quiet country gardens seem to have escaped the bonfires of officialdom. There are massive double white forms as well as three or four shades of scarlet, rose and pink. Some forms have fringed flowers as an added decoration. The large pepper-pot seed pods are thought to be most attractive by flower arrangers, especially those who seek to emulate the compositions of the Dutch flower painters of the seventeenth century.

***Reseda odorata* (Mignonette)**   David Crichton wrote in *The Australian Horticultural Magazine and Garden Guide* of March 1877:

The Mignonette is a well known plant that has become a general favourite owing to its sweetly perfumed flowers, though they do not possess the dazzling beauty of many other kinds that are esteemed less. It is a native of the North of Africa, and is said to be found growing naturally over a large portion of both Egypt and Barbary. When introduced to Europe it first found its way to the South of France, where owing to the delightful fragrance of the flowers it soon became very popular and received the name of Mignonette (Little Darling).

It is fortunate that some of the older scented kinds have recently been reimported to Australia from New Zealand and elsewhere, for it was thought until very recently that we had lost all traces of scent in this otherwise undistinguished plant. Besides the low and scrambling scentless rusty-green form that had become commonplace, there are now several white forms and taller green varieties getting about among gardeners. So far they appear to be only in the hands of home gardeners, but as news of their arrival spreads, no doubt an enterprising seed merchant will seek them out in the wholesalers' catalogues and make them more widely available. All are easily raised from seed; however, if this is sown where the plants are to grow, seedlings will need thinning to about 30 cm apart. Seed is best sown in autumn.

***Tropaeolum majus* (Nasturtium)**   Too often this cheerful flower is despised and cast out as being altogether too common. Yet in a difficult dry spot it will grow and flower happily, covering a multitude of sins with a dense mass of leaves and bright blooms. As children we loved to play in a garden where the long trailing stems of some unknown form of nasturtium covered mounds of builder's sand, grit, pea gravel and dirt. Beset with unsightly rubble and junk? Disguise it in a trice with this rampageous plant. There are dwarf and bushy forms too that fit better into mixed borders. Sadly, the general strains available are not particularly inspiring, but some enterprising seedsman will surely latch on to some of the fine colour groups that are found in Europe. In Monet's garden at Giverny there grow some elegantly coloured kinds—a lovely warm brick pink, a soft buff-coloured apricot and a superb pale creamy-lemon kind. Please let us have some of these here. Those not usually inclined toward freaky food can sample sandwiches filled with cream cheese and nasturtium leaves with complete safety.

***Viola tricolor* (Johnny Jump-Up)**   Recently there have been released onto the market a number of superior hybrids of the viola. Varieties such as the white, blue, yellow, red and apricot strains, often sold as 'Space Crystals', are leaders in this group, but they are too big to be Johnny jump-ups. Newer and even smaller kinds such as 'Prince Henry' (purple), 'Prince Edward' (yellow), 'Cuty' (purple and white), 'Bowles Black', 'Tinkerbell' (blue), 'Blue Carpet', 'Alpine Summer' (yellow and white), 'Maroon Picotee' (yellow heavily brush-marked with deep red), 'Lutea Splendens', 'White Perfection', 'Yellow Charm' and 'Chantreyland' (apricot) are much closer to the mark. They are all most endearing to a cottage gardener, even though they are all comparatively modern kinds. 'Jack-a-Napes' is a genuine old variety which has only recently been reintroduced to general cultivation. David Thomson of Summertown in South Australia has good, vigorous stocks of this ruby-red and golden-yellow viola. The combination sounds rather garish alongside the purer one-colour varieties, but the tiny flowers sparkle like jewels scattered at the feet of larger plants. It is a plant of rare character. All are useful, but there is still a place for the clown-faced original *Viola tricolor*. Children love its funny face of white, yellow and purple. It is a willing seeder; the progeny of a few plants will soon populate an entire garden. Excess plants are easily dealt with by hand-weeding. The few plants that come up in odd corners and cracks in paving always look so much at home that they should never be pulled out; 10 cm.

Biennials

Even more so than many other old-fashioned flowers, those that are biennial in nature, (i.e., taking two years to flower from seed) have not been part of the recent revival of the plants from yesteryear. This is due, no doubt, to the long time taken between planting and flowering, during which the garden where they grow is a relatively dull patch. It is not our practice, as is done in England and Europe, to interplant young biennials with bulbs or annuals; instead there is a general antipathy towards growing them. We rarely see now beds of wallflowers, Canterbury bells, stocks or sweet william, which were once the most popular kinds of biennials. Some of these are making a comeback in the role of potted flowering plants for sale, but on cost alone these plants can never become major garden features. The biennials that do remain with us are those that have attractive foliage and strong architectural qualities as well as attractive flowers. Almost all of them were the strong favourites of nineteenth-century garden writers William Robinson and Gertrude Jekyll and were recommended by them for the very qualities we appreciate still.

***Digitalis purpurea* (Foxglove)**   Long popular with gardeners and garden writers who all appreciate its many fine attributes. It will grow happily in sun or shade, in the open or under trees, and can be relied on for months of colour in late spring. There are several modern strains getting around, as well as some older hybrids such as 'Sutton's Apricot' and *Digitalis* × 'Mertoniensis'. These are worth growing, but they do need to be kept well apart to keep the plants from cross-pollinating. There are also other species worth growing such as *D. lutea*, *D. lanata* and *D. laevigata*, but best of all are the splendid silver-leaved variety *D. heywoodii*, available from David Glenn of Lambley Perennials, and the superb white-flowered form *Digitalis purpurea* 'Alba'. Heights are variable; as a guide, expect between 1 m and 2 m for most kinds.

***Eryngium giganteum* (Miss Willmott's Ghost)**   A fairly recent arrival in Australian gardens as far as can be discovered, yet it has been known since the late 1800s as a very attractive, if somewhat prickly, garden flower. The first year sees the formation of a broad rosette of plain spoon-shaped basal leaves. In the second summer a stout stem clad in a few prickly leaves appears and bears aloft a dense cluster of grey-green and white thistle-type flowers. It is a very dramatic plant and useful for dried arrangements. The plant got its unusual name from the habit of the famous gardener Miss Ellen Willmott of scattering a few of the seeds in gardens she visited. The prickly ghosts of her visit would appear to remind her hosts of her call; 75 cm.

***Oenothera biennis* (Evening Primrose)**   A roadside weed in many parts of south-eastern Australia, especially in the wetter parts, and in ditches and run-offs. In spite of its weedy reputation it is worth looking at for the wilder parts of the garden. It grows to over 1.5 m tall and shows enormous pale yellow flowers for months on end. Each flower lasts only one evening, opening in the late afternoon and turning to mush the following morning. If you plan to bring in plants from the roadside, make sure you get the right one. Check the flower colour, for the more common bright yellow variety is a positive thug; the pale yellow *O. biennis* has larger flowers on taller plants. *Oenothera trichocalyx*, introduced by Thompson & Morgan, is a low-growing trailer which sometimes acts like a biennial and sometimes like an annual. It produces masses of translucent large white flowers. Tracking it down can be bothersome but it is worth the effort; 30 cm.

Verbascum broussa   One of the better members of the mullein family for growing in gardens. During the first season of growth it makes a massive rosette of silver felted leaves, followed in the second year by a towering spire of heavily felted silver from which emerge a long succession of small clear yellow flowers. A few side branches carry the flowering season on even longer. It seems not to seed heavily, but there are usually enough volunteers to carry on from year to year; 2 m and more.

Verbascum olympicum   In many respects similar to *V. broussa* but produces a many-branched flowering stem which resembles a Liberace-style candelabrum. It would look out of place on a piano, but in a garden it is superb, either as a background plant in a border or as a bold eye-catcher rocketing out of surrounding low-life ground-covering things.

Annual Climbers

Annual climbers are not used as much as they once were. Some, like sweet peas, are thought to take too much effort and to require too much garden space for their culture; others are now declared to be weeds—especially the many forms of morning glory that populate large areas of wasteland on the eastern seaboard; yet others have fallen from grace just by being old-fashioned and not spectacular enough to have claimed the attention of new-wave enthusiasts. The changes in garden design and use have also taken away many of the features where once climbing annuals found a home: the woodshed is gone, the henhouse demolished and the vegie patch miniaturised if it exists at all. For those who want to grow some of the old annual climbers, there is now the challenge of finding new ways of using them that will show them to advantage in association with other flowers and without their traditional supports.

Some can be adapted as ground covers to scramble among other perennials and bulbs; others will readily scale shrubs and small trees; and others will only be happy on some large structure such as a verandah or carport. In part the trick is to select plants which will blend or contrast effectively with the plants around them. This is a task which must be looked on as part of the pleasure of rediscovering old-fashioned flowers. It demands a sense of adventure and a willingness to try different combinations until a number of successful partnerships have been effected. There are many other climbing annuals apart from those listed here; the search for new ways of using them will undoubtedly lead to the introduction of other kinds from the wholesalers of Europe and America.

Cobea scandens   Known to many lovers of old-fashioned flowers as the cup-and-saucer vine. In its natural habitat in tropical America it is a perennial climber; in warmer parts of Australia plants will last for several seasons, but many find it best to treat it as an annual. It certainly is not a disadvantage to grow it this way, for in one season it will scale a 4 m wall or tree with no difficulty. The ropy stems and indifferent foliage are nothing to look at, but by midsummer the large flowers begin to open. Beginning pale green, they quickly pass to a dull purple colour. In shape each flower is similar to a Canterbury bell, although they are carried individually on a long, strong stem. The show is carried on well into autumn, by which time large oval seed pods are apparent among the growth. Although not a sparkling star in the garden, *Cobea scandens* is good value, especially for giving a quick effect. *Cobea scandens* 'Alba' has pale green flowers (it would be foolish to say they are white), which gradually develop yellowish tones as the flower ages. Attractive in a quiet way.

Eccremocarpus scaber   This also has the ability to be perennial and evergreen in warm situations. Like many of the other annual climbers mentioned here, it comes from South America (Chile in this case) and is capable of very rapid growth. Most of these quick-growing and semi-evergreen climbers with softwooded stems are liable to rot in cold weather, which is why they are best treated as annuals. You can never tell when established plants are going to conk out, so it is as well to have new plants each year. The foliage is plain, dark green and slight, so the plant is not much in itself. It can be used as a light creeper to cover a fence or shrub but it will not be a useful disguise for ugliness. When the flowers commence, the plant asserts itself as a garden personality. Loose clusters of waxy tubular flowers appear at the end of all the growths and attract the eye with their brilliant orange-red colour. There are other colour forms which can be just as attractive given the right plant associations. *E. scaber* 'Aureus' has bright golden-orange flowers that can pick up the colours of other yellow flowers such as rudbeckias, spray chrysanthemums and heleniums. Dark red dahlias, purple-leaved plants such as berberis and cannas would set off the dark-red-flowered form *E. scaber* 'Carmineus'. These colour forms should be available in separate seed strains from discriminating seed merchants—try Sarah Guest of Specialty Seeds. Like *Mina lobata* and *Cobea scandens*, this plant also does especially well if it can be given an early start under glass.

***Lathyrus odoratus* 'Busby Sweet Pea'**   This plant has had an amazing journey through the years to the present. It was brought to Australia in 1823 by the wife of an engineer employed by the Colonial Office. Descendants of this couple have continued to grow this 'Painted Lady' type sweet pea over the generations to the present day. The seed has been re-exported to England, where Thompson & Morgan list it from time to time. Other Painted Ladies have been reintroduced by members of the Hardy Plant Society in England via their extensive seed distribution program. The Busby Sweet Pea is not a tall grower—about 2 m seems its limit—and the growth is not so lush as in modern sweet peas. The flowers are usually carried in twos on short stems that are held clear of the foliage. The wings (back petals) are

a warm rosy-crimson and the keel is almost white. The perfume is glorious. Keep this and all other old sweet pea varieties well separated or they will cross-pollinate and in one season the strain will be lost, at least in your garden.

In some parts of southern Australia the wild form of *Lathyrus odoratus* will be found rampaging over wide areas of wet ground. It will scale massive blackberry patches and spread in sheets down embankments and over streamlets. The flowers are a bold crimson-purple colour that would be hard to place in a garden even if the plant were less ambitious. There is another form which is slightly less vigorous but so very attractive that it is worth the care of weeding out excessive volunteers. This is *L. odoratus* 'Gloriosus', which has very pale pink wings and a bright rose-pink keel. The perfume is strong. *L. odoratus* 'Wiltshire Ripple' has maroon flowers flecked with pink and grows 3 m tall, which is about as much as most gardeners can comfortably manage.

Mina lobata   A popular annual climber ever since it was introduced from Mexico in 1841. It needs warm weather to do really well. Provided danger of frost is past, it can be started under a piece of glass in the spot where it is to grow. The longer the growing season the better the display of flowers. Experienced growers know that a glass wine-flagon (demijohn) with the bottom removed can be used to provide a sort of miniature glasshouse that will get seedlings established as early as possible. It is also useful for raising other slightly tender seeds. Mina lobata was written up this way in C.F. Newman's nursery catalogue for 1894:

A charming climber for covering arbors, trellises, etc. The flowers appear on long racemes, and in colour they are both singular and attractive, the buds being at first vivid red, but they turn to orange yellow before opening, and when fully expanded are creamy white. The plant, which attains a height of from eighteen to twenty feet [approx 4.5 m], is strikingly beautiful, and produces flowers from the base to the summit.

***Tropaeolum peregrinum* (syn. *T. canariense*)**   Another beauty from the New World, this time from over a large area—Mexico to Chile. It was first brought to Europe in 1810. It has the rare ability to flourish in poor soils in sun or shade and flower regardless. Delicate twining growth to about 3 m produces a constant display of small heavily fringed yellow flowers. It is cold sensitive and prefers areas fairly free of strong breezes, as its tendrils have not much of a grip on things and are easily torn down. Needs some watering to keep it performing into the autumn. Some old gardeners remember it as canary creeper. It is again appearing in seed lists which go beyond the everyday and commonplace.

8 Roses of Yesteryear

This chapter contains a selection of the better varieties from among the many hundreds of old roses now being reintroduced by commercial and amateur growers. Where do they all come from? The answer is not hard to find: look around any old village, town or hamlet on any weekend in early summer. You are likely to find people collecting cuttings and suckers from the oldest gardens, from churchyards and from the long overgrown gardens of derelict homesteads. Such activities are not unique to Australia—similar things are happening in South Africa, New Zealand, the United States and across Europe, and have been since the period between the wars. There have always been at least a few keen gardeners interested in collecting, growing and identifying the rose treasures of yesteryear. From these private endeavours lost rose varieties are being reintroduced to our gardens.

Usually the first step is for the newly discovered plants to be shared around by cuttings under some convenient name— for example, Bradshaw's Farm Rose—but as the plant circulates, some will try to identify it by comparing it against descriptions of named varieties in old gardening books and magazines. Now it might be thought that such information would be extremely hard to come by. But, as in many other areas of study, the microcomputer is being used by amateurs to store any information found, and extensive banks of rose descriptions are being built up and shared around. Eventually a short list of possible names will circulate among the rose detectives, photographs and budwood may be sent abroad for comparison with known varieties in foreign rose collections, and at last a tentative name may be put alongside the 'lost' rose. At this stage nurserymen may take the rose into their stock and distribute it widely; unnamed roses and those with only local names are not looked on with favour by most nurserymen, as there is too much potential for confusion in distributing roses with no

provenance. Even when old roses are entered into the catalogues of commercial growers there is no absolute guarantee that the rose is correctly named; it is only that a large body of keen collectors have agreed on a 'most likely' identity.

The lack of a name is not in itself a very significant reason for not growing a plant, and it would be foolish to ignore, or destroy, a special rose simply because no one living can recall its name. What makes a rose special? It could be a rose that has grown at the family home since the days when great-grandfather took up his land, or it might be the particular favourite of an aged aunt; it may even have been brought over with your ancestors when they migrated here from the old country, or it may be a complete stranger that appeals simply on account of its beauty. Above all it has been a survivor, having grown and flowered without fuss and bother for many, many years. By all means preserve such roses and pass them round among gardening friends. Beauty alone is sufficient recommendation.

Care and Usage

The care of roses has been the subject of whole books. It would be impossible to reproduce all that information here. In regard to old roses it could be said that they will respond to every care and attention, giving good growth and ample flowers in return for feeding and spraying. In a general way the varieties that have survived our years of neglect are very tough plants tolerant of hard conditions and resistant to disease (though not repelling it) and they will perform quite adequately with minimum care. They do better with the usual care given to other roses.

It is possible to choose plants that resist disease better than others and to avoid varieties with bad habits (especially 'balling', where the outer petals turn mouldy and prevent the flower opening). In this way a good collection of old roses can be made without recourse to varieties that need more care, the only disadvantage being that some otherwise desirable varieties may have to be excluded. The best way to find out which are the good performers in your area is to visit gardens and nurseries where old roses are grown. Considering the popularity old roses now enjoy, this should not be as hard to do as it was a few years back.

One other thing that must be remembered about old roses is the many ways in which they can be used to decorate gardens. Beginners with old roses all too often think of them only as replacements for modern roses used in the same settings. Borders and beds of roses are all very well, but there are many other ways of using old roses depending on the habits of growth of the particular varieties. Stop thinking of roses as rather twiggy, gaunt bushes about 1 to 2 m tall which are grown free of other flowers in straight rows, in blocks of the same variety or a mixture of twelve of the best. Old roses may be grown as hedges, bowers, scramblers, climbers, trailers, in borders of mixed shrubs and among flowers. Happily, many gardeners are renewing their acquaintance with these decorative ways of using roses. Visiting gardens and looking at magazines may help you get a few ideas.

Some Ancient Survivors

Among the earliest roses to bring pleasure to colonial gardeners were the autumn damask (*Rosa* × *damascena* 'Bifera', or 'Rose de Quatre Saisons') and the perpetual white moss ('Quatre Saisons Blanc Mousseaux'). Both are very ancient varieties, the former being cultivated by the Romans, and are also extremely tough. They are found frequently throughout the long-settled south-eastern section of Australia as well as in many other colonial settlements. Even where no other roses will grow untended, this pair will bloom year in and year out. As bushes they are not very tidy, but the repeated crops of highly scented flowers are reward enough. They make sprawling shrubs (2 m × 1.5 m) with few branches and sparse foliage. The leaves are large, greyish and downy. The thorns are long, thin and hooked, intermingled with a few needle-like spines. The bark is light green at first, maturing to grey, while the thorns are fawn, slowly darkening and then going grey. The best identifying features are the very large heads of blooms and buds which appear on watershoots with each growth spurt. As both varieties are remontant (i.e., bloom again), several crops of blooms appear each year. The autumn damask has large loosely crumpled petals of clear pink. The rose is extremely good for making potpourri and other rose-scented products. 'Quatre Saisons Blanc Mousseaux' is easily identified by the very thick, hard, bronze-green-coloured mossing on stems, twigs, the back veins and rims of leaves and on the buds. The flowers are loosely double and paper-white.

At about the time these roses were introduced to Australia (*c.* 1840) two Chinese roses were also brought here, via England. These may also be found in the gardens of long-inhabited houses and cottages and occasionally in the wild. Their habits and growth are very different from the previous pair—a pair of Chinese maidens alongside some rather rugged Europeans. The roses are 'Old Blush' (1798) and 'Slater's Crimson China' (1792). Growth in both bushes is densely twiggy, at first slow in developing, but gradually building up into substantial bushes (2.5 m × 1.5 m) and covered with dark green foliage. The stems are smooth and dark with a few scattered broad dark thorns and no bristles. The flowers are semi-double, pale silver-pink flushed deeper at the outer edges in 'Old Blush' and clear crimson in 'Slater's Crimson China'. Such attractive roses could scarcely pass through the hands of countless admiring gardeners without being given some additional names—'Old Blush' is often called 'Parson's Pink', 'Monthly Rose' and 'Pallida', and 'Slater's Crimson China' has been known as 'Semperflorens' and 'Old Crimson China'. While the pink rose is highly scented, the red one, disappointingly, has only a slight perfume to enhance its attractive colour.

There are quite a few other roses that were widely distributed during the early days of the colonies and doubtless survive here and there. Two that are frequently found are old varieties that besides being garden roses were also widely used as rootstocks for other roses. One is the most attractive climber *Rosa* × 'Fortuneana', an ancient Chinese garden rose introduced to English gardens by Robert Fortune in 1850. An attractive double white flower is enhanced by glossy dark green leaves. A strong grower and extremely easily propagated, it quickly spread through the gardening would, at first as a plant in its own right and later as an obliging understock. Now it is often found in derelict gardens, the budded rose having died years ago and the suckering understock still thriving mightily. In Australia it was specially valued as an understock for planting in very sandy soils. Very large specimens appear in many old gardens, covering spaces as large as 6 m × 3 m and even more, with arching canes and intertwined brown-barked stems as thick as a small tree trunk.

To these few roses, many others could be added, for example, 'Lady Banks Rose' (*Rosa banksiae* 'Alba-plena', 1803) and its very widespread yellow form *Rosa banksiae lutea* (1824), some of the gallica roses—'Belle de Crecy' (pre-1848), 'Charles de Mills', or even the rambler 'Russelliana' (1840) with its heavy spreading canes, sturdy foliage and masses of small crimson-purple full-petalled pompons.

One other commonly met rose must be mentioned: 'La Reine' (1842). Among gardeners inexperienced in the older types of roses this is most often given the highly descriptive name of cabbage rose. The flowers certainly are large and many-petalled, and the perfume strong and sweet, but the plant and the flowers do not bear comparison with the genuine cabbage rose (*Rosa centifolia*). 'La Reine' is coarser in all aspects, though not nearly so coarse as to render it vulgar or ugly. The telltale characteristics of 'La Reine' are supple but very upright growth, scattered stubby thorns, large leaves and small flower heads of round sharply pointed buds which open to a very full flower of bright cerise-pink, fading only a little and reflexing into a large globular flower. The perfume is heady; little wonder this rose has been treasured in many old gardens and been equated with the most rosy of roses.

China Roses and Tea Roses

Of all the kinds of old roses that can be found in the remains of our early gardens, the China roses and tea roses are the most widespread. The reason is not hard to find—these roses are well suited to our climate and were *the* roses of the gold-rush period and the spread of rural settlement which followed. Across southern Australia countless thousands of these hardy, ever-blooming roses may be found populating old gardens, derelict home sites, cemeteries and cottage yards. Time and again they rise from floods, droughts, sprayings and repeated tidy-ups to bring forth their delicately coloured blooms and delightful perfumes. The sight of an enormous bush of 'Safrano' smothered in golden-apricot blooms, each flower nodding gently among red-bronze leaves, never fails to set the sentiments stirring among the lovers of the rose. These are roses that can be relied on to produce bushels of flowers in their long season; roses with colours and tints which can range from exotic old golds to all the delicate tints of dawn, and roses that given time will make massive bushes covered with hundreds of blooms at a time. They can be pruned down to conventional rosebush size and so treated will flower heavily, but never so heavily or with such amazing splendour as when let alone from the beginning and grown as a shrub. Remarkably few years are needed to produce a respectable tree-rose. The job is easily accomplished if all that is done is feeding and watering and the removal of dead and spindly growth.

There were literally thousands of roses in these two classes. The greater part of these are lost to us, yet many remain growing wild and with long-forgotten names. To these may be added many nameless home-raised seedlings and the family roses passed down from generation to generation bearing familiar aliases such as 'Granny White's Rose', 'Aunt Ethel's Rose', 'Graetz's Farm Rose'. All of them are worth growing, but the following are a selection from these two generally carefree and reliable rose families.

CHINA ROSES

China roses are known by their compact twiggy growth well covered with smallish smooth green leaves, often tinted red and copper shades when young, and by their small flowers borne in large clusters. Perfume is usually good, and the colour range includes shades of copper, gold, flame, rose, scarlet and crimson. The bushes need little pruning and, although slow to get started, with eventually grow into large and solid shrubs. The distinctions between these and the tea roses have been blurred by interbreeding, so some varieties have characteristics belonging to the two groups.

Papillon (1822)   A very strong-growing rose which is almost the personification of gay abandon—it truly does fling its branches out and up, tossing skyward large clusters of scrolled semi-double blooms of bright rose-pink shot with gold and orange tones reflected from deeper-hued tones on the reverse side. 2 m and more.

Duchesse de Brabant (1857)   A rose met under many aliases, among them 'Countess Bertha', 'Comtesse de Labarthe' or 'Comtesse Ouwaroff'. It is one of the most widespread of old roses. It has cupped semi-double blooms borne in small clusters and coloured a fine pale pearly pink merging to cream at the base of each petal. The leaves are large and the bush is well clothed. 2 m.

Mme Joseph Schwartz (1880)   Virtually a paler coloured form of 'Duchesse de Brabant' and most often found under the name 'White Duchesse de Brabant'. The elegant cream blooms retain the form and pearly sheen of the former rose and occasionally show hints of rose-pink around the edges

of the petals. Equally as fine as 'Duchesse de Brabant' and a good companion for it. Lovely underplanted with *Geranium pratense* and *Anchusa italica*. 2 m.

Hermosa (1840)   Another rose found now and then in old gardens, where it was often employed as a bordering rose, its low, compact growth and prolific flowering habit making it especially suited for this purpose. The leaves are smaller than usual among this group. The flowers emerge from fat, round buds which open to show fully double cupped blooms of pure pink. 1 m, less if pruned regularly.

Comtesse du Cayla (1902)   A very brightly coloured rose of vigorous habit, open growth and strongly scented. The flowers vary in colour from season to season but always show tints of copper, orange, flame and bright pink. They are semi-double and very freely produced. 2 m.

Tipo Ideale (pre-1896)   An older rose as distinctive as 'Comtesse du Cayla'. The flowers show a similar range of colours but are single and carried on growth that is very twiggy and compact. Given time, the bushes will mound up to 2 m or more. Pruning seriously hinders the production of flowers. Often sold as *Rosa chinensis* 'Mutabilis'.

Cramoisi Supérieur (1832)   An outstanding rose of almost perfect habits—leafy compact growth, prolific flowering and a good solid red colour—ideal as a specimen or treated as a hedge rose and requiring little pruning. The flowers are semi-double and carried over twelve months in warm areas. 2 m and over after some years.

Le Vesuve (1825)   Another typical China beauty, this time with rather open, almost double flowers in shades of silver-pink, tending darker on the outer petals. Reputed to be more frost-tender than the others, but it still makes 2 m and more in most Australian gardens.

TEA ROSES

Tea roses, so named for their perfume, which is said to resemble the aroma from a newly opened packet of China tea, are more robust and vigorous than their China cousins. The foliage is larger; so too are the thorns. Strong watershoots are a common characteristic, as are large heads of flowering buds. In many instances new growth has a decided reddish tinge; the leaves and twigs are often covered with a slight silvery meal which usually wears away a month or so after the growth appears. From the hundred or so still in cultivation, the following short list of teas is but a personal selection of good doers:

Mme Charles (1864)   Although the flowers are small in comparison with other tea roses, those of 'Mme Charles' are borne in such large clusters that their lack of size is insignificant. The tall, arching growth, ideal for running up a shed wall, carries prodigious crops of flowers, semi-double silver-pink and darker on the reverse. A very free and vigorous rose. 2 m and taller.

Antoine Rivoire (1895)   A delightful rose in shades of pearly pink and cream which varies from season to season. The flowers are fully double and carried in small clusters. The growth seems to be spreading rather than tall with glossy dark foliage. Flowers are produced over a long season. 1.5 m.

Dr Grill (1886)   Vigorous tall growth is topped with extra large flowers in clusters of five or so blush-pink buds which open to show coppery-cream colours. The flowers are deep and well petalled and have a delightful perfume. As with most other teas, the intensity of colour seems to vary with soil conditions and the time of year. 2 m and over.

Rich scent, healthy dark foliage and abundant flowers are hallmarks of 'Boule de Neige'.

Shell-like, cupped and quartered roses such as 'Reine Victoria' gave their form to the tea roses of old-fashioned gardens.

Grüss an Aachen (1909)   A low-growing tea-type rose often credited with being the first floribunda rose. The large flowers open flat and come in shades of richest cream with tinges of pink at the outer edges. Good foliage, plenty of perfume and strongly remontant. 1.5 m.

Monsieur Tillier (1891)   A rather controversial rose in light of some recent expert opinions; but the original descriptions being rather scant, the 'proof' is subject to many interpretations. I believe this rose to be distinct from 'Archduc Joseph' (1872). Densely packed rich rose-pink petals with deeper shades on the outer petals and the whole shot with coppery and brassy tints. The flowers are cupped and quartered and open flat, and the central petals are quilled somewhat (i.e., rolled together in a tubular fashion). Strong perfume, vigorous growth and masses of flowers all year round in warm areas. 2 m and more.

Mrs B.R. Cant (1901)   A glorious rose in the old-fashioned tradition, deeply cupped and quartered and well perfumed. Outer petals are a rich deep pink; the inner ones are paler rose-pink. Vigorous growth and prolific flowering habit. 2 m and bushy.

Grace Darling (1884)   Named for the heroine of a dramatic shipwreck rescue, this rose is a very fitting tribute. It has tall, upright growth and produces masses of large globular flowers in shades of pale pink flushed with cream. Delicate colours belie its tough constitution. 2 m and over.

Rubens   An angular and sparse bush which produces very fine cream semi-double flowers throughout the summer and autumn. The petals have the appearance and texture of carved ivory. A lovely flower which benefits from an underplanting of a simple perennial to set off the fine colouring and to give the planting some bulk; *Teucrium chamaedrys* and *Silene wherryi* are good. Recognised in Australia from unknown semi-wild plants by Peter Beales and Clair Martin III. 1.5 m.

Safrano (1839)   A very popular rose since its introduction and often found illustrated in early garden magazines and books. For some unknown reason it seems to have been very popular in the gold-mining areas, where hoary old bushes still bloom in many cottage yards. Strong, healthy growth with an abundance of reddish-tinted foliage that sets off ideally the heavy crops of soft old gold to cream flowers. The flowers are loosely semi-double, and the flower colour varies according to the time of year. Teamed with the deep blue of *Cynoglossum nervosum* and *Clematis heracleifolia* 'Davidiana', it makes an easy and splendid garden picture. 2 m.

Isabella Sprunt (1865)   A sport of 'Safrano' and exactly similar but for the colour of the flowers, which in this case is a soft sulphur-yellow that quickly pales to almost white during hot weather. The autumn flowers are especially fine and well coloured.

Perle des Jardins (1874)   A rose often recommended for culture under glass in Europe and America but well able to flourish and produce excellent flowers outdoors in our warmer climate. Exceptionally refined, fully double creamy-white flowers are very fragrant and freely produced. In cooler weather the flowers take on slightly deeper yellow shades. 1.5 m.

Homere (1858)   An old-timer recently reintroduced and one that seems to have some highly desirable qualities; healthy growth and the capacity to produce large heads of buds that flower for weeks in succession. Individual flowers are medium in size but lovely still. The buds open from rose-pink outer petals to show an almost white heart. They are double and fashioned in the old style. 1.5 m.

Baronne Henriette de Snoy (1897)   A strong grower that produces masses of beautifully formed flowers over an extended season. Each bloom is large, double, cupped and quartered and well centred. The colour is a pleasant mid-pink but darker on the reverse of each petal so that a darker shadow is present to liven up the blooms with additional highlights. 2 m and more.

Jean Ducher   Another rose which is frequently treasured in old gardens, often without its name being known. Very fragrant flowers varying in colour between shades of salmon, pink and peach are produced freely over summer and autumn. Growth is strong and hardy. 2 m.

Mr Dudley Cross (1907)   One of the later teas to be introduced, this rose quickly became popular and established itself as a firm favourite with an earlier generation of gardeners. It has many attributes to recommend it: glorious double flowers, perfume, a long flowering season, healthy foliage and almost no thorns. The flowers are a delicate blend of soft creamy-yellow tinged with pink at the edge of each petal. 2 m.

Princess de Sagan (1887)   Almost approaches a modern cluster-flowered hybrid in its production of flowers. The two-toned flowers are rose pink distinctly rimmed with a deeper purplish-crimson colour, and the bushes are always in bloom.

Rosette Delizy (1922)   A late tea that is unusual for the large clustered heads of flowers it typically produces. Each flower is loosely semi-double and coloured yellow with shades of crimson. Continuously in bloom.

Hugo Roller (1907)   Throughout coastal New South Wales this boldly coloured rose is found among the remnants of old gardens. The striking combination of crimson and creamy white is rather coarse but is the distinctive signature of this widespread rose.

Kronprinzessin Viktoria (1888)   Bred from 'Souvenir de la Malmaison', this rose has also been known as 'Souvenir de la Malmaison Jaune', which seems misleading since it is not a yellow form of the parent. The conformation is similar to the full-blown, quartered beauty of Souvenir de la Malmaison and it is also very fragrant. The colour is almost white with lemon shades at the centre, especially in the autumn.

Kaiserin August Viktoria (1891)   Is remembered in many gardens as K.A.V. The growth is compact and spreading and well clothed with dark, glossy foliage. It is one of the best of all whites, has had a long career as an exhibition rose, and is wonderfully fragrant.

Single Roses

Single roses are so rarely seen nowadays that even though they are not particularly old they would fit happily into any garden up to about Federation style. Although they are hybrid teas, their simple form and clear colours are far removed from the complex blends and harsh contrasts of many of that class that are regarded as 'modern'. Used with restraint, they can be a great attraction in a flower garden, and while they are not long lasting they are beautiful indoors too. These roses need the same pruning as any other modern roses. Most of them are vigorous growers and should therefore be sited towards the rear of the garden bed. Choice varieties still available are:

Dainty Bess (1925)   A very well-known soft pink rose with five large petals offset by distinctive dark red stamens at the centre of each bloom. Lovely with pink *Salvia involucrata* 'Bethelii', *Gaura lindheimeri*, *Iresine herbstii*, *Nicotiana sylvestris* and *N. affinis* hybrids.

Ellen Willmott (1936)   Named after a famous and extravagant patron of gardening, this flower is a subtle blend of pink, white and lemon-yellow. The form is ruffled, and the golden stamens set things off to perfection.

Irish Fireflame (1913)   A rose that appears every now and then in old gardens and is usually much admired and treasured even though the name has mostly been long forgotten. The butterfly blooms are a blend of pale apricot, orange, old gold and cream, laced with veins of soft yellow and red. The overall effect is that of a coppery sheen. Strong perfume.

Irish Elegance (1905)   Very similar to the above but with more reddish and pink tones which create a bronze effect at a distance. Can be happily fronted with bronze heleniums, purple fennel and other copper and orange autumn flowers.

Mrs Oakley Fisher (1921)   Slightly lower in growth than the others, this bush is covered for most of a long season with rich gold blooms that pale to old gold within a day of opening.

White Wings   One of the last of this group to be bred (1947) and one of the best. Large single white flowers with dark red stamens. Very tall growth.

Squatter's Dream (1923)   A rose bred in Australia by Alister Clark and propagated from plants found growing, complete with labels still attached and legible, at Old Anlaby homestead, near Kapunda in South Australia. The bushes are spreading and covered in dense dark green foliage that is glossy and disease resistant. Masses of single yellow and old gold flowers bloom early and late on a plant that is everblooming in warm areas.

Mrs Frank Guthrie (1923)   A vigorous single pink which is most prolific and sweetly scented. The flowers are mainly borne in small clusters of buds, from three to seven per stem, so that the succession of bloom is good. The petals are slightly ruffled. Compact growth. One of Alister Clark's roses bred at Bulla, north of Melbourne.

Hedge Roses

Using roses to make hedges or growing them on fence lines is not nearly as common as it used to be. Nevertheless, it is not unusual to see dog roses (*Rosa canina*), *Rosa multiflora* and *Rosa indica* 'Major' growing in profusion along boundaries and at the roadsides in the country. These roses may appear to be growing wild but are usually the remnants of hedges planted years ago and now fallen into disrepair. While the line of plantings will have been blurred by some self-sown seedlings, most often the general line can be easily discerned. Early settlers planted hedges as a cheap, quick alternative to fencing their land-holdings. Their choice of roses and briars was partly based on the plants' use in the old countries (hawthorn was used similarly), partly because the plants would thrive and deter cows and horses from wandering, and partly for sentimental and economic reasons: roses were beloved by all, were useful for making jams and perfumed waters and could be a source of income if the householder could sell the canes to nearby nurserymen as understocks or even bud their own roses for local sale.

Aside from the wilder sorts of roses commonly used for field hedging, use was also made in some areas of *Rosa bracteata*, the 'Macartney Rose', named for Lord Macartney, who made a diplomatic mission to the Chinese Emperor's court late in the eighteenth century. This rose was part of the booty from that expedition. It is a climber but can also be grown as a very tough, thick and well-armed hedge. It has glossy dark green leaves, fawny-buff stems which feel velvety, very strong thorns and quite large single white flowers. Elsewhere, smaller more decorative hedges were sometimes grown in old gardens from the widespread 'Old Blush'. This rose makes a fairly open hedge that is more useful for the continuous show of flowers it produces than for the slight protection it would afford a garden. Occasionally short garden hedges may be found of 'Slater's Crimson China' or a dwarf China rose called locally 'Lady Brisbane Rose' (possibly a rose called 'Fabvier' of 1832). As no one knows for sure what this last rose might properly be called, few nurserymen will stock it; nevertheless it is very attractive and worth having if cuttings should come your way.

To these few may be added other old roses which are really beautiful, reliable and custom-made to be used as flowering hedges inside a garden. The best sorts come from two distinct groups of roses; the spinosissimas, or Scots Burnet roses, and the hybrid musk roses raised by the Reverend Joseph Pemberton—there are others of this class too, but they are not as good for making a hedge.

SPINOSISSIMAS

The spinosissimas are by nature very shrubby, thicket-making plants which produce a mass of canes and plenty of small ferny leaves. In early summer a large quantity of small flowers is followed eventually by a prolific crop of round black berries. The flowers are globular in the double forms and open flat in the single varieties. Perhaps the very best way of growing them is in a hedge of mixed varieties so that the pastel-coloured blooms can make a tapestry of muted colours. In the eastern states, especially in southern New South Wales, Victoria and Tasmania, these hardy colonisers can be found in many unknown forms with colours ranging through white, cream, soft yellow, flesh-pink, lilac-pink and plummy tones. It could be that they are self-sown seedlings, although they could equally be old varieties whose names have been forgotten.

Among the best named sorts, any of the following are attractive flowering shrubs for hedge making or for more general use:

William III An old variety of dwarf habit (1 m) with semi-double flowers of a rich plum colour that eventually fades to a slatey magenta tone.

Mary Queen of Scots A single rose of pale pink overlaid at the outer edges with 'brush-marked' lilac and maroon. 1.5 m.

Irish Rich Marbled A semi-double rose of melded shades of pale pink, lilac and pale silver-grey tones. Utterly charming. 1.5 m.

Falkland A semi-double pink and lilac blend which fades almost to white in strong southern light. 1.5 m.

Mrs Colville Not quite single with a few petaloids but not enough to be semi-double. This rose is purplish in colour though fading to a more delicate colour in our strong light. 1.5 m.

A few of the true species from this family could be added to further increase the intermingled pastel tones of a hedge made from these roses. Roses such as these could be included:

Rosa spinosissima 'Altaica' A rather taller growing kind reaching 2 m and more with large single creamy-white flowers.

Rosa spinosissima 'Andrewsii' A semi-double kind with rich pink blooms and growth that reaches 1.5 m.

Rosa spinosissima 'Bicolor' Semi-double pink blooms with a paler reverse that shows as the flower expands and reflexes; at the same time the upper edges of the petals fade too, so the effect is of a two-tone flower. Like most of its tribe, this bush will grow to 1.5 m.

When looking for these roses in catalogues, make a note that they are sometimes listed as varieties of *Rosa pimpinellifolia*, not so much to confuse customers as to please botanists who are continually debating which name—*spinosissima* or *pimpinellifolia*—was the first to be used to describe these ferny-leaved and fine-spined roses.

INTERPLANTINGS

If the thought of only one season of flowers (in the main) is not pleasing, then a hedge of such plants can be used as the base for other plantings which will give a further season of bloom. Low climbers can be interplanted among the roses that will flower after the roses and finish before the hips (seed pods) begin to ripen. First class for such treatment are the small flowered kinds of clematis, such as *Clematis viticella*, *C. campaniflora*, *C. heracleifolia* 'Davidiana', *C.* × 'Venosa Violacea' and *C.* × 'Margot Koster'. Alternatively a choice could be made from among the three of four forms of perennial sweet pea that are available—*Lathyrus nervosus, L. latifolius, L. pubescens*—or the annual forms such as 'Painted Lady' and 'Busby Sweet Pea'. The clematis have an added attraction in that they form typical fluffy seed-heads that will add to the quiet display provided by the ripening rose hips. Once their season has finished, all these plants may be cut down completely to tidy up appearances and to make way for unimpeded growth in the next year.

PEMBERTON HYBRID MUSKS

Finally among the hedging roses are the Pemberton hybrid musks, blessed with all the good qualities roses need to be good garden plants—healthy growth, vigour, plentiful flowers, attractive colours, flowers that stand well in the weather and good perfume. Their beautiful names and appealing form make them even more attractive. They are all good roses, carefully selected by Pemberton to meet his own exacting criteria. They nearly all bloom heavily in late spring and on and off throughout the summer with a final strong flush of blooms in the autumn. The long canes can be tied easily to a simple three-strand wire 'fence' in a garden and will make a glorious sight within a few years of being planted. Again, the muted colours make a tapestry hedge an appealing idea, but single colours or a limited choice could be attractive if particular colour schemes are being developed. Make a selection from among the following; they are all highly recommended:

Buff Beauty   Vigorous spreading growth carrying large clusters of fully double flowers in varying shades of buff-yellow to apricot and primrose. Strongly scented and always admired. 2 m.

Cornelia   By the time the fully double flowers are wide open, a small centre of golden stamens is revealed, adding to the considerable charms of this pink rose delicately tinted with a hint of apricot. 2 m.

Prosperity   Fairly upright growth which is weighed down by masses of creamy-white flowers set amid dark green leaves. The flowers are large and double. 2 m.

Pink Prosperity   Possible a sport from the above, although introduced by another breeder. Nicely scented blooms are fully double and a good clear pink. 1.5 m.

Thisbe   Seems often to be ignored, possibly because it comes at the end of most nursery lists and gets overlooked. It is a very good light yellow with masses of semi-double flowers. 1.5 m.

Penelope   Somewhat larger flowers than many of the others and coloured in shades of pink and cream. Scented. 2 m.

Felicia   A great attraction in any garden with double flowers of salmon, rich pink and pale pink. With age, more silvery tones develop, adding to the charms of an already lovely flower. 2 m.

Danae   Although one of the older Pemberton hybrids, this hybrid musk is not seen as often as it deserves to be. Semi-double flowers of bright yellow quickly develop cream and buff tonings as the flowers open. 2 m.

Francesca   Another of the less well known kinds, this time with large semi-double apricot to yellow flowers and strong spreading growth. 1.5 m.

Moonlight   A blessing to those who love white flowers and are getting bored with 'Iceberg' everywhere! Semi-single flowers are at first creamy and then chalky white. They come in very large clusters and continue to bloom for ages. Nicely scented and good growth. 2 m.

There are other hybrid musks too, such as 'Pax', 'Will Scarlet', 'Nur Mahal', 'Vanity' and several more, but they do not have the qualities of floriferousness, cane growth and foliage to make them good choices for inclusion in an informal hedge of roses. Their place is in a shrub border, perhaps as a specimen or even up a small tree.

Climbing Roses

Of all the kinds of roses, it is the climbers that have shown the greatest decrease in numbers and use in recent times. Along with all other climbers—except perhaps ivies, which have become hanging basket plants—climbing roses have suffered a serious decline in popularity. How great has been the loss to our gardens as each climbing rose, capable of producing thousands of blooms every season, has been grubbed out and replaced with some dull native shrub or tizzy subtropical glamour plant. Slowly there is emerging a renaissance of the climbing roses—not the stiff and semi-naked sports of hybrid teas but the genuine old climbing roses, roses covered in foliage and flowers with

supple stems capable of being gracefully trained over sheds and archways, around tripods, over fences and into trees. It is climbing roses such as these that are listed here:

Fortune's Double Yellow (*Rosa odorata* 'Pseudindica') (1845)   Introduced from Chinese gardens by Robert Fortune. Masses of small coppery-yellow blooms overlaid with rose-pink, produced in one enormous flush. The growth is dense, fine stemmed and well foliated. Resents pruning in its early years and needs very little even in old age.

Crépuscule (1904)   A really fine apricot-gold, semi-double in form and a very prolific shrubby climber. Ideal for training on verandah posts and on archways. Good repeat blooming and healthy growth.

Lamarque (1830)   A fond favourite with many connoisseurs of old roses and of fine garden plants. Shrubby climbing canes are best treated as subjects for tripods, on low fences or on verandahs. Fully double soft creamy-yellow blooms are beautifully set against rich green foliage.

Sombreuil (1850)   One of the finest white roses ever introduced, which attracts much favourable comment from first-time viewers and from those who grow and love it. Creamy-white flowers are packed with a solid mass of slightly crimped petals which have the appearance of having been sheared off with pinking shears to make a flat-topped rose. Extra fine perfume. One of the choicest roses we have. Sombreuil has been sold in the USA and New Zealand as 'Colonial White'; the name is spurious and should be discontinued.

Nancy Hayward (1937)   An Australian-raised hybrid of *Rosa gigantea* (1889) with vigorous growth and stunning tomato-red single flowers. It has one flowering season, usually very early in the rose year. Raised by Alister Clark, who also gave us 'Lorraine Lee'.

Jessie Clark (1915)   Another Clark rose and possibly one of his best. It is a hybrid of *Rosa gigantea* and blooms once, early in the season. The large flowers are a soft silver pink with somewhat darker tones on the backs of the petals. Glorious.

Maréchal Niel (1864)   A member of the Noisette group of climbers which are mainly noted for their low climbing growth, rich foliage and usually white or yellow blooms. This one is one of the best. Large fully double blooms are yellow at first, passing to cream and white as the days go by. Simply superb and deservedly so since its introduction.

Alister Stella Gray (1894)   Another Noisette with smallish flowers and rather shrubby low growth. Yellow and then paler shades after a few days of sunny weather. A very long flowering season.

Claire Jacquier (1888)   A very strong growing Noisette with abundant small flowers in good-sized clusters. Individual blooms are semi-double and appear in shades of cream and white.

Mme Grégoire Stachelin (1927)   A lovely Spanish rose with huge pale pink flowers richly scented and prodigiously produced, followed by a good crop of large pear-shaped orange fruits. Once-flowering but magnificent and richly scented to boot.

Lady Hillingdon (climbing) (1917)   A climbing sport of a well known bush rose. The same red-tinted foliage and lovely old gold colour. The blooms are loosely semi-double and produced in amazing numbers. Well scented.

Devoniensis (climbing) (1838)   Known also as the magnolia rose, which should be indication enough of its immense blooms and creamy-yellow shade similar to the large Bull Bay magnolia (*Magnolia grandiflora*). The perfume is likewise very strong and lemony. Make sure you obtain the climbing from, as there is also a bush form. A proved performer over 150 years.

Ramblers

Roses often appear along the roadsides of old country towns and even along railway embankments and cuttings in the suburbs. Most often the plants are very low and scrambling, with shiny foliage and bright pink pompon flowers that fade quickly to a pallid pink. At a later date the observant passer-by might notice that the same plants are disfigured with mildew. Just about everyone will recognise these plants as 'Dorothy Perkins' (some may recognise the form 'Red Dorothy Perkins', which really should be called 'Excelsa'). But all too often these are the only representatives of a once very popular class of roses known as ramblers, even though dozens of varieties are still in cultivation in Europe, and lesser numbers in other countries.

Whatever use ramblers are put to, they all need similar pruning. After three or four years the long canes will have produced the best displays they are capable of; at this time they should be completely removed to allow room for new canes to develop. This usually means that about one-third of the total number of canes are removed annually. Alternatively, the plants can be left alone for a number of years, after which time a slaughter will be necessary to remove all the dead and unproductive canes that will have formed a massive thatch at the centre of the plant. This sort of treatment will mean that one year's flowering may be completely lost; however, it has its advantages for busy gardeners.

Most varieties produce one splendid crop of flowers, but the better ones also have lesser displays over an extended season; performance depends in part on the amounts of food and water that the plants get after the main flush of bloom is over. As a general guide, growth can be expected to be between 5 and 6 m.

SELECT VARIETIES

Bloomfield Courage (1925)   Most often seen as a weeping standard, for its bright crimson flowers with their bold white eyes seem to have had a devastating influence on modern rose nurserymen. The flowers produce in sheets of colour but are short-lived and rather too startling for comfort.

Paul Transom (1900)   A superb fully double flower of salmon-pink with bronze in the opening buds. Strong perfume, glossy dark foliage and very free flowering. Almost like a miniature version of the tea rose 'Monsieur Tillier'.

Rambling Rector (date unknown)   A fine loosely double white flower. Very vigorous growth able to top tall trees and buildings. Beautiful scented. One of those favoured by the fastidious Gertrude Jekyll.

American Beauty (1902)   A very sunny flower of bright pink with a white eye and larger than usual for ramblers. Glossy dark green foliage and vigorous growth. Some think it too bold but others find it attractive, especially when grown together with the paler 'Apple Blossom'. Once among the top ten of popular roses and consequently still found frequently in old gardens.

Hiawatha (1904)   A small-flowered variety with cherry-red single blooms with a conspicuous white eye that retains charm because of its diminutive size where similar large-flowered kinds become too obvious. Very thin, supple canes and vigorous growth.

François Juranville (1906)   Larger-than-usual flowers of salmon-pink with some yellowish tints at the centre. Sweetly perfumed and very healthy growth. One crop of flowers is produced, but it tends to be later than other varieties and so can extend the flowering season.

Tea Rambler (1904)   Noted for its especially long flowering season and the considerable charm of its soft salmon-pink blooms. These are loosely double and very fragrant. Rather light foliage with copper and bronze tints which set off the flowers perfectly.

Violette (1921)   One of those amazing purple-coloured ramblers which usually become known as 'blue' roses. In this case the colour is dark and slatey and on the reddish-maroon side. The fragrance is good. It makes a good companion for 'Veilchenblau'.

Veilchenblau (1909)   Commonest of all the purple-coloured ramblers and often found in country gardens and at the roadsides. The colour rapidly develops strong grey and lilac overtones and can be rather wishy-washy unless accompanied by some other plants which will enhance the subtle colours. Very fragrant.

Goldfinch (1907)   A yellowish flower tending to creamy-white in bright sunshine but valuable nonetheless for its colour, which is scarce in this group. A very noticeable perfume and semi-double flowers. Growth tends to be slightly shorter than usual.

Alberic Barbier (1900)   A fine fully double creamy-white with good foliage and a very strong fragrance. Growth is strong and flowers are produced over a long season.

Aviateur Blériot (1910)   Another of the yellow-coloured ramblers, this time tending to the apricot shades and then developing softer cream and light yellow tones as the flower opens fully. Nicely set off by glossy dark leaves. Well scented.

Sanders White (1912)   An extra vigorous white, fully double and fragrant too. Most often used as a white weeping standard because it is reliably recurrent but useful where a strong growing variety is wanted to cover a pergola or shed.

William Allen Richardson (1878)   Small apricot yellow blooms that fade to pale creamy shades and compact growth. This rose is ideal for growing on a verandah post or over an arch. Usually classed as a Noisette rose, it needs less disciplinary training than most ramblers. Delightful with small clematis such as *Clematis viticella*.

Milkmaid (1927)   Another compact climber with small, clustered flowers that are semi-double and cream to white. This is strictly speaking a Noisette rose, but it is well suited to training on a post or over a gateway.

The few dozen old roses listed in this chapter represent a cross section of the varieties popular with our gardening ancestors. Many may still be found in older gardens where they have been treasured from generation to generation; others have been recently reintroduced from overseas to please the many avid collectors of old roses; all are good performers in a garden setting mixed with annuals, perennials and bulbs. Used according to their habits of growth, they can enhance our gardens with flowering hedges, bowers, archways and shrub-like growth.

The Pelargonium Society
·PALMAM QUI MERUIT FERAT·
AWARDS THIS
FIRST CLASS CERTIFICATE
PELARGONIUM
RAISED BY
EXHIBITED   BY
CHAIRMAN   SECRETARY

9 Simply Geraniums

It is hardly surprising to discover that Australian gardens have never been without geraniums. They have been so widely grown and treasured through generations of gardeners that they have passed into our garden lore as plants ever-present, hardy, tough, adaptable and colourful, easy to grow and reliable. Even on the First Fleet there were plants of geraniums, though we are not quite sure just what sort they were—scented-leaf or fine-flowered—but they were there when the fleet landed at Sydney Cove and the first European settlement began. The plants in question were the property of Arthur Bowes-Smyth, surgeon on the Lady Penrhyn. *On 5 January 1788, just two days before the fleet had its first sight of Australia, he wrote in his diary: 'This night it was so very hot I was obliged to throw off the bedcloathes. There are now in the Cabin geraniums in full blossum and some grapes which flourish very much.'*

They may have been brought all the way from England, though it seems doubtful whether even such hardy plants could have survived the 36-week voyage. More likely they were collected at Cape Town, when the First Fleet stopped there for fresh water and provisions and to collect plants for the orchards and fields of the new colony. During the month-long stay, many of the officers and officials sailing with the fleet travelled to inland farms to make private purchases of stock, feed, plants and fresh food to take with them on the last leg of the journey out. The animals and plants were intended to be the beginnings of private enterprise once New South Wales was reached. No doubt some First Fleeters visiting the well-established gardens of the Cape of Good Hope were attracted to the idea of taking with them cuttings and plants of hardy flowers to beautify the new homes they planned to make in the new settlement. Among these were members of the pelargonium tribe, which have been commonly known as geraniums for several centuries.

There are those who think it most likely that these geraniums were *Pelargonium capitatum*, the rose-scented geranium. There are several reasons for thinking this way. One is that fine-flowered geraniums were only just being introduced in England and France and would not have been imported to the Cape by 1787. Another is that the rose-scented geranium may well have been grown at the Cape as part of the extensive trade in homeopathic remedies conducted by the Dutch East India Company with its colonies and trading stations in Indonesia, South-East Asia and Japan. Yet another reason is that plants of *P. capitatum* have long been naturalised on the Kurnell Peninsula on Botany Bay. This is all open to question, of course, but it serves to introduce the scented-leaf geraniums as old-fashioned plants that have never really waned in popularity. During the middle and late years of the nineteenth century, several state governments sought to alleviate the crisis of rural depressions by broadening the base of the agricultural economy to include, among other things, growing plants for the perfume industry. For one reason or another the extraction of essential oils from perfumed plants failed to establish itself as an alternative rural industry, but at least the experiment indicates how hardy such plants are!

There may have been among those first garden makers some who were inclined to the habits of gardening in the Old Country; they would have grown their geraniums in pots; may even have sheltered them under glass or brush according to the old ideas of the plants being tender, but it could not have been long before the realisation came that in the milder climate of Australia geraniums would grow perfectly well outdoors in most places. They do have a degree of frost tenderness but do not generally need the cosseting afforded them in much colder climates. Indeed, before many years had passed several early diarists and letter writers noted the hedges of geraniums which were a feature of many small gardens in Sydney Town and at Parramatta.

Scented-Leaf Geraniums

The scented-leaf geraniums grow best in sunny spots where the soil is moderately rich, well drained and friable. Most of them will make quite large bushes within a few years of being planted out, and all but a very few are well suited to growing among flowers and shrubs as part of a mixed border. Grown this way they make a valuable contribution to a cottage-style garden, giving a variety of perfumes and foliage shapes to the picture created by the gardener. Another really attractive way of growing them is in a halved wine barrel. Given the usual attention to drainage, feeding and after-care in taking off dead leaves and flowers, a selection of scented-leaf geraniums can bring perfumes and flowers to any sunny courtyard, doorway or paved area.

Any pruning or repotting that needs to be done is best done in the spring. Pruning the woody-stemmed varieties can be done quite 'hard', while some of the softer-wooded small varieties can be given a light all-over clipping. All are easily grown from cuttings, and many will send up a few suckers from the roots as well—especially where they have been severed to over-close digging. Although the plants are hardy, they do attract some pests which must be controlled to keep the plants looking attractive. Attention to watering, feeding, grooming and setting the plants where there is a good movement of air will do much to minimise the attacks of pests and diseases. Occasionally it may be necessary to use a commercial spray to control heavy infestations of aphids, looper caterpillars, red spider mite or white fly, but *never* use sprays on plants whose leaves are to be used for culinary purpose, such as flavouring jellies, jams and cakes or for perfuming finger bowls and potpourri.

Not all the varieties that follow in the listing of recommended varieties are genuine old species and cultivars; some are quite recent introductions from breeders who are still producing distinctive originations not wildly dissonant with the original kinds. It seems that the scent of the leaves could scarcely be improved, but there are certainly some very attractive new flower colours being brought into the old colour range (which was mostly pale lavender and mauve with darker veining and dark spots on the upper petals).

It is hard to know the best way to present the plant descriptions. Some would adopt a straightforward alphabetical approach, others would conform with modern botanical 'families' within the pelargonium tribe, yet others would describe the plants according to the perfume and scents of their leaves—but my nose isn't entirely reliable on that score (though I am not anosmic). As I am a gardener at heart, I have plumped for an arrangement which groups the plants according to the garden positions they best occupy. Before getting started on that task, it is as well to pause a moment and learn just a little of perfume, fragrance and scent.

Many of us would use the words almost interchangeably. However, there are differences. Many things have scents, but they are not always fragrant, and flowers which perfume the air from a distance are not always sweetly scented close up. Those who are hyperosmic—that is, have a sharp sense of smell—will be able to detect many nuances and complexities in the smell of any flower; some, heaven help us, even get carried away like winetasters with their immense vocabularies of descriptors.

Most of us must get along with rather less discriminating noses, though we could, with practice, differentiate fragrances which are balsamic, spicy, heavy, sweet, honeyed, fruity, violety, rosy, or the unique fragrances of sweet pea, lilac, lily-of-the-valley, bearded iris and wistaria. Canon Ellacombe, an early writer who investigated the qualities of scents and perfumes (see *In My Vicarage Garden and Elsewhere*, 1902), was followed by Eleanour Sinclair Rohde with *The Scented Garden* in 1931 and posthumously by Gertrude Jekyll in *A Gardener's Testament* in 1937. A thorough modern discussion can be found in *The Fragrant Year* by Helen van Pelt Wilson and Leonie Bell (1967).

Returning to the scented-leaf geraniums, I have arranged them from the largest growers down to the smallest, as best as can be judged from their performance in this part of the country. In frosty areas it is doubtful whether the larger varieties would grow to the dimensions given here unless sheltered by some protective wall or corner or covered with sacking when frost threatens.

RECOMMENDED VARIETIES

Pelargonium quercifolium (pre-1800)   Often called 'Royal Oak' on account of its massive growth, stout woody trunk and large oak-shaped leaves which are glossy and marked with a dark reddish stain at the centre. Bushes almost 2 m tall and over 2 m across are quite common. The plant suckers freely from the roots and can spread over large areas, though it is very easily controlled by pulling up unwanted growths. The flowers are larger than in most other species and are a medium mauve-purple with darker maroon veins on the upper petals. The leaves and stems are covered in slightly sticky glandular hairs which give off a pungent medicinal scent which some consider rather unpleasant. According to Kate Greenaway's Book, *The Language of Flowers* (1884), the oak-leaved geranium is symbolic of true friendship.

Pelargonium denticulatum (1789)   Finely cut glossy leaves, slightly rolled inwards at the edges, are sticky to the touch and pungently perfumed. The growth is slender and erect, though it tends to flop over unless supported by surrounding plants. The small flowers are a soft mauve-pink. Very similar is *filicifolium*, which has very finely cut leaves which give rise to its common name of skeleton-leaved geranium. Both varieties are intolerant of wet, cold soils and can rot off in winter unless planted in a light, free-draining soil.

Pelargonium graveolens (1774)   The rose-scented geranium loved by herbalists, cooks and potpourri makers since its introduction. It is said that in the language of flowers it indicates preference. The leaves are twice divided and cut and are of a mid-green with a sparse covering of short hairs. Each leaf tends to roll under a little at the edges. The small flowers are carried on hairy stems and are borne in

tight clusters. Petals are a uniform lilac-pink with very thin dark veins. A well-known variant is *P. graveolens* 'Lady Plymouth', which has leaves splashed and edged with cream variegations. Growth overall tends to be rather more spreading and shorter than the 1.25 m of the parent.

***Pelargonium* × 'Dr Livingstone'**   A very large-leaved version of another rose-scented geranium, *radens*. It also grows more vigorously than many others. It is a very popular plant for use as 'stuffing' in the cut-flower trade and is grown in vast quantities for this purpose overseas. Here it seems to be relegated to use in the borders of posies and nosegays. Similar too is 'Pheasant's Foot'. The flowers are insignificant lilac-mauve affairs with some darker veins. The growth can reach 1.5 m in all dimensions. Strong water-shoots which develop extremely large leaves are occasionally produced.

***Pelargonium* × 'Mabel Grey'**   Instantly wins admirers when garden visitors are invited to crush its leaves and smell their fingers. Of all the scented geraniums, 'Mable Grey' must surely have the most powerfully lemon-scented leaves of all. It seems to have a lingering quality that lasts both on the skin and in the air. The leaves are large, acidic-green, shaped like vine-leaves and rough in texture owing to the presence on the surfaces and veins of short stiff hairs. Growth is strong, often unbranched, and upright to the point of appearing stiff and a little ungainly, especially when the plants get woody and old. This is easily remedied by judicious spring pruning to encourage fresh new growth from low down on the plant. A few suckers may spring up from the roots at some distance from the plant. 'Mable Grey' has a reputation as a rather slow grower in cooler areas but will eventually reach 1.5 m or a little less. The plant originated in Kenya and is intolerant of cold, frosty weather.

***Pelargonium* × 'Dark Lady'**   A hybrid of *P. tomentosum*, with more upright growth, slightly less perfume and a dark patch around the veins at the centre of each hairy leaf. It will make a good bush to 1.5 m given good conditions. It is certainly more tolerant of dryness at the roots than its parent. The flowers are insignificant and pallid lilac. It is a fairly recent Australian hybrid but fits in comfortably with any of the older varieties.

Pelargonium tomentosum (1774)   Usually called the peppermint geranium, this has been popular with gardeners and cooks since it was introduced from the Cape of Good Hope by the plant-hunter Francis Masson. He introduced at least fifty new pelargonium species as a result of his travels in Africa, botanising for Kew Gardens at the direction of Sir Joseph Banks and King George III. An interesting aside is that Masson met some of the officers of the First Fleet while resting between expeditions in Cape Town and expressed a wish to accompany the fleet to botanise in Australia. As it happened, he stayed in the Cape and introduced many marvellous plants. *P. tomentosum* is well known for its sprawling growth clothed with large velvety vine-shaped leaves redolent of peppermint. My nose tells me that the strongest perfume issues from the undersides of the leaves. Although it is less often used in cooking these days, it gives a special lift to jellies and custards (consult Lady Jekyll, *Kitchen Essays*, for several good recipes). The flowers are almost insignificant, being very small and white. The plant may grow to about 75 cm in height, over 1 m if it can scramble over adjacent plants, and can easily spread 2 m and more, which makes it a good ground cover in temperate areas. It resents dryness.

Pelargonium* × *nervosum (1820)   Enjoys the reputation of

ABOVE
Healthy old bushes of common geraniums in a cottage garden.
TOP
Red geraniums by the windowsill—an essay in old-fashioned style.

closely resembling the lime in its perfume. It makes compact upright growth to 75 cm and has greyish-green leaves that are rounded, slightly toothed and rimmed with a hint of red, especially when grown fairly hard. The flowers are large and carried in small heads. The overall colour is lavender with some darker markings on the upper petals. The lime-scented geranium is not as widely grown as it should be, though it appears from time to time at garden shops and nurseries in batches of mixed scented-leaf geraniums bought in for sale in the herb department from specialist wholesalers. Like many other scented-leaf geraniums, *P.* × *nervosum* doesn't look much as a young plant in a 10 cm pot and often gets overlooked in favour of some gaudy-flowering thing.

***Pelargonium crispum* 'Major'**   This plant indicated an unexpected meeting, according to the old nineteenth-century language of flowers, and the plant is something of a surprise in its foliage and habit of growth. It has very small rounded leaves that appear crimped at the edges; these are sported alternately up erect, unbranched stems that can reach up to 1 m. The leaves are loosely arranged in two opposite files, which adds to the eye-catching 'flatness' of the fastigiate growth. The scent is strong and lemony and the flowers are very pale lilac-pink with two large upper petals and three narrower lower petals.

***Pelargonium crispum* 'Variegated Prince Rupert'** (1767) A variegated version of *P. crispum* 'Major' and although a little diminished in scent and vigour from its parent it is still a good doer. It makes a useful garden or pot plant and is much in demand for floral decorations. Some dealers label it with the alternative American name 'French Lace', which seems another example of the tendency to change the names of plants to suit something perceived as 'buyer preference'.

***Pelargonium crispum* 'Minor'**   All the characteristics of *P. crispum* 'Major' in a miniature form. The growth is very compact with the leaves so close-packed that very little stem is visible. Growth tends to be so thin and wiry that the bushlet becomes a little inclined to floppiness, making it splendid for trailing over the edge of a garden bed onto a pathway. It will grow to 60 cm or a little more.

***Pelargonium odoratissimum* (1724)**   Delights all who know it with its crisp apple-scented leaves of bright yellow-green. It is similar, though a little larger, in appearance to the nutmeg-scented geranium (*P. fragrans*). Those with a keen sense of smell declare it to smell strongly of Granny Smith apples; most, however, decline to offer an opinion on which side of the hill the orchard was sited! The flowers are carried on trailing stems that project well beyond the dome of foliage and are white with some small red markings. Occasional seedlings will appear spontaneously in sunny spots near mature plants. It can also be propagated from the close-joined stems which support the crown of leaves. An all-over trim is the only pruning this variety requires.

***Pelargonium fragrans* (1897)**   Signifies an expected meeting and is certainly a welcome and pleasant thing to meet in any garden. The bush is a compact mass of small ruffled grey-green round leaves on succulent stalks. The actual growing shoots are very short-jointed. Slender stalks of tiny white flowers emerge from the tight dome of foliage from the warm days of summer and into the autumn. The leaves are invariably described as nutmeg-scented, although those who pride themselves on the keenness of their proboscis sometimes pronounce aromas of pine and eucalyptus—a fair warning to the dull-nosed majority! There are a number of other closely related hybrids which have varying degrees of fruitiness, spiciness and resinosity. Look out for 'Fruit Tingles', 'Apple Cider', 'Old Spice' and 'Tutti Frutti' (I kid you not). There are also at least two variegated kinds; one with all-over splashes of creamy-white and the other with a variable margin of yellowish-green. One of the most eye-catching ways to grow them is as pot plants displayed on an old-fashioned, three-tiered semicircular wire pot stand. At Beaumont House in Adelaide an arrangement such as this was a feature during the 'Gardens in Time' exhibition held in 1987. All members of this group are best pruned by clipping the plants all over into a neat bun shape.

Pelargonium betulifolium   Very rarely seen, which is a shame as it is a fine plant for the edge of a bed, especially when it can trail over and down the rocks of a low wall. The growth is very low and spreading with small spatulate leaves which are greenish-grey, scalloped and red-rimmed at the edges and lightly scented with a vaguely medicinal perfume. The lilac-pink flowers are upstanding and rather larger than expected for such a lowly plant.

***Pelargonium grossularioides* (1789)**   Thought of as the coconut-scented geranium. It is a low-growing evergreen herbaceous plant with round scalloped leaves on long stems radiating from a central growing plant. It is ground hugging, rarely getting more than 5 cm tall but spreading in a neat circular mat for 30 cm or so. It produces minute purple-red flowers and self-seeds prolifically. The perfume is quite attractive, but the plant can be invasive among small perennials, etc. It can be grown quite happily on the edges of gravel paths and other hard, sunny environments. The only pruning needed is to cut off the dead flower stalks.

Uniques, Laras and Other Species-Derived Geraniums

Although they have perfumed foliage and are quite similar in growth and flowers to the scented-leaf geraniums, the Unique and Lara breeds of pelargonium are usually thought of as sufficiently different to be grouped apart, first and foremost because they are all hybrids, but with the important difference from the likes of 'Mable Grey', 'Both's Snowflake' and 'Dr Livingstone' that their flowers are larger and more colourful than the species and their immediate hybrids. Their treatment is exactly as for any other geranium. The Uniques are an ancient race dating back to the 1880s at least. On the other hand the Laras are very new, having been bred by the Geelong enthusiast Cliff Blackman from 1974 onwards. Most of the species-derived hybrids are productions of the nineteenth century; nearly all make fairly moderate-sized bushes.

***Pelargonium* × *blandfordianum* (1892)**   A curious plant with finely cut silver foliage supported by rambling scrambling stems that never make a really satisfactory contribution to the garden. Despite this, it is still something to treasure. It produces small loose heads of tiny flowers, each one smartly marked on the upper petals with maroon blotches and a clean white central stripe; the lower petals are plain. There are two distinct varieties, one with a base colour of white and the other with a base colour of bright rose-pink. William Robinson, writing in *Flora and Sylva* (vol. 3, p. 137), reports that old writers also call this plant 'Lady Betty Germaine' but is not forthcoming on whether this applies to the pink or the white version.

***Pelargonium* × 'Clorinda' (1907)**   Long a popular variety, so much so that other lesser varieties are sometimes sold in place of it. However, it is most distinctive and could not easily be mistaken for anything else. The leaves are large, divided into three big lobes and somewhat hairy. The large flowers are carried in small clusters and are a clear pink with some light feathery marks in purple on the upper petals. The leaves give off a resinous, piny scent when they are rubbed.

***Pelargonium* × 'Countess of Stradbroke'** (pre-1800) This could be a member of a group of hybrids called angel pelargoniums, which have the small growth and leaves that characterise *P. crispum*. It is a very old variety and was identified for me by Mr Rob Swinbourne from a plate in Sweet's *Geraniaceae* of 1820. It is rather difficult to grow from cuttings but is worth trying if a source can be located. It has small rounded dark green leaves tinted with a reddish margin, dark red stems and a very refreshing light citronella perfume. The flowers are rather like a miniature Regal pelargonium with a pair of dark rose-pink upper petals and three slightly paler pink lower petals. The stems are at first erect but they flop over as the growth elongates; 30 cm × 45 cm.

***Pelargonium* × 'Crimson Unique'** A rather straggling hairy creation that simply covers itself with a mass of bright crimson flowers from early summer until autumn. The flowers are carried on multi-branched stems and keep up a succession of blooms for several months. Individual flowers are full-petalled and rather angular in outline, and the upper petals have darker scarlet veins and a small central patch of the same colour. The hairy, bright green leaves are palmate, i.e., rather like a grape leaf. The plant seeds freely in warm sandy soils, but few suckers are developed; 60 cm × 60 cm.

***Pelargonium* × 'Endsleigh'** A hybrid which seems to carry the characteristics of *P. quercifolium* and *P. capitatum*. The leaves are covered with fine hairs, are oak-shaped and sometimes incurving and have a dark blotch in the centre of each leaf. Growth is low and prostrate and the flowers are not especially noteworthy.

***Pelargonium* × 'Lara Jester'** and ***Pelargonium* × 'Lara Starshine'** Two of a growing number of a new race of pelargonium hybrids slowly percolating from the world of the exhibitor-collector to that of the plantsman and garden maker. The breeding involves *P. radens*, which has some similarities with the rose-scented geranium (*P. graveolens*), so the foliage is sweetly scented and divided into many fine 'fingers'. The flower colours vary within the broad range of rose-pink with some darker veining and darker lavender tinges on the top petals. A bush of 'Lara Jester' in my garden threw a sport which has much larger frilled petals. It is being watched carefully to see if the variation is stable. Others in the family are 'Lara Ballerina' and 'Lara Starshine Improved'. Grown in the open garden, the plants easily reach 1 m in height and 1.5 m across. Pot-grown specimens would require a large pot to develop to their full flowering potential. Not all have well-scented foliage.

***Pelargonium* × 'Pink Pet'** Looks for all the world like a paler version of 'Scarlet Pet', a refinement that endears it to many gardeners where the brilliance of the latter repels. It may be a sport or a remake of the same cross that gave rise to 'Scarlet Pet'. Whichever, it is a very attractive plant that is being badly overshadowed by its gaudy relation.

***Pelargonium* × 'Rollison's Unique'** (*c.* 1800) Comes in a shade of glowing cerise-purple unique among geraniums. It has rangy growth that scrambles around, climbing if given some support, and clothed with hairy dark green crinkled leaves that look decidedly soft. The flowers are borne in small, fairly tight clusters and look good coming out between similarly coloured pinks, *Allium acuminatum* and as a foreground to *Salvia involucrata* 'Bethelii', *Monarda*,

lythrums and any other mauve, purple and dark red coloured perennials.

***Pelargonium* × 'Rose Bengal'** Another angel pelargonium and though slightly larger in all respects than 'Countess of Stradbroke', and a stronger grower, the similarities are obvious. The growth habit is mat-forming and trailing with erect flowering stems. The rounded leaves have a light clean smell reminiscent of citrus blossom. 'Rose Bengal' flowers heavily and produces large full-petalled flowers that are dark rose at the top and pale pink—almost white—at the bottom; 45 cm × 60 cm.

***Pelargonium* × 'Burton's Unique'** This plant came to me from Coralie Thomson of Summertown in South Australia. It is similar in its foliage to 'Scarlet Pet' and Pink Pet', but the flowers have a marked difference in that they are very full-petalled where the others are rather gappy. The colour is a strong rose-pink with dark feathering and spotting over a white central zone, and there are two conspicuous patches of lilac overlay at the centres of the top pair of petals—a very singular appearance not met in many other geraniums, though the Laras show similar patterns. The growth is sprawling, and mature plants achieve about 1 m in ground-cover and 45 cm in height.

***Pelargonium* × 'Scarlet Pet'** The most commonly grown of all old varieties of geranium. It is propagated in large numbers for use as a ground cover and 'filler' in landscaping projects. It has even been used alongside highways to cover the scars of cut-and-fill operations. Wide-spreading brown stems carry a dense cover of deeply cut and divided rich green leaves that are slightly hairy and redolent of spicy aromatic tones. The medium-sized flowers are bright scarlet-red, veined much darker on the upper pair of petals. Dimensions are 75 cm tall by 1 m and more in diameter.

***Pelargonium* × 'Scarlet Unique'** Large full-petalled flowers with very bold black-red feathering on the two uppermost petals. The flowers are carried on branching stems which produce flowers over an extended season. The bush is upright and rather woody with slightly hairy palmate foliage. Although frequently seen in the collections of exhibitors, this variety is very easy to grow and should be more widely seen as a garden plant. Growth can be up to 60 cm tall.

***Pelargonium* × 'White Unique'** Oak-shaped leaves and pure white flowers of a fair size. The upper petals have several very fine maroon veins; dark red stamens. As the flowers age they develop some pink tones, but this does not detract from the effect. The bush is spreading and a strong grower to about 75 cm tall and 1 m across. It suckers readily if the roots are damaged by digging.

Coloured-Leaf Geraniums

Coloured-leaf geraniums are separated according to the colour patterns on their leaves; thus the Bronze Zonals have yellow-green leaves with a ring of bronze around the centre of each leaf, the Gold Zonals are an all-over yellow-green marked in some varieties with a green 'butterfly' splash at the centre of each leaf, the Silver Zonals are banded with a broad margin of white variegation around the edge of each leaf, and the Silver and Gold Tricolors have a base colour of white or yellow with red, bronze, black and/or green rings and splashes at the centre.

The brilliance of the colours, their comparative ease of culture and uniform habits of growth made them attractive plants to use *en masse* for creating beds and borders of colourful plants laid out in geometrical and other designs. The plants could be grown from cuttings in cool greenhouses, with minimal heating over the winter, and be planted out in late spring ready for a stunning summer display. In this they were much easier to manage than tender semi-tropical foliage plants and the thousands of annual seedlings that were otherwise needed for such schemes. As the plants were yearlings, their growth was compact, with foliage right down to the ground and the colours strong and clear. The only grooming they needed was to have the flowers nipped off before they opened and spoiled the carefully-thought-out colour schemes of the displays. At the end of the year the plants could be dug out, cuttings made of the best pieces and the plants thrown away. They were also used as colourful pot plants, a method of growing them that is still popular with collectors and exhibitors.

In the milder climates of Australia the fancy-leaved geraniums will grow well outdoors in frost-free areas and can make quite large bushes. They are, however, inclined to be rather gaunt and leggy with very little foliage on the old stems and are best grown anew from cuttings every two years. They need (with very few exceptions) an open, sunny, airy position and produce large leaves and strong colours in response to feeding. Most people like to leave the flowers on the plants instead of pinching them off as was once the case. Like all geraniums, they suffer from white fly, rust, loopers and red spider mite. They should be controlled by whatever means you find most effective and acceptable. There are a good many old varieties still available because they have not been bettered in coloration or vigour by modern breeders. Singular in their appearance are:

Freak of Nature   Green leaves with a large white splash at the centre of each leaf. This is sometimes so large that the leaf has only a narrow rim of green to perform the functions of photosynthesis. The result of this extensive variegation is that the plant is not easy to grow or to propagate and remains in the hands of a few collectors. Sometimes new growths appear that are all green; these should be removed at once or they will rapidly outgrow the variegated parts of the plant so that it appears to revert to all green. The single flowers are single and bright vermilion.

Distinction (*c.* 1870)   Grown widely in parts of Australia for many years. A lot of gardeners would not know the plant by name, but the description will put the plant in mind for quite a few. The dark green leaves are almost perfectly round with small serrations along the edge. Each leaf has a distinctive narrow black zone running around it, rather nearer the outer edge than the centre. The dark red flowers are small, rather narrow in the petals and carried in small clusters. Over the space of several years the plant can grow as large as 1 m tall.

A Happy Thought (1877)   Often seen in gardens as a large, rather dishevelled bush. When grown as a small plant it is much more attractive than an old bush. The green leaves have a striking central splash of creamy-white. Sometimes, especially on new growth, an intermittent reddish-brown band appears where the green and white parts adjoin. The rather small flowers are a cheerful red.

Bronze Queen   At first looks rather uninteresting—a middling green with an indistinct brush-marked bronze-coloured ring in the middle of the leaf. Closer inspection reveals that the leaf is not plain green but splashed and streaked with several shades of yellowish-green extending from the centre of the leaf to the edges. The flowers are a soft dark red colour.

More conventional with the groupings described are:

Black Douglas (Bronze Zonal)   A good grower which develops large, well-coloured foliage. The base colour is bright golden-yellow and over this is a broad band of light bronze-red. The flowers are bright red. Similar, though with smaller red flowers and a narrower band of bronze-brown colouring, is 'Maréchal McMahon' of 1862. He was one of Napoleon's generals.

Crystal Palace Gem (Gold Zonal)   Forms a low spreading plant with dainty yellow-green leaves, each one marked with a butterfly splash of a slightly darker shade of green at the centre. This marking is irregular in shape but always comes from the centre. The single flowers are a very clear scarlet. Very popular in England in the 1850s.

Golden Harry Hieover (Gold Zonal)   Also a low-growing plant but is lax in growth where the former is sturdy. The almost trailing stems carry very rounded leaves with shallow scalloped edges. The background colour is a rather soft yellow colour and there is a chestnut-red zone brushed over this. The leaves appear thin and rather lacking in substance. The small flowers are vermilion. Needs more care than most of the other varieties listed here.

Madame Salleron (Silver Zonal)   The compact little edging plant that everyone grew in the fifties. It does not flower and can easily be propagated by dividing up the clusters of short stems which make up each clump. First listed in France in 1845, it has often been given the name 'Little Dandy'.

Mrs J.C. Mappin (Silver Zonal)   Mid-green leaves with a wide margin of white. Like many other silver variegated kinds of geranium, it will develop puckered and cupped leaves if grown in the open garden. Tradition has it that garden-grown plants have access to more nutrients than potted plants; thus the green centre of the leaves grows faster than the white borders, causing the distortion. This sounds plausible, but there are, no doubt, other explanations. The flowers are of the phlox-eye variety; palest pink with a small darker eye at the centre of the flower and dark stamens. A similar plant with lovely bright red double flowers is 'Caroline Schmidt'. The fairly common silver-variegated double pink is 'Chelsea Gem', which is sometimes sold as 'Lady Churchill'.

Lass O'Gowrie (Silver Tricolor)   A round-leaved geranium with creamy-white borders and a centre that is a combination of bronze, brown and red zones around a centre splashed with cream and green. It has single red flowers but is not so brilliantly variegated as 'Miss Burdett Coutts' (Silver Tricolor—1860) with which it has strong similarities. 'Lass O'Gowrie' is reputed to be the easier of the two to grow. Both are only suited to growing in pots, as they suffer badly in the open garden in summer.

Italia Unita (Silver Tricolor)   Palmate leaves with a narrow creamy-white border around a broad grey-green centre and a rather narrow brown zone. The flowers are red.

Mrs Pollock (Gold Tricolor)   First introduced in 1858. It produces flat palmate leaves which are a good clear yellow, paler towards the edges, which are boldly marked with intermittent red splashes and some lightly washed purplish-brown shadows. The flowers are bright red.

Sophia Dumaresque (Gold Tricolor)   Rounded and somewhat cupped leaves of creamy-gold splashed with irregular zones of red, bronze and brown. The colour is best in spring and autumn when the new leaves are not susceptible to bleaching by the strong sunlight. Not really vigorous enough for growing in the garden but ideal as a pot plant. The flowers are a soft red.

10   Fuchsias

The Australian Horticultural Magazine, Published in Melbourne between 1877 and 1878, is especially valued by garden historians because it gives detailed information about the plants then cultivated in southern Australia. The issue for March 1878 (Vol. II, No. 3) has a lead article on fuchsias which provides some useful information both on the history of the fuchsia in cultivation and on the state of development of the flower:

There is, perhaps, no other plant that has been more improved by the art of the horticulturalist than the Fuchsia, and the florists' varieties of the present day afford a striking contrast to the species from which they have originated. The number of varieties that have been raised from seed are innumerable, and include among them flowers which it is impossible to surpass according to their respective type. Those who remember the old varieties that were once grown and highly prized, and will mentally compare them with the flowers of the present day, must acknowledge the immense difference between the flowers of the past and the present . . . It is difficult now for florists to produce flowers superior to existing ones.

Such bold claims should be enough to arouse the interest of modern gardeners and send them scurrying back to their books and catalogues to see if any of these unsurpassable delights are still being grown. And provided a carefully written and researched catalogue is at hand, it can easily be seen that there are indeed many old varieties of fuchsia still being grown by fuchsia enthusiasts; living testimony to the claims made for them by Mr David Crichton, editor of the *Australian Horticultural Magazine* way back in 1878.

What is especially interesting in Mr Crichton's article is the number of fuchsia species that he lists as good garden subjects having strong growth and attractive flowers. The following is a summary of the species recommended by him:

Fuchsia excorticata
F. *coccinea* (syn. F. *magellanica* according to J. Shirley Hibberd in *The Floral World* [1870])
F. *lycioides* (syn. F. *rosea*)
F. *macrostemmon* (= F. *magellanica* 'Macrostemma')
F. *gracilis* (syn. F. *magellanica* 'Macrostemma')
F. *gracilis* 'Globosa' (= F. *magellanica* 'Globosa')
F. *syringaflora* (syn. F. *panniculata*)
F. *corymbiflora*
F. *corymbiflora* 'Alba'
F. *serratifolia*
F. *fulgens*
F. *arborescens*
F. *conica* (= F. *magellanica* 'Conica')

Thanks to the general interest in all sorts of old plant varieties, specialist nurseries are gathering as many of the original species and old cultivars as they can muster. All of the fuchsia species listed by Crichton could be assembled from the catalogues of two or three comprehensive fuchsia nurseries.

Somewhat later, in 1893, Mrs Margaret Browne, adopting her husband's pen-name as Mrs Rolf Boldrewood (he wrote *Robbery Under Arms*), was even more enthusiastic about fuchsias in her very successful book *The Flower Garden in*

Australia—A Book for Ladies and Amateurs Dedicated by Permission to the Countess of Jersey:

We have no plants more profitable to gardeners: being easy of propagation, and flowering in a comparatively short period. Plants that almost anyone can grow. If sheltered from frost will bloom beautifully, grow well out of doors, also in frames and greenhouses, in the form of bushes and standards. With good management they can be made to bloom six or eight months of the year, yet doing as well as they do in gardens and verandahs.

Mrs Boldrewood was introduced to the pleasures of gardening early in life and as a child had her own patch in which she grew capsicums and jonquils; as a schoolgirl she visited Mr Guilfoyle's nursery at Double Bay in company with her cousin and often carried home a small pot plant as a gift from the proprietor. It is quite likely that she would have seen there, among other newly introduced plants, fuchsias such as *Fuchsia boliviana* (1875), *F. fulgens* 'Rubra Grandiflora', *F. loxensis* (1823) and *F. cordifolia* (1841). The several variants of *F. magellanica* could also have been on display to whet the interest of the many fashionable customers of the place—*F. magellanica* 'Molinae', *F. magellanica* 'Gracilis Variegata' and *F. magellanica* 'Riccartoni', and also *F. procumbens* and *F. splendens*. These plants from the foggy valleys and hillsides of the southern Andes mountains are all pretty and perfectly adapted to most sheltered outdoor gardens. They mostly grow into large shrubs whose nectar-rich flowers are the delight of small honeyeaters. All of them are readily available.

Wild South Americans

Fuchsia arborescens   A native of Mexico occasionally found in old gardens in areas where frosts and winter cold do not damage it. It makes a substantial shrub to 4 m (puny alongside the 8 m recorded for it in its habitat). The dark green glossy leaves have dark red veins and stems, and the flowers are carried upright in large heads. The individual flowers are very small and of a rosy-mauve colour. The minute corolla is lavender.

Fuchsia boliviana (1875)   Produces spectacular hanging racemes of very long, thin, dark blood-red flowers. Many flowers are borne on one stem, so the display goes on for a month or so. The foliage is large, rich green and heavily veined. It sometimes seems almost velvety in texture. It is a native of Bolivia, Argentina and Peru. Growth is fairly upright and will reach 2 m or so. There is a similar hybrid called 'Mark' and another *F. boliviana* hybrid named 'Scarlet Ribbons' (1984), very vigorous and tall, which produces enormous scarlet long-tubed flowers.

Fuchsia corymbiflora (1877)   Has been equated with *F. boliviana* by some authorities (Ron Ewart, *Fuchsia Lexicon*, Blandford, 1987), but local sources assure me that plants raised from field-collected seed and distributed in Australia are different. To an untrained eye the flowers certainly look quite distinct from those of *F. boliviana*. Leaves are very large and covered with fine hairs. Growth is vigorous; tall (3 m plus) and upright until weighed down by the enormous racemes of heavy flowers. The individual flowers are about 8 cm long and very slender, opening to a small star of sepals and a small corolla. The overall colour is scarlet. It is a native of Peru.

Fuchsia corymbiflora 'Alba'   A highly attractive form of the above species in which the tube is almost pure white. The sepals are tinted on the inner surface with rose-pink and the corolla is scarlet. Something quite special and keenly

ABOVE
Fuchsias at home in a damp, shady corner.

TOP
My lady's eardrops—old-fashioned fuchsias of the nineteenth century.

sought by many collectors. Like its brethren, this fuchsia tends to produce many flowering shoots but not a lot of growing shoots. This means it will always be in short supply as the nursery people can never get enough cuttings to meet the demand. They also have the reputation of being rather difficult from cuttings.

***Fuchsia fulgens* 'Rubra Grandiflora'**   Produces the most outstanding display of brilliantly coloured orange-red and scarlet blooms which are extremely long and carried in large clusters. The foliage is hairy, mid-green and broad, making the bush a mound of foliage against which the pendant flowers are shown off to great advantage. Eventually this denizen of Mexico will make a shrubby upright bush of 2 m or so.

Fuchsia loxensis (1823)   Originated in Ecuador and has become a favourite shrub among collectors in mild-climate areas. It produces lush medium-sized foliage of a mid-green colour, somewhat hairy and lightly veined. The flower heads are produced at the ends of the growing tips and contain a modest number of medium-length flowers. The tube is a very bright scarlet-orange, as are the sepals, and the corolla is a darker dull red. Against the green foliage the flowers look very attractive. The bush is upright, well clothed with leaves and bushy to about 1.5 m.

***Fuchsia magellanica* 'Gracilis'** (1823)   Now called *F. magellanica* var. *macrostemma* by those in the know, but most people will recognise it by its familiar name 'Gracilis'. It features small, delicate, grey-green leaves, reddish stems and prodigious quantities of small red and purple flowers on thin, drooping stems. Growth is upright and slender, eventually reaching 3 m or more.

***Fuchsia magellanica* 'Gracilis Variegata'**   Green, cream and silver shades of variegation on the diminutive leaves and the usual red and purple flowers. Growth is not so vigorous as in the plain forms but is still quite strong; the plant will build up to a shrub of 1.5 m or so, arching and slender.

***Fuchsia magellanica* 'Gracilis Tricolor'**   Pleases many gardeners with its variegated plummy foliage with white margins and red rims, which combines well with the familiar red and purple flowers. Strong growth to 2 m and more.

***Fuchsia magellanica* 'Molinae'**   The pale-pink flowered form of this family of South Americans. The bush grows very tall, often over 3 m, and becomes a woody shrub with peeling tan bark. The brittle branches are liable to break in windy situations, especially when weighed down with wet leaves. Sometimes offered for sale as *F. magellanica* 'Alba'.

***Fuchsia magellanica* 'Riccartoni'** (1830)   The most commonly seen variety of this group, with strong growth to 3 m or more and sometimes found naturalised in damp gullies and along watercourses in Victoria, South Australia and New South Wales. Leaves greyish-green, larger than the type, and masses of tiny red and purple flowers. It is thought to be a hybrid.

Fuchsia splendens (1841)   Seems to be regarded as identical with *F. cordifolia*. This plant from Mexico and Costa Rica has rather sprawling and untidy growth, although it is reported as growing to 2.5 m—possibly it would, given the support of other plants for its scrambling stems. The foliage is green, reddish at the edges and on the stems. The rounded leaves are slightly hairy and very heavily veined. The startling flowers are made up of a flattened scarlet tube, green sepals and a short yellow-green corolla. It has something of a firecracker in its coloration and appearance.

Varieties

The species fuchsias from Central and South America may well have given Mrs Boldrewood and David Crichton a great deal of pleasure with their colourful flowers and easy growth, but it was the hybrids which really took hold of their enthusiasm and turned their admiration into a degree of excitement at the latest productions of the hybridists of France, Germany, England and America. Since the introduction of the first few species by the captains of clippers trading in the lucrative guano markets, the fuchsia had attracted the attentions of plant breeders who were quick to achieve outstanding improvements in flower size and colour. Varieties such as 'Phenomenal' are as large and prolific as the very newest varieties. Today many old varieties still compete successfully with the very latest creations from Holland and California. Among them are:

Bon Accord (1861)   A French variety which some time during its history has picked up the much less appealing name of 'Erecta Novelty'. Could some careless nuseryman have lost the label and thought up this shocker of a synonym? Indeed it does carry its flowers in an upright position, something of a novelty among the pendulous fuchsia tribe, and its flowers are rather unusually coloured too, but 'Erecta Novelty'? Too dull for words. The bush is very compact and the branches are upright as well as the flowers. The tube and sepals (back petals) are waxen ivory-white. The corolla is a delicate shade of pale mauve-pink. Hardy and easy to grow.

Canary Bird (1873)   The name alludes to the yellowy-green colour of the foliage, not to the flowers. Given bright sunlight, though not direct sunshine, the leaves of this fuchsia develop a uniform yellow tint all over. The bush is low and spreading, but not floppy, and looks especially good trained over a low wall or spreading across the edges of a pathway. The flowers provide a rather startling contrast to the foliage; the tube and sepals are deep scarlet and the corolla is dark purple.

Colossus (1841)   An early variety prolific with large flowers, and a hearty constitution that endears it to the many who must garden in hot places where many modern highly bred fuchsias fail to thrive. The short tube and sepals are red and the corolla is a bright purple with pale red veins.

Countess of Aberdeen (1888)   This lady-like plant needs a lightly shaded spot to do well but is otherwise a good old-timer; dense shrubby low growth of mid-green that sets off nicely the small pale flowers. The overall colour is pale pearly pink, almost white; the reflexed sepals turn back just a little and show the white corolla.

Countess of Hopetoun (1888)   Another aristocratic lady but with the distinction of being a local. She was first noticed in the Melbourne Botanical Gardens and is a sport of 'Phenomenal'. Her lady namesake was the wife of a Governor of Victoria. Very appealing crimson flowers with a white corolla.

Dominiana (1852)   This is one of the long tubular fuchsias that sometimes see service outdoors jammed into an odd corner against a fence or between standard roses. They are known in the trade as Triphylla hybrids and usually rate a separate section in a catalogue or sales area. This particular cultivar is a rich red all over, with a very long tube and short, stumpy sepals. The dark flowers glow against the dark, reddish foliage. Dense, upright growth to about 1.5 m.

Earl of Beaconsfield (1878)   Long drop earrings are called to mind by the form of this old British variety which has always been popular for its strong healthy growth and pleasing colour combination of salmon-pink and vermilion. The outer parts of the flower are a delicate pink and the inner skirt is a bright luminous red. The growth is upright but slightly spreading; it makes a very useful shrub for bush-houses and shady areas.

Eclat (1874)   A tall upright bush that is popular for its profusion of small red and white flowers. 'Eclat' is very hardy and will grow to 2 m if well cared for with ample food and water. Branching and foliage are light and airy and the bush is often bent over with the weight of flowers.

Heinrich Henkel (1897)   A Triphylla type with long pendulous flowers of pale crimson and a brighter-coloured corolla. The foliage is green, heavily tinged with red, and sometimes showing purplish shades if the light is bright, especially so on the undersides of the leaves. Expert opinion tells us this should be given the full title of Andenken an Heinrich Henkel, though most dealers continue to use the shortened version.

Lord Lonsdale   A fine upstanding fuchsia with large and beautiful flowers of pale pink with a striking orange-red centre. Quite a dandy. Growth is shrubby and slightly spreading, making a compact and tidy bush.

Mary (1894)   Another Triphylla type; very long tube-like flowers of an intense crimson colour throughout. The foliage is a rich dark green with reddish-purple tints on the undersides and in the veins.

Meteor (1892)   The big thing about this plant is the unusual bright reddish-copper colour of the new foliage; as it hardens off, the mature foliage turns to a quieter bronze-red—quite an eyecatcher amid the usual greens of most fuchsias. The spreading, almost horizontal growth makes it ideal for trailing over rock edgings in bush-houses, or for growing in a hanging basket, but a typical nineteenth-century way of growing it would be to plant alternately with the yellow-leaved 'Canary Bird' in a shrubby version of bedding-out. Their flowers are much the same: scarlet on the outside with a purple corolla. It is sometimes sold as 'Autumnale', but my information is that 'Meteor' was its first name.

Mrs Marshall   Another grand old performer which will grow where many modern cousins wouldn't have the heart. Creamy-white tube and sepals set off a flaring rosy-cerise skirt. Another champion for the bush house or the shady garden of an inner-city terrace house.

Muriel (1877)   At first glance the flower hardly rates a second look, for it is the old familiar combination of scarlet and purple—but stand back and look at the growth. This is a fuchsia that you can train over archways and up verandah poles, or along the roof of a bush-house. It has long, pliable growth that can be tied and trained to perform in a variety of ways. Prolific flowering and hardy. The aged barky branches will continue to make good flowering growth for many years.

Phenomenal (1869)   The description of E. & W. Hackett's catalogue of 1898 captures the fine qualities of this still popular plant: '*Phenomenal*, short tube and reflexed petals of rich crimson, enormous corolla, very double, of a beautiful azure violet flaked red. The largest double Fuchsia.'

Sunray (1872)   The Victorian fascination for any plant with variegated foliage found its mark with this fuchsia which, when given good light, will produce an attractive display of light green foliage heavily edged with creamy-yellow and with a pink tinge right on the rim of each leaf. Growth is

low and spreading and the flowers are typically fuchsine cerise and rosy lavender.

Caring for Fuchsias

The wild fuchsias described earlier need very little in the way of attention to keep them happy and performing well. A situation where the soil can be kept damp, though the drainage must be good, some light shade and shelter from blistering winds suits them best. Fertiliser applied in the form of a mulch of stable litter will ensure a steady show of flowers and vigorous growth, and an occasional squirt over the foliage with a hose will be about all that is needed. As the plants mature, any dead twiggy growth will need to be removed so that the strong basal watershoots that appear will be able to grow unchecked by the thatch of dead sticks.

Some of the varieties which tend to sprawl can be helped to make a better bush if the young growths are supported by careful staking. Alternatively these varieties could be planted among other upright-growing shrubs which would offer them a degree of support. Such attentions need not be given if the natural habit of the plants is followed and they are interplanted with other low things such as the hardy ferns *Polypodium australe* 'Cambricum' (the Welsh fern), *Doodia aspera*, *Blechnum penna-marina*, *Pellaea rotundifolia* and *P. falcata*. Grown this way, the scraggy stems can wander where they will and push up growing tips where they can, flower and be admired without the detraction of twisted, gaunt stems. *Fuchsia splendens* and *F. procumbens* are very attractive when grown this way. The ferns and the fuchsias have the same requirements for water and light and form an almost natural association. The dead fronds of fern need to be cut to the ground every so often and at this time the stable-litter mulch can be applied; the new growths will push through the mulch with ease.

The more complex hybrids need a little greater care and attention, as they do not have the same easy-growing habits as the fuchsia species. In particular they need fairly frequent propagation to produce good flowering specimens and to avoid the tendency of old plants to suddenly die off. Many of the twiggy, large-flowered varieties, such as those most often grown in hanging baskets, produce very brittle growth that snaps under the least stress; a puff of wind, a sudden shower of rain or even the weight of flowers is enough to cause damage. This is not a disadvantage if there is ample time to make daily checks on the plants, but a busy working person may not be in the garden much from one weekend to the next. In my selection of old hybrids I have tried to avoid such risky varieties; even so, it is a good idea to take some cuttings from time to time just to be sure. The extra plants always make welcome gifts for other gardeners, or for trading tables, if they are not needed.

STANDARD TRAINING

Much has been said of the manner of growing old fuchsias as large flowering shrubs that are ideally suited to shady areas and bush-houses. Mention has been made of the nineteenth-century fashion of interplanting the trailing coloured-leaf forms 'Canary Bird', 'Meteor' and 'Sunray' with other low-growing foliage plants in a bedding-out scheme, but I have made no mention of using fuchsias as standard bushes to add height and accent to the same horticultural carpeting. The production of standards is not beyond the skills of most gardeners, but it is time-consuming. Several years can pass between starting with a rooted cutting and producing a final product worth looking at. Standard fuchsias always need a solid stake to support their weak stems, and this must be in place from the start. Mucking around with light bamboo sticks and progressing through ever stouter grades is asking for trouble, in particular the disaster of a broken main stem while one stake is being removed and another inserted and the plant retied. All that anxiety can be avoided by starting out with a good stout stake. Tomato stakes are not necessary —in fact they are too heavy and ugly—but a small hardwood stake about 1.5 cm × 1.5 cm should be adequate.

Most beginners will want to start by growing a standard plant in the ground, as it is so much easier to stand the stake securely in the soil than it is in a pot. Start with a small plant chosen for its good strong-growing lead shoot. Once planted, all the side shoots should be removed and the plant encouraged to establish and grow by regular feeding with a weak liquid fertiliser and by being well watered. As the plant grows, all the side shoots that appear should be rubbed out until the plant has reached the desired height. Don't be over-ambitious in this; no fuchsia that naturally grows to 75 cm can be made to turn into a 2.5 m giant by training it as a standard.

For standards of 1 m or so, fairly low-growing varieties should be chosen, while taller specimens can be obtained by starting out with varieties that are naturally strong, vigorous growers. 'Eclat' can be relied on to grow to 2 m and more as a standard, but 'Countess of Aberdeen' will make only 1 m or so. As the plant grows, its single sappy stem will need to be tied to the stake. The best way to do this is to use plastic-coated wire twisties, making a loose loop around the stem with the tie and then making another knot around the stake. Once the desired height has been reached, the plant

should be permitted to make four or five pairs of side-shoots and the top should be pinched out. Subsequent growths should have their growing tips pinched out until the required shape and size have been attained. Then the standard can be left to flower in glory! Follow-on care should include careful watering and feeding and attention to the state of the ties which secure the plant to its stake.

As autumn draws to an end, a fuchsia will slow its growth and begin to lose its leaves until winter dormancy sees growth halt altogether. Pruning should be delayed until all danger of frost is past; in fact it can be left until there are signs of tiny new green growths on the stems. The plant can be pruned back hard to a framework of old wood and should break into strong new growth for quite a few years provided a good feeding and watering program is followed. Eventually the growth and flowers will begin to deteriorate and the plant will not be attractive to look at; this is the time to start again with a new plant.

Fuchsias get very few diseases, especially when they are grown in gardens of mixed flowers, but they do suffer from aphid infestations and red spider mite attacks and from the depredations of looper caterpillars. These can be controlled by regular checking, hosing water over the foliage and applying your choice of control agents, chemical or herbal, according to your preference.

For as full a listing as is possible of old fuchsia varieties, readers should consult *The Checklist of Species, Hybrids and Cultivars of the Genus Fuchsia*, edited by Leo Boullemier for the British Fuchsia Society (Blandford Press).

A primrose from England. This hand-coloured newspaper illustration from the Australasian Observer *(c. 1856) was copied from an original painting by E.J.W. Hopley. The sentimental theme of plants from 'Home' was taken from a* real event: the arrival of the trial shipment of plants in Wardian cases. The primrose was in full bloom when the case was opened, and such was the public excitement that it was necessary to put a guard on the plant.

11   Jonquils and Tazettas

When the first rains of autumn sweep over the land, accompanied by the squalls and thunderstorms of March and April, even the most uninterested home-owner is stirred by the smell of damp soil and the sense of freshness on the air and heads instinctively for the outdoors and a spot of gardening. Easter weekend seems to be the local turning point in the change of seasons; garden shops and nurseries all mark the long weekend as the time when business picks up after the doldrums of late summer. Seedlings, shrubs and bulbs appear, and a few days of feverish activity produces gardens from weedy lots during an annual tidy-up. Gardening taken care of for the year (or at least until the football season is done) its active pursuit is left to those dedicated to the craft. For those of us who do enjoy gardening year round, those early rains set in motion the cycle of the year— summer-affected shrubs and trees lift up their tatty leaves, seeds begin to germinate and bulbs begin to grow. Within a few days of the first rains the tiny Zephyranthes *and* Habranthus *open their flowers; not long after, the first leaves appear from the bulbs of the bunch-flowered narcissus, commonly known as the jonquil.*

Even in places where gardening has been forgotten for decades the green spears of jonquil leaves return following the autumn rains, marking the spots where gardens once were made and then forgotten. Even in the dry and dusty interior, in places such as Wilpena Pound and the Hay Plains, jonquils can be found growing near ruined shepherds' huts and in long-deserted farmyard gardens. They are just there, and always have been, uncared-for and lowly, despised and common—altogether a plant to avoid in a fashionable garden.

How often jonquils are cried down and ignored. But what pleasures are gardeners who eschew these members of the narcissus family denying themselves? Let me tell you.

Jonquils are an ancient flower that have long been used in religious ceremonies in the Middle East and the East. They were known to the ancient Egyptians, to the Romans, Greeks, Persians, Moguls, Moors and Chinese. Even in the short history of Australia they seem to have been always with us. It is a sad comment on our time that the jonquil is now so out of favour, for it is such an obliging plant, hardy, adaptable, prolific, graceful and beautifully scented. The Prophet Mohammed appreciated its unique qualities; he wrote of it: 'Let him who hath two loaves sell one, and buy flower of narcissus: for bread is but food for the body, whereas narcissus is food for the soul.'

Surely it must be the pure far-carrying perfume which is the soul-food contained in the jonquil; the flowers are sweet, modest and charming, but the perfume is heavenly. There are those who decry the perfume as overpowering and condemn the flowers as cemetery-dwellers, harbingers of death and generally morbid things. This attitude seems rather shallow in light of the appreciation the flower has been accorded across the ages.

For me the jonquils are something special. Their first signs of growth in the dog-days of late March never fail to cheer as we clean up the tat of crisp brown leaves and shrivelled twigs left by yet another hot, dry summer. Their flowering season begins with the first days of winter and carries through until the daffodils march in with the spring. They fit in odd corners under tall shrubs and on dry sun-scorched banks, places where not much else would grow, and come again and again to start the gardener's year. They see out the tiny blooms of *Cyclamen hederifolium* and *Colchicum speciosum* 'Album'; they are still going when the hellebores expand their broad bells of white, green and dusky purple in midwinter, and they see in the first daffodils, such as 'Peeping Tom', 'Cyclades' and 'Beryl'. No winter garden in Australia is complete without them.

As a group, the jonquils have become rather confused in the minds of many gardeners. Generally the name applies to any bunch-flowered narcissus; this is certainly so in Australia, but if some thought is given to the various plants that are blessed with the name *jonquil* it becomes fairly apparent that there are several groups whose distinct features indicate they could be separate branches of the narcissus family.

Rush-Leaved Narcissus

One group that is fairly easily recognised contains the rush-leaved narcissus. These have dark green leaves, round in cross-section, small heads of clear yellow flowers that are usually dainty and often starry. The corollas (petals) and the corona (cup) are uniform in colour, and the corona is short. The perfume is exceptionally strong and very sweet. This group originates in the damp high mountain meadows of southern France, Spain and Portugal, and the Atlas Mountains of Tunisia and Morocco. As a rule the bulbs are small, very round and have a shiny rich red-brown coat. Plants in the group do not relish hot, dry conditions and will sulk if planted in places where they do not get some water during summer.

Of the rush-leaved jonquils, we can still grow the following kinds:

Narcissus jonquilla Probably the most widespread of all the diminutive forms of narcissus. Although quite a strong grower given good conditions and ample water, its flowers are always small. Characteristically the petals are broad and bluntly pointed, and the cup is very small and somewhat incurving. Overall height at flowering is about 30 cm. Compared with *Narcissus cyclamineus* and *N. triandrus*, this variety is fairly common; even so it is not usually found growing wild as are many others of the jonquil group. Recently *N. jonquilla* 'Henrequesii' has been available from one specialist in small bulbs. It is regarded as an exceptionally good form of the species.

Narcissus × odorus Most often sold as *N. odorus*

'Rugulosus' or *N. odorus* 'Campernelli' or some combination of these. Great is the confusion of names applied to the same plant. Nurserymen, being the conservative people they are, refuse to sort things out so that the same name is applied to the same plants, and the gardener must tread warily when stepping down the jonquil path. As a guide, look for stocks with names including *odorus*, *rugulosus* and 'Campernelli'— though with some of the spellings adopted in the trade, even these guides will be found inadequate!

Whatever the name and whatever the spelling the plant is readily identified by vigorous tubular foliage of deep green. The flowering stalks are about 45 cm tall and usually carry 5 to 8 flowers. Young bulbs or those that are overcrowded may produce single flowers. The flowers are large, about 3 cm across, with broad, pointed and somewhat twisted petals and a cup that is lobed and flaring at the rim. The colour is a uniform soft yellow. It is a little less particular about summer dampness than *N. jonquilla*.

Narcissus × odorus 'Plenus' A double form of the above which attains much the same size as the plain variety and is just as easy to grow. The flowers are fully double with alternate row upon row of petals and cups packed inside each other. So great is the number of petals that the flowers sometimes split down one side, in the fashion of the old dianthus 'Mrs Sinkins'. The flowers are much heavier than the single variety and are prone to having their supporting stems snapped off by winds or the flowers weighed down to the ground by rain and splashed mud. Snails seem to find them delectable too! Each stem bears 4 or 5 flowers. The buds are greenish on the outside and take some time to open fully. The developing buds swell to become round and fat before they finally pop open. This variety increases more slowly than the single form; so if bulbs of the two are mixed to achieve a cottagey effect, the singles will gradually overtake the doubles and it will appear that the doubles have 'gone back' to the plain kind. The remedy is simple: keep the different sorts apart.

LATTER-DAY JONQUILS

There are also fairly recent jonquil hybrids with larger flowers and flat foliage, such as 'Golden Perfection', 'Juane A'Merville' and 'Sweetness', which could pass for inclusion as members of this group, though their flowers and growth are much larger, reflecting their complex parentage with other branches of the narcissus family.

Several miniature hybrids are also getting about— 'Hawera', 'Sundial', 'April Tears', 'Xit', 'Tête-à-Tête'. These are not really suited to growing in the open garden as they are very small and easily lost among more vigorous plants. They can be grown happily in a well-tended garden with other small treasures—'Alpine garden' is the term that could be applied to such a place, but that conjures up visions of ugly rockwork, moss-rocks, cement-rendered streams, gurgling cascades, and other such monstrosities. A plain flat bed with some shelter from nearby tall trees and some small shrubs can be an attractive setting for masses of species: cyclamen, dwarf bulbs of all kinds, small campanulas, alpine phlox, small thymes and even small ferns. That is more the kind of garden needed to set off these tiny jonquils. They seem rather inclined to set single flowers. 'Hawera' is the only one which, in my experience, regularly produces two flowers per stem.

All-White Tazettas

Another group of jonquils are those with all-white flowers. Technically speaking, these are botanically separate from the rush-leaved jonquils discussed previously. They form part of a very large and widely scattered group called tazettas, a name by which they are commonly known in Europe, America and England. The name is almost universally accepted in the bulb trade, though in out-of-the way corners of the Dandenongs they are still called jonquils by growers. The white-flowered tazettas are pure white in the cup and the petals. There are no off-white shades or soft lemon tints, just pure crystalline white.

***Narcissus papyraceus* (The Paper White)**   This is reputed to be the most widely grown of all narcissi. It is grown in the millions for the cut flower trade in Europe and for forcing indoors in cold climates. It has naturalised itself in many parts of south-eastern Australia, in California, South Africa, and in the Gulf states of the United States of America. It is thought to have originated around the western end of the Mediterranean, though it is so widespread that it is impossible to localise it to any particular area. The silver-green foliage emerges with the first rains of autumn, and the starry white flowers, carried 10 to 12 per stem, appear in early winter. The texture of the flowers is rather thin and papery, but this does not seem to be much affected by bad weather; the flowers will last many days despite rain and wind. The perfume is strong but not overpoweringly sweet.

Narcissus panizzianus   Sometimes offered by bulb dealers, but there seem to be few easily recognisable differences between this and the former variety. Authorities generally state that it is somewhat smaller than *N. papyraceus* but also very variable, so that distinguishing the two is difficult to the point where some say it is simply the same plant showing the normal degree of variation that is found in most wild plants.

Narcissus niveus   Similar to *N. papyraceus* but immediately recognisable, having more slender foliage and much smaller, more pointed flowers. The pollen is bright golden-orange and quite striking—a small difference but an important one in identifying the species. The small bulbs are very round and fat, with almost no neck, and the outer tunic is a very dark, highly glossy mahogany-brown. Not everyone could get excited about what the underground parts of a bulb look like, but these are, in their own way, quite attractive. This is a good doer; even though it is not a big grower, it can hold its own in any garden bed. It is not sufficiently strong to do well naturalised in rough grass.

Narcissus pachybolbus   From Algeria, this is something of a curiosity, for its main attractions are said to be found in its extremely large bulbs! The smallish flowers are white with rounded petals and small incurved cups. They are scarcely different from those of *N. papyraceus*; however, the bulbs are something else. They are large for a narcissus, bigger even than most large-flowered daffodils, but would anyone dig them up just to look at them? Stranger things have been done by gardeners, no doubt. Nevertheless, buying bulbs simply to enjoy their size does seem a trifle bizarre. Like *N. niveus*, the bulbs are dark brown and aglow with a rich sheen. Perhaps this tazetta is better regarded as a botanical identity than as an essential garden plant.

Bicoloured Tazettas

The largest and most varied group of tazettas comprises those tazettas which have bicoloured flowers; combinations of white, cream, yellow, gold, orange and red. Many are complex hybrids, some natural but most manmade, and all of them exceptionally hardy, prolific and colourful. The earliest varieties are rather mixed up. In the 1800s seventy-five named varieties were listed. Although their names survive to confound us, almost all of them disappeared during World War I when the Dutch bulb industry was devastated, many of the bulb stocks being totally destroyed by lack of care and several harsh winters. Descriptions of many of these varieties are not sufficiently detailed to be helpful in identifying the unknown old varieties which are sometimes found. Even at the time they were being introduced, the close similarity between many varieties was commented upon by gardening writers. Read what David Crichton had to say in *the Australian Horticultural Magazine and Garden Guide* in July 1877: 'This section is very showy, and includes flowers with white, orange, yellow, lemon, and cream coloured petals and cups. Numerous varieties are to be found in nursery catalogues but many differ only in a slight degree.'

Narcissus tazetta   First among the tazettas would be this one—the Chinese Joss Flower, or Chinese Sacred Lily. These are the flowering bulbs frequently seen on Chinese scroll-paintings. The bulbs are grown in small pots, forced into flower early and used as traditional New Year flowers. The bulbs are very vigorous and multiply rapidly. The bunch-flowered flower stems carry as many as twenty blooms per stalk; the flowers are broad-petalled and white with a pale yellow cup. The perfume is sweetly scented and typical of all tazettas. This bulb is frequently found naturalised in the old goldmining areas and in many other long-settled places.

***Narcissus aureus* 'Soleil d'Or'**   Probably the most recognisable of all tazettas, but it is not quite so common as the Chinese Joss. Most are familiar with its bright golden-yellow petals and bold orange cup. The flowers are carried about ten per stem, and a clump of bulbs will produce a strong spotlight of colour in any dull wintry garden. It is among the hardiest of the group and is usually found in association with the Joss in deserted gardens, churchyards and old gardens. It is widely grown as a cut flower around the world.

Narcissus tazetta* ssp. *lacticolor   The third of the common tazettas most often found in gardens and naturalised in the countryside. It is easily identified by its large heads of starry flowers. The pointed petals are a rather grubby coloured white and the small cup is lemon yellow. This variety is inclined to grow very tall and the flower stems tend to flop in wet weather. It is a useful plant in areas where conditions for plants are hard: under hedges, along laneways, among large shrubs and small trees, in rooty ground and orchards; it will thrive where other plants perish. While not among the front ranks of desirable flowers, this plant should be valued for its willingness and adaptability.

That very popular florist's flower, the tazetta that looks like a tiny waterlily or formal camellia, is a fairly recent sport of *N. tazetta* which originated in New Zealand. It is called 'Erlicheer'. It has good strong stems and will hold up well against rain and wind. The bulbs are vigorous and healthy. It will grow almost anywhere but does best where water can be applied until the foliage ripens and dies in early November. Much superior to the commonly found 'Double Roman' for planting in a flower garden.

Just where 'Double Roman' fits into the scheme of things in the narcissus family is hard to determine. It appears to be a mutation of *N. tazetta* ssp. *lacticolor*; it has similar pointed petals with the same muddy colour, and the brighter-coloured cup segments which are layered between the

ABOVE
'Tête-à-tête', *a modern jonquil with all the appeal of the* forms of yesteryear.

ABOVE LEFT
When the jonquils bloom, can spring be far off?

LEFT
Whether grown in a potager *or in the flower garden, garlic produces striking flowers.*

TOP RIGHT
Galanthus x 'Elwesii' *is one of the easiest snowdrops to grow.*

ABOVE RIGHT
Crocus speciosus *is hardy, but watch for birds scratching up the sweet bulbs.*

RIGHT
Crocus chrysanthus *brightens a dull winter's day.*

FAR RIGHT
Colchicum autumnale '*Album*' *is reliable and prolific.*

FAR RIGHT TOP
Cyclamen repandum *in late winter.*

doubled petals are the same colour as the cups of *N. t. lacticolor*. Bunches are offered for sale in florists' and on roadside stalls in early winter and find a ready market. In the garden the plant is notorious for flopping the flowers face-down in the mud at the least hint of rain. It does not stand wind well, as the stems are too thin and pliable to hold up the large heads of heavy double flowers. The scent is good, but there are better double tazettas for garden display.

Narcissus italicus A starry-flowered tazetta with reflexing narrow white petals and a small incurving bright orange-yellow cup. It has short grey-green foliage and is not as tall or as vigorous as the other tazettas described. It is a perky little flower of a size that suits it well for growing with other small plants. It is quite hardy and will even thrive among the roots of Japanese cherries. There is some resemblance to the frequently sold but rarely flowered *Narcissus canaliculatus*, but it is altogether a much more satisfactory plant. At full stretch it is about 30 cm tall.

Survivors from the Past

In the middle years of the nineteenth century, Dutch bulb breeders were busy trying to improve the tazettas as well as working with their better-known products, tulips and hyacinths. During this time many new varieties were introduced, but not all that many have survived the intervening years. The reasons are not too hard to find; the tazettas are not winter-hardy in the areas where the Dutch bulb merchants found their main markets—England, northern Europe and the eastern shores of the United States of America. In these climates the bulbs were treated as pot plants and kept in cool greenhouses where frosts and snow could not kill the cold-tender bulbs. Stocks of many varieties were lost through enforced neglect and destruction of the growing fields during World War I. In a few places removed from the war, where the climate was warmer, some of the old varieties survived. It is from these sources that our present supplies of tazettas have been grown. Varieties such as 'Medusa', 'Geranium', 'Xerxes', 'Grand Monarch', 'Cragford', 'Bazelman Minor' and 'Trawalla' are among those that have survived in the sunny climates of California, the Gulf Coast of the southern United States, Australia, New Zealand, the Cape Province of South Africa and the Scilly Isles in the English Channel.

'Medusa' produces very starry flowers with white petals and an intense burnt-orange cup. It is not very often seen, mainly because all the known stocks in Australia have come from one garden near Beaufort in western Victoria. Several commercial growers have small numbers of bulbs so it is worth asking for, even if the name does not appear in catalogues and lists. Growth is slender and tall; even so, the flower stems seem sufficiently strong to hold up the flowers despite wintry storms.

The rest—'Geranium', 'Xerxes', 'Grand Monarch', 'Cragford', 'Bazelman Minor' and 'Trawalla'—are all cast in the same mould, having broad petals almost circular in outline and very short open cups. 'Geranium' is one of the best; it has white petals and a glowing orange-apricot coloured cup. The petals are usually slightly crumpled like a poppy flower, an effect which is most appealing in a slightly less than perfect old-fashioned kind of way. This variety has perfectly cyclone-proof stems. Some unkind critics think them clumsy, but who cares? The flowers are gay and look marvellous against the fresh new green of grass in spring. 'Xerxes' has only two or three flowers per stem, but they are very large for a tazetta, a clear indication of the *N. poeticus*

blood in the breeding lines. The flowers are crumpled like those of 'Geranium' and have soft buff yellow petals and a red cup. In brilliant sunlight the cup can scorch, though the protection of a few leafing branches will fix that problem. When the flowers have finished and the tree's leaves are fully developed, the foliage will get enough light to build up a good flowering bulb for the following season so long as it is remembered that bulbs under trees need good fertilising to keep going amid the far-reaching mass of tree roots. Likewise, extra water should be applied in early summer to keep the bulbs growing as long as possible. 'Grand Monarch' seems to be a superior version of *N. tazetta*, and though it is a prolific bloomer it seems rather dull alongside its brighter-coloured cousins and lacks the wild appeal of its natural forebears. Clean white petals and a pure yellow cup on strong stems; good increase from very large bulbs but lacking distinction or charm. 'Polly's Pearl' is similar with white petals and a pale primrose cup, but cannot compete alongside 'Silver Chimes' (see below).

A good companion for 'Xerxes' and 'Geranium' is 'Cragford'. The three planted near each other, separated by grassy paths and other spring bulbs, seem to come closest in a home garden to the fabled world of Keukenhof, the wonderful bulb display garden in Holland. Tulips and hyacinths can make that picture an even closer copy of the original, but these are by no means necessary or desirable unless you can get some of the wild forms and species which would make the picture more like the famous Nut Walk planted by Sir Harold Nicolson at Sissinghurst Castle— something to be even more ardently desired than the whizzbang show in the Netherlands. 'Cragford' has white petals and an orange cup that pales to cream towards the centre of the flower. If it, and the others, can be set amid drifts of *Muscari armeniacum*, *M. neglectum*, *M. tubergenianum*, the forms and hybrids of *Tulipa greigii*, *T. kaufmanniana*, *T. fosteriana*, and spring-flowering crocus, the dream is well on the way to becoming a reality.

Two very old varieties are 'Bazelman Minor' and 'Trawalla'. They are both further variations on the white and yellow theme but have the distinction of age and, in the case of 'Trawalla', local interest; 'Trawalla' came from the property of the same name near Ballarat. Years ago bulbs were received from the gardens there by a keen collector of daffodils and narcissi. No known names were attached to the large white and yellow tazetta so it was simply labelled 'Trawalla' and the name has stuck. In cases where there are many similar varieties, this sort of locality name can be the best way of giving an identity to a plant antique. At least this avoids the frustrations of having innumerable slightly different plants attached to one plant name, as has been the case with some old roses and dianthuses.

At the lowest part of our garden grows an enormous pear tree; its fruit is small, hard and unpalatable, but in spring it is covered for a week or so with a mantle of pure snow-white flowers. To stand under it and hear the drone of bees working the flowers is a real pleasure; a sunny lazy time for snatching a few moments of daydreaming before returning to the more humdrum work of pulling out weed seedlings. Underneath the tree and flowering at the same time is the last daffodil of the season. It is a lover of damp and cool places and carries two very broad-petalled white flowers with a small pale yellow cup. The petals are slightly twisted but that just adds to the charm of the flowers. They are sweetly scented with hints of ripe fruits rather than the cloying sweetness of the most common tazettas. The clump has been there for ages but has not lost any of its capacity to flower strongly and seems to have found just the right spot to live. The bulb is sometimes known as 'Twin Sisters' but even by this common name it is neither common nor widely grown. Botanically it is known as *Narcissus × biflorus*, a natural hybrid that has been found growing in the wild where *tazetta* and *poeticus* (Poet's Daffodil or Pheasant's Eye Daffodil) varieties grow side by side. These are always among the last to begin blooming, which explains why *N. × biflorus* flowers so late. Although not a top-flight performer, this daffodil will grow and flower well under established trees, extends the season and provides sweet flowers for early summer posies.

Modern Varieties

There have been some modern tazettas bred too, though the pace of introduction seems to have slowed considerably since the ninety-eight varieties purchased by the Lord Proprietor of the Scilly Isles when he established the cut flower trade there in the 1870s. In appearance they are not significantly different from their surviving ancestors though each one has its own distinctiveness and all are worthy of a place in any spring flower garden.

Of all the newer tazettas, 'Silver Chimes' is most likely the one to become widely grown, for it is exceptionally robust and an excellent increaser. The flowers are frequently carried more than twelve to the stem and are very long lasting. They are thick textured and almost pure white but for the cups which are barely tinted with cream. At a short distance the slight colour variation between the petals and cup is not visible, giving a garden effect of clean white colour against dark green leaves. The scent of the flowers is good but does not carry on the air as the more strongly scented common types do. It is reputed to be infected with some sort of virus. This seems to be confirmed by the marked striping of the leaves, but it has not affected the vigour of the plant at all. There are those who believe such apparently diseased plants should be kept isolated from others of the same family to prevent cross-infection. Though no such contamination has been observed in this case, it would seem a wise precaution nonetheless. Although the variety has been available commercially for more than twenty years, the bulbs are still moderately expensive. This is probably because a lot of growers prefer to leave the bulbs in the ground and make their profits, year after year, from the cut flowers rather than dig and sell the bulbs. Even so, a few bulbs purchased one autumn will rapidly multiply into a pleasing clump. The rate can be increased by digging up the bulbs each year, taking off the small side bulbs ('chips') and replanting them in a well prepared and fertilised spot.

Double Tazettas

Double tazettas, like most other double flowers, have their enthusiasts and their detractors. Three modern double varieties have received their share of attention and criticism: 'Cheerfulness', 'Yellow Cheerfulness' and 'White Marvel'.

'Cheerfulness' and 'Yellow Cheerfulness' are two look-alikes; one variety being a neat combination of cream and soft yellow, and the other two slightly darker shades of primrose-yellow. The flowers are double, but not bursting with petals, and are globular in shape. Each stem can carry up to eight flowers in good soil; in hard conditions, or where no fertiliser has been used for many years, the number of flowers is much reduced. The white form seems less vigorous than the yellow, and both kinds need good soil to do well. They are not candidates for the dry, dusty corners of your shrubberies or for the hurly-burly of life in the root-filled ground under fruit trees. In their modest way they are two charming varieties and scarcely likely to offend anyone.

Not so 'White Marvel'! It is one of nature's curiosities—damned by horticultural purists and adored by the lover of freakish flowers. It is a Dutch-raised plant and it shows; their bulb growers have an eye for the odd and quaint and a penchant for introducing them. 'White Marvel' usually has only two quite large flowers per stem. There are the familiar six petals and a fair-sized trumpet-shaped cup. The startling thing is that inside the cup there are dozens of other cups tightly packed one inside the other like a mass of frilly petticoats. Now you could lift up a flower and be charmed by such a cute sight or you could raise a top-heavy bloom from the dirt, whisk off the spattered mud and curse the thing for its crudity. Weird it may be, cute and quaint possibly, but it certainly is not the carefree soul that Wordsworth admired. The texture of the petals is rather thin, so they do not last particularly well in bad weather. Fortunately, or unfortunately, it is quite a sturdy plant, and the bulbs increase steadily. It would probably have caused a sensation had it been seen by Parkinson or Gerard but these days it seems to be of strictly limited appeal.

For many years jonquils and tazettas have been relegated to the most distant parts of garden, if admitted at all. No doubt there are many who consider the best place for some of the really common kinds is the outermost limits of cultivation, but this should not blind anyone to the really fine forms slowly becoming available now that the cottage garden revival has encouraged dealers and growers to offer them once again. The tazettas need not be confined to the cottage border. They can be combined with summer-flowering perennials to give early colour among the emerging foliage of later developing plants. Provided selection is made carefully with regard to vigour and foliage, they can be planted in company with many small spring bulbs in endless combinations or they can be massed in broad, shallow azalea pots to brighten outside living areas and entrances. The more finely scented kinds could even be taken indoors for short periods to decorate hallways and sunrooms. Such accommodating and cheerful flowers should be included to brighten every garden of choice winter flowers. Nothing more surely shows the first signs of renewal in a gardener's year and nothing could be more welcome.

12 Some Permanent

Bedding-out Plants

'When the bedding system first came into vogue, it was no doubt its extreme brightness, or what we should now call "gaudiness", that caused it to hold the position it did; but it was soon done to death. Only scarlet geraniums, yellow Calceolarias, blue Lobelias, or purple Verbenas were used; and the following year, by way of a change, there were Verbenas, Calceolarias and Geraniums—the constant repetition of this scarlet, yellow and blue nauseating even those with little taste in gardening matters, whilst those with finer perceptions began to enquire for the Parsley bed, by way of relief.' (William Robinson, The English Flower Garden, *1883)*

The general idea had been established many years before as 'ribbon bedding', in which the pattern was simple ribbons of colour laid out in long beds. These schemes depended for their colour on many hundreds of identical plants being raised or over-wintered in heated glasshouses, to be planted out as they approached the summer flowering season. All the plants had to be a uniform height so that the pattern could easily be seen, and the plants were kept within the bounds of the pattern by continuous nipping, pinching and clipping. Such ideas needed many skilled gardeners and vast behind-the-scenes resources to put them into operation, so the style was pretty well limited to the gardens of the very wealthy and to large public parks.

Competition among the plutocrats being, as it was, all-pervasive, they strove to outdo each other in various ways, including the creation of elaborate gardens around their mansions. Aided by that once proud race, the head gardeners, they began to improve on the simple ribbon border.

At first it was enough to interlace some of the flowery ribbons and then to tie them into complex knot patterns,

which drew in part for their inspiration on the old Tudor knot-gardens made with hardy herbs. But they went far beyond the old patterns and were soon laying out multicoloured schemes featuring coats of arms, family mottoes, heraldic beasts and symbols and even the names of their estates. The number of plants needed for such plans was staggering. It was not unusual for a large garden to use over seventy thousand individual bedding plants, while really large ducal and royal demesnes would demand hundreds of thousands of plants. The consumption of labour in setting out, watering, feeding and maintaining such gardens was huge. Often the bedding-out schemes were timed to be at their peak for some special social event when the mansion house would be the centre for house parties, balls and the like. Ascot Week, the opening of the hunting season and the arrival of the family to take up residence for the summer were key events in the head gardener's management schedule on every estate from Cornwall to Rhode Island.

In time the idea went over the top when elaborate multicoloured interwoven 'carpets' were contemplated and created. American millionaires, and doubtless others too, went for even more complicated designs which their gardeners called 'mosaiculture'. It was about this time that Robinson and others began their public protests against the excesses of 'carpet bedding', but it was not so easily finished off. By the end of the century three-dimensional schemes constructed of galvanised wire stuffed with damp moss began to appear, in the shape of crowns, baskets and cornucopiae—the whole being covered with living flowering plants. Such things can sometimes be found today at horticultural expositions.

Such excesses would probably have been passed off as the harmless foibles of the very wealthy had not the idea spread downward through the classes until the popularity of bedding-out became almost a mania. The rapidly expanding horticultural technology of the mid-nineteenth century enabled many middle-class home owners to indulge in the fashion too. Books such as Charles Francis Hayward's *Geometrical Flower Beds for Every Body's Garden* of 1853 claimed that it would 'enable those who may be unacquainted with the science of gardening, by referring them to the diagrams, to make [gardens] without difficulty, and, at the same time, to give the flower-beds style and proportion pleasing, symmetrical and durable'. The gardening magazines of the day carried detailed descriptions of the newest bedding schemes from all the great houses and also told amateurs which of all the hundreds of newly discovered plants could be used to create floral tapestries. To achieve the full colour range they desired, gardeners began to use coloured sands and gravels, crushed glass and pebbles in their designs. They took as their precedent the earlier gardens of the Dutch and the Tudors—revivalism was another hallmark of the age. The results were colourful, but it is hard to understand how gardeners could happily use such inert materials.

Although Robinson gives us a very short list of four basic bedding plants—geraniums, calceolarias, lobelias and verbenas—a much wider range of compact, low-growing half-hardy annuals provided an enormously varied palette for the horticultural carpet-weavers. Ernst Heyne, a South Australian nurseryman who trained at Dresden Botanic Garden and was chief plantsman at the Melbourne Botanic Gardens, gave a good list of bedding plants suited to Australian conditions in his book *The Amateur Gardener for South Australia* (1871). Heyne's list includes bulbs and perennials as well as annuals and shows the range of plants that could be included in bedding schemes. Popular bedding plants were ageratum, antirrhinums, *Beta vulgaris* (coloured-leaf beetroot), *Begonia semperflorens*, celosias, eschscholtzias, fuchsias, gaillardias, gazanias, heliotropes, *Iresine herbstii* and *Iresine aureo-reticulata*, lantanas, limnanthes, perilla, pyrethrum and thymes. Heyne also has a few well-chosen words about the 'Arrangement of Plants According to Colour', or bedding-out:

On lawns, ribbons, stars, or more or less elaborate designs as taste or fancy may direct, are cut out, the edges being either left natural as cut from the turf, or what is preferable lined with edging tiles, which not only gives the whole a more finished appearance, but also greatly facilitates the work of keeping the creeping roots of the grass forming the lawn in order. The design having been formed, it has to be planted, and here the taste of the gardener has ample scope of showing itself by selecting plants which in size, shape, and colour of leaves or flowers and otherwise properly blend together so as to make the whole a uniform and ornamental mass. A variety of annuals, bulbous or tuberous plants, or those having coloured or otherwise ornamental foliage may be used for such purpose, which is sown or planted on the spot where they are to grow. Where the system, however, is to be carried out to perfection, a larger number of plants of the same sort,

as may have been selected, are grown in pots and cultivated in them till they are nearly ready to flower. They are then planted out as the design may require and immediate effect is thus produced, which can be kept up by repeating the operation with a fresh set of plants grown again for the purpose.

Scarcely more than twenty years later Mrs Margaret Maria Browne, writing under her husband's alias as Mrs Rolf Boldrewood, was not quite so effusive, though she did admit: 'Ribbon borders are most attractive, but the designs must be well carried out and the colours artistically blended. They require much clipping and trimming. Carpet bedding is also effective, but the same remarks as to colour and design apply.' Could it be that the lack of skilled labour and the harder Australian conditions quickly put paid, for all but the wealthiest, to this exuberant fashion?

It is pretty plain that carpet bedding, ribbon borders and the whole idea of flowers as architecture are things of the past. A few examples still persist in such curios as floral clocks and the patches of bedding which seem to flock around municipal council chambers in the older suburbs and towns of our country, and even in the rather staid set pieces around the finishing posts of racecourses and in company names spelt out in flowers as factory gates. But is there a place for such horticultural dinosaurs in these hurried times? There are those who believe so and argue, and demonstrate, their case strongly.

The acknowledged leader of these latter-day revivalists is Christopher Lloyd, who writes a weekly column in *Country Life* and often reminds his readers of the pleasures that can be had from experimenting with bedding-out. His book *The Well-Chosen Garden* has a swag of ideas for fun with bedding. There must be some local gardeners who derive pleasure from trying new schemes too; it would be very surprising if there were not. One that comes to mind is a small bed in the gardens of Kennerton Green near Moss Vale in New South Wales. A previous owner had made a star-shaped bed with a sundial at the centre. The rays of the star were outlined with silver-leaved succulents, and carefully chosen low-growing flowers were used as infill—almost as in colouring-in with pencils or paints.

It is the careful choosing and planning from year to year that can be so challenging and enjoyable for those prepared to indulge in a little bedding-out. The massive displays of yesteryear are gone, but something of them can be recaptured by the imaginative use of annuals combined with other hardy plants within a set framework. A permanent framework of plants at once gives some constraints within which the gardener must seek to build an attractive, balanced and colourful display, reduces the level of intensive maintenance necessary and reduces the number of plants that must be renewed annually. I could imagine that succulent edged star filled with pink forget-me-nots interplanted with the deep claret tulip 'Eisenhower'; dark pink hyacinths such as 'Jan Bos' could be used one year. The pink forget-me-nots could be replaced with white ones, or the new strains of pale pink pansies and white violas could be tried. For a summer blaze it would not be difficult to combine yellow or cream dwarf French marigolds with dot plants of variegated spider plant (*Chlorophytum* sp.) and the variegated yellow-flowered canna. As the area to be filled is only small, the costs would be quite reasonable for the pleasure of mucking about with bedding-out.

In warm climates alternanthera is often used as a border, or a dwarf form of coleus. In such situations much use could be made of the many pastel-coloured forms of dwarf cannas now available, as well as the colour strains of larger coleus that can be had. A bolder red-coloured scheme might be built around the dark red sempervivum 'Malby Hybrid', the very dark red-leaved miniature geraniums 'Black Opal' or 'Red Black Vesuvius' and the red-leaved and red-flowered single bedding dahlia 'Bishop of Llandaff'. It would perhaps be foolish to risk the ire of Robinson's ghost by going into detailed blue and purple schemes, but the possibilities are innumerable if you look out for plants with colours and dimensions that suit each other and the space available. Keep to single-colour groupings and try to keep the shapes as simple as possible. A simple rectangular or oblong bed is a good starting point for beginners. The other vital point to remember is that the bedding-out plants cannot be allowed to go on from year to year getting bigger—the success of the idea is largely controlled by everything staying neat, tidy and in proportion with the outline of the design. Regular overhauling is essential.

Echeverias and Sempervivums

As the strains of annuals change frequently there can be little point in recommending any one in particular. So long as you remember to select single-colour selections rather than mixed, things should work out well. It is some of the other more permanent bedding plants that may need some detailed description, for by and large they are no longer found in the stocks of general nurseries. Fortunately after their fall from grace at least some of these plants were taken up by other enthusiasts and specialist collectors who love succulents, variegated geraniums or herbs. Among these most useful, adaptable and easily grown plant antiques are the echeverias and sempervivums. They make neat small rosettes, are very hardy and are tolerant of dry conditions. Propagation is so simple it is child's play. The plants send out short stolons with baby plants already growing from the tip. Within a few weeks of appearing these have sent out their first roots and begun to grow into larger plants. It is a simple matter to sever the offsets and grow them on in a sandy potting soil or to plant them directly where they are wanted. They suffer from very few pests—mealy bug and looper caterpillars which can be treated by whatever means you prefer.

ECHEVERIA VARIETIES

The varieties best suited to making edges and borders are:

Echeveria secunda   Makes flat rosettes of silver-grey leaves that do not appear especially succulent. It is often known as 'hen and chicks', although this name has traditionally been associated with several European members of the sempervivum family. In late winter short croziers of orange and yellow bells are displayed. One of the toughest.

Echeveria elegans   An its name indicates, more elegant than most. This is because each leaf has a band of translucent tissue around the edge which imparts a jewel-like quality to the plant. The rosettes are more cupped than in the former plant and reach about 10 cm in diameter. The leaves are flat and bluntly rounded at the end and besides being silver-grey are covered in a fine white powdery meal which increases the elegance of the plant. The short flower stalks appear in late spring and bear silvery-pink bells that are orange and yellow inside. This species looks magnificent when grown in the cracks of a dry-stone wall; allowed to multiply and spread undisturbed, it will make a large clump of dozens of silver rosettes.

Echeveria pulidonis   Rather brighter than the others, for its thick silver leaves are rimmed with dark red. The individual leaves are slightly incurved and round at the tip. The flowers are a bright yellow colour. Like all the other species described here, this plant comes from the dry

hillsides of central Mexico, where it grows partially shaded by rocky outcrops.

Echeveria albicans   Included because it has foliage that is whiter than white. A covering of dense powdery white 'farina' covers the silver-grey leaves. This will wash off in hard rain. The plant is susceptible to 'ankle rot' in wet, cool climates, which means it should not be treated as an outdoor plant except in places like Burra and Hay. Elsewhere it does very well as a multi-clumped specimen in a special pot standing beside a doorway. The flowers are yellow and orange.

SEMPERVIVUMS

The sempervivums appear similar to echeverias, at least until they flower, but are a separate family which occur naturally in the mountains of southern Europe from Spain to Turkey. In the days of Queen Victoria, intrepid travellers frequented the more out-of-the-way corners of Europe and Asia Minor to see the ruins of ancient cities, to hunt exotic game, to tread where Homer and the Greek heroes trod, to make religious pilgrimages and to study natural history. Quite often they would carry home with them bulbs, seeds and small plants collected during their travels. There was not such thing as plant quarantine, so it was simply a matter of popping the plants into a sponge bag and carrying them home.

Among the plants that were collected in this way were many of the endless variety of sempervivums. They have attracted many common names over the centuries which applied to only one or two common European sorts known since Roman times—live-for-ever, house leek, hen and chicks, joubarbes, and old man and woman among them. In some places they were thought to offer protection against lightning strikes and were encouraged to grow on mossy rooftops and in thatch. The old names were applied to all the foreign introductions too, and collecting them became quite an important hobby, especially among the enthusiasts for the new fashion of rock and alpine gardening. There are many small differences between hundreds of cultivated species and hybrids. The selection described here offers a good variety of colour and is large enough to use in bedding-out schemes. There are many others which are small and best confined to pot culture. Like the echeverias, they reproduce by offsets attached to short runners from the parent plant.

Sempervivum × 'Malby Hybrid'   An old garden hybrid raised in England by Reginald Malby, an early rock-gardener who was especially famous for his photographic close-ups of alpine plants. The rosettes are about 10 cm across and a vivid ruby-red for six months of the year; for the remainder they assume a quieter red-green colour. The flowers, which mark the end of the plant's life, appear on a short spike and are pinkish-coloured stars. The plant offsets freely and is very tough.

Sempervivum × 'Raspberry Ice'   A star quality about this one. It is a large plant with good deep red colour all over; the entire surface of the leaves is covered in a dense coat of long, glistening silver hairs, giving it a very glamorous appearance. It produces offsets readily and is hardy, though liable to scorching if planted in really hot exposed places. Occasionally it can become infested with mealy bug, which needs to be controlled to keep the plants looking attractive.

Sempervivum × 'Lavender and Lace'   Presents a change from the red shades of the others, for it has lavender-coloured leaves that are tinged with purple at the edges and the heart. Each leaf has a rim of fine hairs along it which catches the sunlight and adds a touch of class to the plant. The rosettes are not so large as the other varieties, about 7 cm across, but it is still large enough to use in the garden without getting lost.

***Sempervivum* × 'Sir Trevor Lawrence'** Offers a contrast with its solid silver rosettes with each leaf tipped a conspicuous black-red. The neatness of the markings and the compact incurving growth makes for a charming plant with a definite character. Thinking of companion plants which could pick up the colourful contrast could form the basis of a challenging piece of small-scale garden planning.

USED AS POT PLANTS

The use of sempervivums and echeverias as potted plants has been referred to as another way of growing these nineteenth-century favourites. The idea is to gather as varied a collection of low pots and seed pans as you can muster and plant them up, one variety per pot, and let them grow until the pots are filled and overflowing with masses of colourful rosettes. Writing in his book *My Garden in Summer*, Edward Augustus Bowles cautions:

The great difficulty in arranging them attractively is to avoid the appearance of a nursery garden produced by so many seedpans. So I have hunted diligently wherever I went for any sort of pots or pans of different shapes or sizes, and now there are scarcely three alike among the lot. Pigeons' drinking bowls, pans with ornamental mouldings, and a few ordinary flower pots of varying sizes did much to help . . . . When I have had a game of chess with them and castled the King, and a fellow too much like his neighbour has made a Knight's move, the general effect is good.

This attractive and easy approach to creating a special interest collection, so typical of nineteenth-century gardens, is not seen nearly often enough in Australia. The entire collection would take up a small space and a little time; it could be shifted from time to time or rearranged as Bowles delighted to do to create instant attractions at doorways, on the risers of garden steps, on balustrades and in courtyards.

Dot Plants

A piece of bedding-out can very easily become rather dull and flat if the idea is carried out with relentless sameness. This design problem was quickly realised by earlier proponents of the style and they came up with dot plants to give height and emphasis to their plans. Quite simply, the flat carpets of low annuals, perennials, succulents and coloured foliage plants were given a lift by introducing taller foliage plants. Quite often these were potted semitropical plants which were overwintered in a glasshouse and brought out when the frosts were past. They were planted—pot and all—in the garden according to the design and removed for safekeeping to a glasshouse in the autumn. Local experience showed that many of these plants could grow happily year round in the warm climate of Australia, so the kentia palms, araucarias, cabbage-tree palms and dragon trees, popular as dot plants, were left to grow unchecked.

That is how there came to be so many old gardens with a pair of one of these unusual plants in the middle or at either side of the front garden—the bedding-out has long since been discontinued but the centrepieces remain, overgrown and so massive that nothing will flourish under them

Dot plants which are more manageable can be found among the perennials and small shrubs. Standards of fuchsias, shrubby lantanas and the variegated sorts of abutilon can be very effective but do need to be pruned carefully to keep them from dominating and outgrowing their places in the overall plan.

Some interesting plants that have been used in the past as dot plants are:

Variegated yuccas These plants can make very arresting centrepieces for a special piece of gardening. Their bold, spiky outlines and colourful cream, white and pink variegated leaves can be a good foil for many planting combinations. You will find that they will outgrow their spot in a few years and will need resetting; that is not quite the problem it may at first seem, as they can be grown easily from large stem cuttings. It is a simple matter to lop off the top metre or so of an overlarge plant and start it off again by rooting it in some dry sandy soil. Within a month or so it will have made new roots and can be set out where it is needed. This is best done in warm weather. The old root and stem need not be cast on to the bonfire or put through the shredder; put in some-of-the-way corner and watered normally, it will most likely send out some new side shoots which can be severed, treated as cuttings and the extra plants thus obtained swapped with gardening friends. There seems now to be no specialist grower of these very hardy plants. They appear now and again in our better nurseries, especially those that deal in architectural plants for landscapers. When you are doing a nursery crawl remember that the plants will often not be labelled, so it is wise to familiarise yourself with the descriptions. These tall plants are all useful for the centrepiece of a bedding-out plan:

***Yucca gloriosa* 'Medio-picta'** A striped variant of the most commonly seen yucca. The leaves are broad, grey-green and only slightly recurving at the tips. The variegated form has a wide gold central stripe which is very regular and clean cut. The whole plant is upright and looks smart and almost military in its precision. With age the centre of the plant will produce a tall spire of creamy coloured bells. The plant takes up about 1 m square and grows 2 m tall.

***Yucca recurvifolia* 'Marginata'** Bold recurving foliage which is not so wide as in the former variety; the plant takes on the appearance of a plume of leaves which is sweeping and dramatic rather than architectural. The wide gold striping is on the outer edges of the leaves. There is a reverse form of this variegation in *Yucca recurvifolia* 'Medio-picta' which I have seen once, at Jenny Walker's nursery in Melbourne. Much to my regret I did not snap it up. Both sorts should occupy a space about 1 m square and 1.5 m high.

***Yucca glauca* 'Tricolor'** Boldest of all yuccas, having a brilliant combination of cream and green stripes with a strong pink border at the edges. The bottom leaves will turn brown and dry off, at which stage they can be carefully pulled off—watch the spine at the tip of each leaf. Groomed this way, the plant takes on the appearance of a standard. Allow it a diameter of about 60 cm to grow in. It seems very reluctant to offset, which is not a habit to be admired when a pair is needed. Brave gardeners desperate enough to try beheading the plant may be rewarded with offsets.

***Cordyline australis* 'Atropupurea'** Another dot plant often found struggling on as a remnant of a long-forgotten piece of bedding-out. It will grow into a tall shrub, even a tree, but is best kept in its juvenile form as a drooping fountain of purple-coloured foliage. The only way to achieve this ideal would be to throw away the plants once they outgrew their usefulness. It is possible to prune them, but the outcome would be a mass of new shoots and an unsightly trunk totally unsuited to the precision required in a bedding scheme.

Some shorter plants are useful for making the transition from low edging plants to the taller central 'dot' plants. A variety of foliage effects can be achieved by calling on any of the following to fill the planner's orders:

***Santolina chamaecyparissus* (Lavender Cotton)** A neat shrublet of 60 cm or so which is pure silver. It can become rather straggly and leggy but given an annual clipping will stay compact for quite a few years. Old plants do tend to collapse and die just when you don't want them to, so it is a good idea to replant from cutting-grown stock every three years. At midsummer the plant will cover itself in small yellow buttons of flowers—the aesthetes snip them off so they don't interfere with the colour scheme, others put up with the discordant note or plan around it.

Senecio bicolor This plant comes in a variety of disguises with combinations of cut and solid leaves. All of them are attractive and easily grown plants. The botanical name seems to change now and then but you may recognise it as dusty miller. In the nineteenth century it was recorded as powdered beau and dusty bob by the gardening writer Shirley Hibberd. There are many cultivars about in the trade, among them 'White Diamond', 'Cirrhus' and 'Hoar Frost'. New plants are compact and neat; frequent pinching out will keep them that way, but old bushes become woody and a mess of tangled stems. The quality of the foliage deteriorates too, so it is best to take cuttings every year and renew the plants when they are used for bedding-out.

Santolina chamaecyparissus* ssp. *squarrosa The diminutive form of lavender cotton is more compact and more finely divided. It still produces the yellow flowers which some find so objectionable, but its value as a very low shrublet cannot be overlooked. It is possible to grow it as a tiny clipped hedge, or it can be left to grow naturally into neat buns of silver foliage.

***Chrysanthemum haradjanii* (syn. *Tanacetum densum* ssp. *amani*)** Frequents many a garden, trailing over low walls and acting as a ground cover. In bedding-out it is invaluable for frontline duty as a continuous border or interplanted with the contrasting leaves of silver fescue (*Festuca ovina* 'Glauca') or *Artemisia stelleriana*. It is easily grown from cuttings at almost any time.

Grasses

Grasses were probably better known to nineteenth-century gardeners than they are to gardeners of today. This situation is changing rapidly as the use of grasses in mass plantings in cities such as Washington D.C. begin to receive wide acclaim among landscape designers. Grasses are very much unknown quantities; gardeners are unsure about their cultural requirements, methods and seasons for propagation and their growth habits. Cautious home owners immediately think of bushfires and snakes when the idea of grasses as garden plants is introduced, yet after becoming familiar with one or two kinds they begin to appreciate the unique contributions that grassy foliage and seed-heads can make. Others may think with dread about such willing growers as kikuyu grass, many sorts of bamboo and, more recently cursed, pampas grass. Wisdom dictates a slow period of acquaintance. However, don't let that put off trying one or two. They can turn that dull, lifeless corner into something rather special and can also be used as dot plants in bedding-out designs. Look out for:

***Miscanthus sinensis* 'Zebrinus'** A tall-growing grass which forms a tight clump of many, many stems. The leaves are long and pendant, and in this case banded crosswise with pale yellow stripes. By late autumn the 2 m tall plants hold aloft their 'flowers'—delicate pronged affairs that come close to resembling lightning conductors. These will last well into winter but can be cut down earlier if a tidy mind prevents enjoyment of their mature charms. *Miscanthus sinensis* 'Variegatus' is similar in all respects but for exchanging its yellow zebra stripes for white bands that run up and down the length of each leaf.

Stipa gigantea A plain enough tufty sort of grass which seems pretty so-so until late spring when its pannicles of heads shoot up and up and up until it is about 2 m tall. Now it is a very majestic plant; one that is beautiful if it can be planted where the golden light of early morning or late afternoon can shine thought its bronzy golden oats. Simply splendid. In late winter the dead thatch of old leaves should be carefully teased away from the emerging new growth. At this stage the flower stems cannot be distinguished from those that will simply produce more foliage, so care is needed; do the work by hand and don't be tempted to get stuck into it with shears or secateurs.

Chasmanthium latifolium The seed-heads of this grass are flattened into one plane and folded into each other so that altogether they have the appearance of minute kites that dance in the wind on the end of threadlike stems. It seems trustworthy, but like all grasses it should be watched lest it become too well adjusted to your garden. The foliage is bright acid-green; a nice light touch in a garden of darker greens. Overall it will attain about 75 cm. Trim lightly at the end of winter.

Sasa veitchii A short, broad-leaved bamboo which is a willing runner. It is often found in large old gardens, where it makes large thickets. Each dark green leaf develops a wide band of dry, buff-coloured foliage creating an unusual and telltale effect. There are two forms, one tall and one short. A deep strip of steel lawn edging will contain the runners; but it does need room to roam, so don't try to make it grow in a small space. As an underplanting to larger bamboos it can create an Oriental feeling in a short time. From time to time thinning of established clumps and clearing out dead stems is necessary to maintain a crisp, clean image of stems and leaves such as would be found in a Japanese scroll.

Arundinaria viridistriata A dwarf bamboo with mainly yellow leaves that have a few darker green stripes. Very dense growth to about 60 cm. It multiplies and spreads but is easily contained with lawn edging or by chopping around the perimeter with a sharp spade or hatchet.

***Pennisetum alopecuroides* (Rose Fountain Grass)** In some areas this grass has naturalised along roadsides and in other gravelly spots where water sometimes accumulates after rain. It is very tough and drought tolerant but seems to need a drenching once in a while to keep it in good heart. The fine grassy growth throws up short pinkish 'pussy-tails'. It self-sows here and there but not prolifically. Mature clumps can be divided in spring and need careful watering through their first season to ensure they get well established.

***Arundo donax* 'Variegata'** A common old-fashioned bamboo well known in its plain grey-green form as a windbreak around market gardens. Its mature stems were often used as tomato stakes. This boldly variegated form is rather less vigorous in growth but does need to have its roving tendencies curbed. Each year in winter all the old stems should be cut to the ground. This removes all the old tatty foliage damaged by wind and summer's drought and

ABOVE

Aloe saponaria *will brighten winter with orange-red bells.*

ABOVE LEFT

The crown of thorns plant *(*Euphorbia milli *'Splendens').*

LEFT

The Japanese sago palm *(*Cycas revoluta*).*

TOP

Echeverias mass their rosettes in tight clusters.

allows the sparkling white and green new growths to be shown to advantage.

Setaria plicatilis A very attractive grass with broad dark green leaves that are distinctly pleated. It has a decidedly tropical appearance. It needs good drainage and damp soil to do well. The fan of leaves spreads wide, creating a low clump. The panicles are green or pinkish but not particularly telling against the striking foliage. It usually needs a good tidy up at the end of winter. The plants are frost tender, and the large leaves are susceptible to wind damage.

Carex buchananii **(Bronze Sedge)** A low dense mound of fine grassy leaves which are an intense reddish bronze colour. A very useful plant for giving a lift to border colour schemes and for creating contrasts with other foliage forms. *Carex* × 'Silver Curls' is rather similar in appearance, but the leaves are silver grey.

Agaves and Aloes

In Audrey Le Lièvre's biography of the great and extravagant nineteenth-century gardener Ellen Willmott (*Miss Willmott of Warley Place—Her Life and Her Gardens*) there is a charming photograph of five gardeners with a pony and cart preparing to move a massive tubbed century plant from its winter quarters to a position outdoors in the garden. Such gigantic plants must have been truly admired to be afforded such manpower and care. The same plant can be found growing all over the drier parts of Australia. *Agave americana* haunts many an old farmyard, cemetery and roadside cutting—so much so that it is regarded as a pest by many country folk and is just as disliked by many sophisticated city dwellers. But for all this, the century plant is very tough and can provide striking foliage and form where nothing else could survive.

Such grand plants should not be so harshly dismissed from playing some part in our gardens. Around swimming pools, atop garden walls and against sunbaked outbuildings these tough plants can be set in tubs, throwing their bold outlines in silhouette against the walls or sky. We have known this for ages from Italian and Spanish gardeners. How is it that we have ignored the possibility for so long? English and American gardeners persist against the threats of frost and snow with tubbed plants. Why have they been so little used in Australia? Let us look again at the possibilities:

Agave attenuata The most useful of all the large succulent plants that can exist happily in large tubs. It has no spines so can safely be used at ground level and where people brush past. The rosettes are usually about 1 m in diameter and made up of broad light grey-green leaves. It takes about ten years to produce a flowering stem, at which time the rosette dies, but in the meantime the plant has made numerous babies around the base. The plant can be grown from a large rosette sawn off and set in sand; roots will soon form and the plant is ready to create an instant effect just where you want it. It is also possible to reduce the height of a tub-grown plant by adopting the same method. Smaller side-growths can be grown this way too but will take a number of years to reach full size. While the plants are very tough, they do need some watering and feeding to keep them looking their best. Old leaves that die can be carefully pulled away from the trunk and discarded. Like all other large-leaved succulents, this plant can suffer from hailstorms lacerating the leaves and from rotting during very cold wet weather.

Agave americana **'Medio-picta'** The most desirable of all the century plants. It is smaller in its overall dimensions than

the other members of the family because its ability to photosynthesise is reduced by the large variegated area of each leaf. Nonetheless it can still make a sizeable plant up to 1.5 m across. The large leaves are recurved, dark greyish-green and have a broad central stripe of creamy-yellow. Plants set in tubs along the top of a garden wall instantly carry us away to the shores of the Mediterranean.

Agave americana **'Variegata'** Too common altogether for many, but it looks spectacular growing in the cast-iron urns atop the gateposts at Forest Lodge in Stirling, South Australia, and it certainly must have been used for exactly the same purpose in many other old gardens across the country. The plant is doing very nicely in the rockeries in lots of public gardens, but confined inside a tub and out of harm's way it can do good service where anything else would curl up its toes. The large leaves are strongly recurved and have a wide cream border down each side. There are dark brown hooked spines along the full length of the edges.

Aloe africana From southern Africa. May have first travelled to our shores as a large stem cutting tied in the rafters below deck on a sailing ship. It has long been in our gardens and it can still be found in farmyards and mining towns and at the seaside; often the last survivor of a long-abandoned settlement. Growth is strong and upright, usually with a few side branches from the main trunk. The crown makes a large round head of downward-curving leaves which are sword-shaped, very succulent and of a soft green trimmed with hooked, dull reddish spines. The flowers in winter are a treat to gardeners and to small honeyeaters and wattlebirds. The tall branched flower spikes are a mass of long coral-red bells which drip nectar. The birds will feed avidly, and the gardener will get a lot of pleasure watching them forage.

Aloe striata Gives an opportunity for low-level planting, as it is completely spineless. It is not, however, cowardly; indeed, it is rather brash and colourful. The large grey-green leaves have a border of opaque white which makes an attractive variegation over the plant. The rosette is low and broad, covering a metre or so, and from this rise tall ramrod-straight flower stems which divide into many side branches for the topmost third. But where the other aloe flowering stems are stout and thickset with flowers, these are slender and hung with well-spaced bells. The effect is much lighter and more graceful. The candelabras of bloom will soar 2 m or so into the air and add more cheerful orange-scarlet flowers to the dull days of winter.

Aloe plicatilis The book-leaf aloe, as it is often called, has a remarkable and unique appearance which immediately marks it for distinction. The leaves are arranged in two opposite files so that they bear a strong resemblance to a fan. The stem divides frequently, in fact dichotomously, that is, always splitting in two, never with a main branch and side shoots. This means that the plant is very shrubby and covered with a dense crown of foliage. The trunk rapidly develops into a very stout affair, and even quite young plants take on the appearance of miniature trees. It looks marvellous as a tub plant and has the most outstanding appearance of all the aloes described here. In midwinter short unbranched flowering stems appear carrying twenty or so large tubular flowers of clear coral-red. Like all the rest this plant grows easily from large stem cuttings, which makes possible the acquisition of a large mature-looking plant.

Appendix: Some Source of Old-Fashioned Plants

Trees, Shrubs and Roses

J.E. and J.P. Acott, 3 Bowen Street, Trentham VIC 3458 (peonies and boxwood standards)

'Badger's Keep', North Street, Chewton VIC 3451 (old apple varieties)

Best Chandler & Son Pty Ltd (Como Nurseries), PO Box 13, The Basin VIC 3154 (rare trees and shrubs)

Bleak House, Calder Highway, Malmsbury VIC 3446 (old roses)

Carmel Rose Farm, 550 Canning Road, Carmel WA 6076 (old roses)

Con's Rose Nursery, 140 Oaks Road, Thirlmere NSW 2572 (old roses)

W. & J. Duncan, Hughes Park, PO Box 18, Watervale SA 5452 (old roses)

Bridget Gubbins, China Walls, Tooma NSW 2642 (clemaris)

Hilltop Cottage, Shicer Gully Road, Guildford VIC 3451

Neville Harrop, 17 Auvergne Avenue, New Town TAS 7008 (tree peonies)

Newman's Nursery, North East Road, Tea Tree Gully SA 5091 (camellias)

John Nieuwesteeg Roses, Tarrawarra Road, Coldstream VIC 3770 (old roses and Alister Clark roses)

The Perfumed Garden (David Austin Roses), Cur Bungower and Derril Roads, Moorooduc VIC 3933

Ross Roses, PO Box 23, Willungra SA 5172 (old, classic and species roses)

Thomas Roses, Kayannie Road, Woodside SA 5244 (old and classic roses)

David Thomson, Gares Road, Summertown SA 5141 (rare Plants)

Weald View Gardens, Lobethal Road, Ashton SA 5137 (fuchsias)

Woodbank Nurseries, RMB 303, Kingston TAS 7150 (rare plants)

Yamina Rare Plants, 25 Moores Road, Monbulk VIC 3793

New Zealand

Camellia Haven, 80 Manuroa Road, Takanini, Auckland

Cross Hills Gardens & Nursery, R.D. 54, Kimbolton (rhododendrons & azaleas)

Dene's Garden Way, PO Box 8019, Havelock North

Harrisons Trees, R.D. 1, Palmerston North

Mark Jury's Nursery, PO Box 6b, Urenui, North Taranaki

'Roseneath', State Highway 1, R.D. 2, Albany, North Auckland (old roses)

Rhodohill Gardens and Nursery, Paradise Valley, R.D. 2, Rotorua (rhododendrons & azaleas)

South Pacific Rose Nurseries Ltd, Shands Road, R.D. 6, Christchurch

Tasman Bay Roses, PO Box 159, Motueka

Tikitere Rhododendron Gardens, PO Box 819, Rotoroa

Top Trees, Ferry Road, Clive, Hawkes Bay

Perennials, Bulbs, etc.

Alberts Garden, 9 Beltana Road, Pialligo ACT 2609

Aridaria Garden Cactus Nursery, Lot 13 Alexander Avenue, Evanston Heights SA 5116

Coffields Nursery, PO Box 102, Creswick VIC 3363 (rock plants, including auriculas and primulas)

Colonial Cottage Nursery, 62 Kenthurst Road, Dural NSW 2158 (perennials)

Diggers Plants Co., 105 LaTrobe Parade, Dromana VIC 3936

Gentiana Nursery, Cnr Coonara and Hackett's Roads, Olinda VIC 3788 (bulbs and rock plants)

Glenbrook Bulb Farm, 28 Russell Road, Claremont TAS 7011

J.N. Hancock & Co., Jackson's Hill Road, Menzies Creek VIC 3159

Honeysuckle Cottage, Lot 35 Bowen Mountain Road, Bowen Mountain NSW 2753

Lambley Perennials, PO Box 142, Olinda VIC 3788

McGraths Cactus Nursery, 102 Hughes Street, Canningvale WA 6155

Meadows Herbs Cottage Nursery, PO Box 57, Mount Barker SA 5251

Nargates Plant Farm, Blackwood Road, Trentham VIC 3458

The Ornamental Grass Co., 75 Ryedale Road, West Ryde NSW 2114

Rainbow Ridge, 8 Taylors Road, Dural NSW 2158 (irises and day lilies)

Sheringa Perennial Plants, Balhannah Road, Carey Gully SA 5144

Tedworth Bulb Farm, PO Box 72, Kempton TAS 7030

Tempo Two, PO Box 60A, Peacedale VIC 3912 (irises and day lilies)

Trewhella House, 33 Raglan Street, Daylesford VIC 3460 (bulbs)

Viburnum Gardens, 8 Sunnyridge Road, Arcadia NSW 2159 (perennials)

Vogelsery Bulbs, PO Box 369, New Norfolk TAS 7140

Wirruna Nursery, Wallington Road, Wallington VIC 3221 (rare plants)

New Zealand

Ashton Glen Perennials, Estate Road, Wairuna, R.D., Clinton.

Bay Bloom Nurseries, PO Box 502, Tauranga

Belle Fleur Gardens, Northope 4 R.D., Invercargill (dahlias)

Bloomin' Plants, 1 R.D., Palmerston, Otago

Clareville Nursery, Main Road, Clareville, Carterton (no mail order)

Coehaven, 150 Rangiuru Road, Otaki (ericas and callunas)

Cottage plants, Freepost 356, Dept. G, PO Box 28006, Christchurch

Daffodil Acre, PO Box 834, Tauranga

Dunhampton Lily Fields, 1 R.D., Ashburton
Hokonui Alpines, R.D. 6, Gore
Joy Plants, Runciman Road, R.D. 2, Pukekohe, Auckland (perennials & rare bulbs)
Karamea Herbs, Tuhikaramea Road, R.D. 10, Frankton (herbs & old roses)
Kauri Creek Nursery, Main Highway, Katikati (old-fashioned annuals, perennials & roses)
Kereru Nursery, Okuti Valley, Little River, Canterbury
Frank Mason & Son Ltd, PO Box 155, Fielding (fuchsias)
Millstream Gardens, Pukehou, Private Bag 9009, Hastings
Moss Green Gardens, R.D. 2, Akatarawa, Upper Hutt
The Old Vicarage Nursery, 12 Opanuku Road, Henderson, Auckland 8 (mail order only)
Parva Plants, PO Box 2503, Dept. G, Tauranga (mail order only)
Peak Perennials, PO Box 8337, 23 Toop Street, Havelock North
The Peony Gardens, Lake Hayes, No. 2 R.D., Queenstown
Princess Garden Perennials, Main Road, Te Roti, R.D. 13, Hawera
Richmond Iris Garden, 376 Hill Street, Richmond, Nelson
The Roseraie, 46 Omahu Road, Remuera, Auckland (perennials, David Austin roses)
St Martins Geranium Nursery, 13A St Martins Road, Christchurch 2
Somerfields, PO Box 10133, Phillipstown, Christchurch (organic herb and cottage plants)
Southwell Plants, Hillend, R.D. 2 , Balclutha
Summergarden, PO Box 890, Whangarei (day lilies)
The Terraces Peonies, Mt Grey Road, Heithfield, North Canterbury
Titoki Point, Taihape, R.D. 1 (no mail order)
Village Green Garden Centre, PO Box 42, Albany (water gardens)
Waitaka Irises, Ellmers Road, R.D. 2, Gisborne

Seeds

Jim and Jenny Archibald, Bryn Collen, Ffostrasol, Llandyssul, Dyfed SA44 5SB, Wales
Chiltern Seeds, Dept R, Bortree Stile, Ulverton, Cumbria LA12 7PB, England
Diggers Garden Club, 105 LaTrobe Parade, Dromana VIC 3936
Gawler Sweet Peas, (M. McDougal), PO Box 63, Meadows SA 5201
Larner Seeds, PO Box 11143, Palo Alto, Calif. 94306, USA
Robinett Bulb Farm, PO Box 1306, Sebastopol, Calif. 95473-1306, USA
Rust en Vrede Nursery, PO Box 231, Constantia 7848, Rep. of South Africa
Seed Savers Network, PO Box 975, Byron Bay NSW 2481

Specialty Seeds, PO Box 34, Hawkesburn VIC 3142
Sunburst Bulbs, PO Box 183, 7450 Howard Place, Rep. of South Africa
Theodore Payne Foundation, 10459 Tunford Street, Sun Valley, Calif. 91352, USA
Kings Seeds, PO Box 19–084, Avondale, Auckland
Vallenders Seeds, 28 R.D., Manaia, Taranaki

Societies

Australian Garden History Society, Royal Botanic Gardens, Birdwood Avenue, South Yarra VIC 3141
California Horticultural Society, 1847 34th Avenue, San Francisco, Calif. 94122, USA
Cottage Garden Club of South Australia, Secretary, Mrs Val Budden, 42 Barrington Avenue, Enfield SA 5085
The Garden Conservancy, Box 219, Albany Post Road, Cold Spring, NY 10516, USA
Hardy Plant Society, Administrator, Mrs T. King, Bank Cottage, Great Comberton, Pershore, Worcs. WR10 3DP, England
Heritage Roses in Australia, Mr C. Rainer, c/o PO Box, Crafers SA 5152
Heritage Roses (New Zealand), Lyn Atkinson, 97 Richmond Hill Road, Christchurch 8, New Zealand
Heritage Roses (USA), Judi Dexter, 23665 41st Street South, Kent, Wash. 98032; or Frances Grate, 472 Gibson Avenue, Pacific Grove, Calif., 93950, USA
Maze Society, 7 Holly Buch Lane, Harpenden, Herts. AL5 4AL, England
Northwest Perennial Alliance, Bob Lilly, NPA Box 45574, University Station, Seattle, Wash. 98145, USA
Pioneer Plant Society, Miss Pamela Puryear, 708 Holland Street, Navasota, Texas 77868, USA
Auckland Garden History Society, c/- 40 First Avenue, Kingsland, Auckland 5
Dunedin Garden History Group, c/- Otago Early Settlers Museum, 220 Cumberland Street, Dunedin.

Many of these businesses are small, personal nurseries and from time to time they change hands or cease trading. Once you have become thoroughly immersed in garden making, you will be aware of these changes and the many new businesses which spring up yearly. I have listed those places I have dealt happily with for many years. I am sure you will be able to add many more. When writing to or visiting these places, it is important to have a short list of things you want and to ask for them. It is equally important to keep your eyes open for other plants which may add to the treasure trove of your old-fashioned garden.

Index

Page numbers in italics refer to illustrations